DANCING FEMALE

Choreography and Dance Studies

A series of books edited by Robert P. Cohan, C.B.E.

Please see the back of this book for other titles in the Choreography and Dance Studies series

DANCING FEMALE

LIVES AND ISSUES OF WOMEN
IN CONTEMPORARY DANCE

Edited by

Sharon E. Friedler

Swarthmore College, Swarthmore, USA

and

Susan B. Glazer

The University of the Arts, Philadelphia, USA

 harwood academic publishers

Australia • Canada • China • France • Germany • India • Japan • Luxembourg
Malaysia • The Netherlands • Russia • Singapore • Switzerland • Thailand

Copyright © 1997 OPA (Overseas Publishers Association) Amsterdam B.V. Published under license under the Harwood Academic Publishers imprint, part of The Gordon and Breach Publishing Group.

First published 1997
Second printing 1998

Amsteldijk 166
1st Floor
1079 LH Amsterdam
The Netherlands

British Library Cataloguing in Publication Data

Dancing female: lives and issues of women in contemporary
   dance. – (Choreography and dance studies; v. 12)
   1. Modern dance   2. Women dancers
   I. Friedler, Sharon E.   II. Glazer, Susan B.
   792.8'082

   ISBN 90-5702-026-2 (softcover)
   ISSN 1053-380X

Cover photograph: Liz Lerman Dance Exchange in *This is Who We Are, c.* 1994, choreographed by Liz Lerman. From the left: Kimberli Boyd, Michelle Pearson and Bea Wattenberg. Photo: Beatriz Schiller.

*Dedicated
to Sharon's mentors Dorothy Harris and Marcia Parsons,
to Susan's mentor Stella Moore
and to all our students*

CONTENTS

INTRODUCTION TO THE SERIES

Choreography and Dance Studies is a book series of special interest to dancers, dance teachers and choreographers. Focusing on dance composition, its techniques and training, the series will also cover the relationship of choreography to other components of dance performance such as music, lighting and the training of dancers.

In addition, *Choreography and Dance Studies* will seek to publish new works and provide translations of works not previously published in English, as well as to publish reprints of currently unavailable books of outstanding value to the dance community.

Robert P. Cohan

LIST OF PLATES

PREFACE

Dancing Female: Lives and Issues of Women in Contemporary Dance reveals the richness and complexity of women's contributions to the art of dance. It explores the intimate and diverse world in which women create, teach, direct, perform and write, providing a resource for looking back at past realities and looking forward to possibilities for the next century. It is about the physical, spiritual, and intellectual nature of dance and how women live in their art, how the writer's voice meets the reader's, what is consonant and what is dissonant.

Despite a rich history and rampant assumptions that women dominate in dance, when we began our research in 1989 we could find little scholarly work linking women to one another, to their heritage and to their professional environments. We are both directors of dance programs in the United States: one at a liberal arts college and the other at an institution with a conservatory tradition. We both administer, teach and create. Some of our work takes shape as performance, some involves the choreography of lectures, proposals or schedules. As educators and dancers we felt the need for literature focused on women in dance, lore that could provoke discussion within and beyond the field and promote further scholarship. No single book dealt satisfactorily with the full scope of women in dance.

We wrote *Dancing Female* with a varied audience in mind: dance educators and students, teachers and students of women's studies and general readers interested in the history and aesthetics of contemporary performing arts. We assume that our readers are interested in dance, in women, or both. Throughout this anthology our contributing authors vary in age, background, experience and writing styles in order to represent diverse viewpoints regarding this vast and multifaceted subject.

Dancing Female is divided into two books. The first concerns the lives of women in dance while the second analyses common issues that women face throughout their careers. Each begins with "Dancers Talk," which establishes the parameters of the discussion and notes various points of view. Through interviews and research we have gathered the opinions of many dancers and have recorded how each issue has affected them. Book I, "Matriarchs, Mentoring and Passing on the Heritage," is a contemporary examination of the ways in which women transmit their art from one generation to the next through their professional and personal relationships. Some chapters explore why women choreographers have chosen to create the dances they do in the manner they do. Others focus on particular women, their motivations and their impact, raising critical questions about women choreographers, dancers, writers, educators and administrators. How do women work independently, and organizationally? How do they set up institutions? How has higher education helped or hindered their efforts? Essays cover a range of major Western theatrical dance genres: ballet, modern, jazz, tap and theatre dance. Book II, "The Physical Body, Theory and Practice and Using the Knowledge," considers the dancer's relationship to her art from three perspectives: her physicality, the theory and practice of dance that impact her career in psychological and spiritual terms, and finally, the cultural context in which she works.

In dealing with some of the tensions, joys, frustrations and fears women experience at various points of their creative lives, the presentations strike a balance between a theoretical sense of feminism and its practice in reality. *Dancing Female* poses and helps to answer basic questions about women, power and action.

The editors are deeply indebted to Choreography and Dance Studies Editorial Consultant Muriel Topaz, who is one of the dance field's most eloquent and sensitive mentors. Her detailed reading and comments about this book forced us to rethink sections that were troublesome and to be forceful in our own editing. As a result of her generous prodding, we know we have produced a stronger and more focused book.

We also acknowledge the enormous support and encouragement of our two institutions: Swarthmore College through a Mary Albertson faculty fellowship; and The University of the Arts. Special thanks also to those friends and colleagues who provided invaluable aid along the way: Robert Ackerman, Edna Cohen, Marion Faber, Judy Lord, Susan Perloff, Marlene Rice, Pat Shapiro, K. C. Patrick and Susan Vigeurs, Telory Williamson, the staff of the Dance Collection, New York Public Library and all our contributors. Our work as co-chairs of the 1989 national conference of the American Dance Guild served as the impetus for this book. The staff of Swarthmore College Computing Services kept us from succumbing to the pitfalls of technology. Above all, we thank our beloved husbands and children, Louis Friedler and daughter Sorelle, and Robert Glazer, Bill and Paula, Ted and Carolyn.

Dancing Female records the current state of women in dance and is our response to our own love of its history. The challenges of organizing space, time, and energy that we have come to know through our bodies in dance directly impact how we negotiate these tasks in other arenas and how we have come to write this book.

Sharon E. Friedler   Susan B. Glazer
Swarthmore College *University of the Arts*
Swarthmore, USA   *Philadelphia, USA*

BOOK I

MATRIARCHS, MENTORING AND PASSING ON THE HERITAGE

PART I

DANCERS TALK ABOUT MATRIARCHS, MENTORING AND PASSING ON THE HERITAGE
Sharon E. Friedler and Susan B. Glazer

When dancers are asked how they learned to dance, they invariably begin by relating an anecdote about one of their teachers, a person to whom they feel indebted, the person who taught them. How and what was taught comes second. Dancers often point to one or two individuals whose influence led them into the field. The relationships they describe are frequently more complex and intimate than those observed in student-teacher relationships in other fields because the study of dance is addressed simultaneously as theory, history and practice in the body.

In dance ideas and imagery are transmitted through physical movement as well as through the written word. Students learn dance by observing, imitating and analyzing. The power of the physicality of the student-teacher relationship is demonstrated in the ways a teacher knows her students. She knows their bodies and what they can and cannot do; she knows their creative potential and how they respond to various intellectual stimuli; she knows their personal histories, their family histories and their relationships outside class.

Dance has developed under the maternal eyes of teachers and choreographers who were largely responsible for the characteristics of dance today. One can argue that most traditions reveal a distinctly feminine pre-eminence despite historically powerful and pivotal male figures in classical ballet such as Petipa and Balanchine.

A matriarch is an elderly, esteemed female leader of a family or group. Who is a matriarch in dance? One who invents a new vocabulary, technique or way of working, one who has a group of followers who then go out to teach the work of their teacher, one who has written about the dance or who has been its subject, one whose personal imprint on dance is so strong that she is inexorably linked to the future of her art.

The term 'matriarch' traditionally has been associated with the development of modern dance; one immediately thinks of the choreographic giants of this century such as Isadora Duncan, Mary Wigman, Doris Humphrey, Martha Graham, Katherine Dunham and Hanya Holm. The contributions of a small number have been readily acknowledged in other writing; the discussions and interviews in this section extend that number to include women whose points of view and work have not been recognized as broadly. From the chronicles of their lives and achievements, these new matriarchs prove to be exceptional mentors.

Mentoring is a close, intense, mutually beneficial relationship between two people. It can be hierarchical or non-hierarchical in nature. Non-hierarchical peer mentoring relationships are characterized by the participants' complementary level of knowledge, experience or expertise. Interaction flows back and forth between colleagues who learn from one another, and, as each has the same level of power, can assist each other in attaining professional goals. In dance schools and companies, journal publications, service organizations and management one can identify pairs or sometimes groups of women working cooperatively in peer mentoring relationships.

In hierarchical mentoring relationships, one person is older, wiser, more experienced and more powerful, and the other is younger and less experienced. The informality and complementary aspects of mentoring are consistent with the reciprocal nature of dance, in which a spirit of cooperation between the teacher and the protégée (a student who is specially assisted; not all students are protégées) is indispensable to the creation of the product. Mentoring is vital to the development of the young female dancer, connecting her to her history, suggesting ways for her to develop her own movement, choreographic and scholarly style and preparing her to become a mentor to future dancers.

Martha Myers, Dean of the American Dance Festival and one of dance's esteemed matriarchs, shares her approach to teaching, coaching and advising: "Mentoring is part of the joy of teaching. It is a word I prefer to teaching. I like to think of this age-old interaction between two people — or one and several — as a dialogue of mutual discovery. Education should always be mutual, a quest, not an exchange of goods. Both younger and older bring their life experiences to this dialogue, but it can't be assumed that wisdom is imbedded in it. Even if it were, it can't be handed out one to the other. The goal is not to fill up an empty vessel, but to work toward an equilibrium in the dialogue with a kind of mutual nourishment." Even in dealing with specific skills, Myers asserts the value of mentoring in combination with an attitude which is open to discoveries made by the protégée: "We should be open to this possibility, even with a simple tendu, as movement science and somatics have demonstrated.

"My role at the American Dance Festival has been as an educator, officially as Dean. When I think of 'vision' regarding an institution, I like to think of it in relation to many angles of that institution, in this case what has gone before (the tradition of Bennington and the days at Connecticut College); of how this interacts with what is currently the scene across the country and globally; and how we can expand the possibilities within this art form, and the public's perception of it. I think of 'vision' as romantic, as in Walt Whitman's 'I hear America singing,' or 'I hear America dancing.' I do see America dancing, as nations before us, and many today, continue to do. Romance in this sense is the steed that pulls the pragmatic chariot. And I like to think that during my tenure at ADF this educational vision has influenced dance in this country in some small way. Specifically, my interest in dance training has always been broader than producing the virtuosic body; that it should aim at the development of an expressive, creative, self-actualized artist, a fully dimensional person with resources to continue growing throughout her career and beyond."[1]

Marion North, Director of the Laban Centre for Movement and Dance in London since 1973, was one of the first educators to systematically utilize mentoring in a curriculum. North, a renowned specialist in movement analysis, was Rudolf Laban's research and teaching assistant during the last ten years of his life. Continuing her teacher's tenets, she created a center for performance, choreography and research based on Laban's philosophy that dance could be for everyone at professional, recreative, therapeutic and educational levels. The Laban Centre, under North's leadership, has advanced the study of dance in Britain, linking the school with international developments in the field. "I have been a mentor to countless young people... my own personal experience of counseling and counseling training has stood me in good stead, both from the point of view of working with the faculty and with the students, both as groups and individuals. Academically of course, and artistically, this is a core area of the work of the Centre."[2]

Peer Mentors

When one artist pairs with a colleague for the purpose of mutual professional support, and the relationship is balanced as opposed to hierarchical, the participants are equally able, responsible and invested. Although such relationships have not traditionally been considered as mentoring relationships, many examples support this expanded definition. Marion North uses all her colleagues' expertise and cooperation for funding,

---

[1] Written statement provided by the artist, June 2, 1994.

[2] Written statement provided by the artist, June 13, 1994.

organization and curriculum decisions but had a special long-term peer mentoring relationship with Bonnie Bird, who was artistic adviser for the Centre's resident Transitions Dance Company for more than twenty years until her death in 1994. Transitions Dance Company serves as a preprofessional apprenticeship assisting dancers in making the shift from student to professional and is the academic manifestation of mentoring. North credits Bird: "I must say that the major support during the 21 years has been Bonnie Bird, who had a wealth of experience in these fields, and I would particularly emphasize her contribution in the artistic curriculum area."[3]

Peer mentors like North and Bird support one another's development over time and present one model of women working together; there are other models. In the 1950's, Shirley Ririe and Joan Woodbury were involved in a Utah-based dance company called Choreodancers. This company provided them and other teachers with opportunities to choreograph and perform with their mature professional colleagues. The company was democratic in nature; participants collectively decided what works they would do, who was to choreograph and where they were to perform. Continuing to work collaboratively, Ririe and Woodbury founded their own company in 1964 and team-taught at the University of Utah. Regarding the challenges of their university affiliations, Shirley Ririe says: "Joan and I started out in half-time appointments. We shared a job. We had to go to the Vice President of the University three times to finally get us both full-time appointments. At the time we were in the Physical Education Department. The dean would not fight for us, we had to do it ourselves. We always taught full-time loads; this is the way we were able to achieve full department status for dance. The administration (all men) would give praise to our international reputation and the influx of students from all over the world. They would recognize that we had built one of the strongest modern dance departments in the nation. Yet the monetary equivalent of this praise never came. I attribute this, in part, to the male chauvinist dominance at the University and to the fact that the Fine Arts Department has never had an important status on campus. We gave of our time generously because we loved and believed in what we were doing."[4] Over the course of thirty years they built both the Ririe-Woodbury company and a modern dance department. Practices and ideals from one experience fed the other.

Jeraldyne Blunden founded the multi-racial Dayton Contemporary Dance Company in 1968 with the advice and encouragement of three peer

---

[3] Ibid.

[4] Written statement provided by the artist, June 1, 1994.

mentors. She credits her business acumen to Josephine Schwarz, her taste for what is presented on stage to Mary Hinkson and her energy and spirit to Thelma Hill. Ms. Schwarz from Ohio along with Dorothy Alexander from Atlanta were pioneers in the development of regional ballet. Mary Hinkson joined the Martha Graham company in 1951 and excelled in roles that showcased her remarkable musicality, strength, beauty and fluidity. Thelma Hill (died 1979), exponent of the Horton technique, former member of the Alvin Ailey company and known as a masterful teacher is the matriarch/ mentor to a generation of African American artists. It was Thelma Hill, says Ms. Blunden, "who throughout my life kept pushing me and told me to keep going and not to ever give up. When she told me I should join National Association of Regional Ballet, now Regional Dance America, I asked her why join a white ballet organization? She told me that they would need companies like mine. She was right. It provided the proper networking."[5]

In the early 1980's in Minnesota, partners Linda Shapiro and Leigh Dillard created and co-directed the New Dance Ensemble, another model of peer mentors at the helm. For thirteen years, the company set a new standard of excellence and professionalism in the Midwest. It hosted numerous nationally known choreographers and eventually created the New Dance Laboratory to encourage its members to work at their craft with as much support and as few restrictions as possible. "By acknowledging the dancers as an essential part of the creative process and then treating them accordingly by giving them power and authority to help shape the Lab we developed a unique and revolutionary model for the time," says Linda Shapiro. Looking back to the beginning of New Dance, Leigh Dillard remembers: "How giddy we were when we made a list of choreographers we wanted to work with. How gratifying that we actually got to work with so many of them... And how naive we were and how much we learned about the working process. What a high... what a gas... what a thrill!"[6]

Refining and defining vision are central concerns for Judith Jamison, Denise Jefferson and Sylvia Waters. Since Alvin Ailey's death in 1991, these three women have directed the Alvin Ailey American Dance Theatre institution. Jamison directs the company, Jefferson heads the school and Waters oversees the Repertory Ensemble. Their mutual support and consultation shapes the organization. Jefferson summarizes the school's outlook as follows: "Dancers are so critical and hard on themselves. They need a nurturing environment so they can open up and explore who they are, what works for them, and what doesn't. They need feedback."

---

[5] Telephone interview, August 9, 1994.

[6] Written statement provided by the artist, April 15, 1994.

Waters affirms the importance of a supportive director in relation
to the young Repertory Ensemble dancers. "They need an outside eye; they
don't yet have the maturity and strength. I try to establish a relationship
where they know they can come to me with problems and things that are
on their minds. I encourage them to be their own people, although they've
certainly got my eye and my attention every step of the way."

Not surprisingly, Jamison, in referring to the first company, also
points to a concern for the whole individual. She says: "The bigger you get,
the less intimate you get, but this company seems to maintain a level of
intimacy and genuine caring. That energy and vitality and caring have
always been a part of this company, stemming from Alvin's idea of what
a dancer should be. You encourage and help your fellow dancers as much
as possible."[7]

Hierarchical Mentoring

In contrast to peer mentoring relationships in which the participants' ideas
carry equal weight, six categories of hierarchical mentoring pairs show
other ways written, spoken and movement heritage are passed on in dance.
An analysis of these six pairs assists us in understanding the distinctive ways
dancers engage in the complex verbal and nonverbal learning process. Each
of these mentoring pairs is influenced by the balance of power between
the mentor and the protégé; the gender, dynamics, age and status of the
participants; the length of the relationship; the participants' goals.[8]

Mother-Daughter Mentoring Pairs

Older women traditionally nurture and counsel younger ones in families but
not in the professional world. Nevertheless, figurative mother-daughter pairs
are common in dance. Women at the highest levels of power, like women in
the corporate world, are few in number. Sali Ann Kriegsman, former director
of the dance program for the National Endowment for the Arts and currently
executive director of Jacob's Pillow, says of her past mentors and present job
that there is no preparation. "You jump off the high board and hope there's
water in the pool. However, in the early 60's, in San Diego, Nancy Johnson,
who is presently the general manager of the San Francisco Ballet School,

---

[7] Reiter, Susan. "The Vibrant Ailey Enterprise: Ailey Women," *Dance Magazine*. Nov., 1993,
p. 52–53.

[8] Jeruchim, Joan and Shapiro, Pat. *Women, Mentors and Success*. New York: Ballantine Books,
Random House, Inc., 1992, p. 23.

and her husband Richard Carter, presently a soloist with Miami City Ballet, were my role models. Nancy was raising three children, building a theatre, developing the school, choreographing, teaching and doing everything alone. She enhanced my understanding of ballet, but more importantly, she demonstrated what it is possible to achieve when you roll up your sleeves and do it. She had a strong commitment and the will to work toward success. She was intrepid, trying to make something grow in soil that was not very hospitable."[9] As director of the N.E.A. dance program during a time of turmoil for the arts, Kriegsman followed the example of her mentor; she also made something grow in soil that was not hospitable.

Bonnie Brooks, executive director of Dance/U.S.A., the largest organization of dance companies, regional service organizations and presenters in the United States, emphasizes the paramount role of mentoring in the future of leadership in dance. This is borne out in her own experience: her first mentor was a woman. "Rhoda Grauer, former director of the National Endowment for the Arts dance program and currently a film and video producer for public television, was my first mentor. I was a little grade-four temporary working at the N.E.A. when I went to her to ask for a job in her department. She rolled her eyes but must have recognized the intensity of my desire, for one year later, when she had an opening, she asked me to apply. During my three years as a program specialist I became thoroughly grounded in dance by being exposed to a constant flow of the most creative artists in the country. This was my university experience and Rhoda was my dance mother."[10]

Mother-daughter mentoring pairs are most common in the dance world due to the pre-eminence of women choreographers especially in modern dance. Bessie Schoenberg is frequently cited by contemporary American choreographers as an influential mentor. In the 1920s, Schoenberg was a member of Graham's fledgling company when she was asked to teach at Sarah Lawrence College. For sixty years she has served as a mentor to administrators, choreographers, performers, scholars and teachers. Among the many protégées from Schoenberg's workshops for professional choreographers held at New York's Dance Theatre Workshop, Sally Hess, a choreographer, performer and teacher acknowledges Ms. Schoenberg's influence:

"I'd been making dances for some time but had just begun to teach dance composition. Over the ten-week course, she taught me a new way of

---

[9] Phone interview, May 12, 1993.

[10] Phone interview, May 24, 1993.

speaking about dance that I use in the classes that I teach now and that will, in turn, help my students speak to each other about the dances that they show in class: an approach which is not personal, not judgmental, but rigorous, accurate and sympathetic to their dances and movement studies. Bessie says, 'You might try…' rather than 'I think you should…'. It sounds obvious but is very difficult to do; to remove the personal pronoun from one's commentary on work in progress. I began to learn to listen and not to jump defensively at what was being suggested. Bessie was continually turning us back to our own inner worlds, prompting us to examine and to trust our own voices, no matter how shaky. Of course she is curious: the process of dance-making is a delight to her, and through her, to me."[11]

Minnesotan Heidi Hauser Jasmin and her mother Nancy Hauser shared a perspective passed from one generation to another. Hauser was mentored by Hanya Holm, who was Mary Wigman's protégée. Each woman's work demonstrates a common commitment to a philosophy of dance that stresses the discovery and development of an individual vocabulary based on universal principles of motion, the right of each person to be both a creator and a performer of dance, and the importance of improvisation as an aid to investigating both. In her book *The Language of Dance*, Wigman advised teachers to: "Speak your own language and try to convey something of what drove you once to the dance: your enthusiasm, your obsession, your faith, and your relentless endurance with which you worked as a student. Have the courage to be yourself and also to help your students find the way to themselves."[12]

Reflecting on her study with Wigman, Hanya Holm recalled: "She was like an ocean that always came back to you and always renewed. Her theories were not yet set. Whatever new vision came to her required a new discovery, and the question was: how shall one go about expressing this idea best?"[13] With respect to her own ideas concerning making dances, Holm said: "Mary Wigman felt that the development of every dance personality should take place in two different directions: the perfection of the performer as an individuality and, on the other hand, the adjustment of this individuality to the group. The dancer who choreographs may bring with him a blueprint of his idea. But this, though it may be necessary, is only the smaller part of his work. …Unlike a conductor whose coworkers play from a printed score, the

---

[11] Written statement provided by the artist, May 26, 1993.

[12] Wigman, Mary. *The Language of Dance*. Middletown, Wesleyan Univ. Press 1966, p. 107.

[13] Sorell, Walter. *Hanya Holm: The Biography of an Artist*. Middletown: Wesleyan Univ. Press 1969, p. 18.

choreographer works with live material, he has to utilize the creative ability without destroying the personality of the individual performer within the group."[14]

Nancy Hauser carried the principles of Holm with her when she moved to the Midwest and settled in Minneapolis, where, after thirty years still influenced by Wigman and Holm, she formed her own modern dance school and company. Her daughter Heidi Hauser Jasmin studied with both Holm and Hauser, became a dancer and choreographer in Hauser's company and, in 1987, became artistic director of the company and the school. Her goal is to preserve and extend the Wigman/Holm/Hauser approach. In an interview conducted one month before Nancy Hauser's death at age 80, Nancy and her daughter complete one another's sentences and echo each other's thoughts. Hauser starts:

"Fortunately, Heidi and I have always been good friends. ...we had a professional relationship that worked because each respected the other one." Her daughter concludes: "Being an artist really has to do with dedication and devotion.... It's about taking chances, not compromising your integrity and not being concerned with success and getting recognition. That's what I really learned from my mother."[15] Wigman, Holm and the Hausers represent a significant four-generation link in the female lineage of modern dance.

A mother-daughter pair that includes mentoring in both performance and administrative expertise is Joan Myers Brown, founder and artistic director of Philadelphia Dance Company (Philadanco), and Kim Bears, principal dancer and assistant artistic director. Recognizing a need to provide not only a performing outlet but also a training program for African American dancers, Brown established a repertory company and school in 1970. Philadanco has become one of the country's premiere modern dance organizations, with an annual budget that ranks seventeenth nationally, a company that tours internationally and a school that instructs over five hundred students annually.

Joan Brown is a fiercely independent woman whose professionalism and competence are well-recognized. Not everyone would want to be mentored by this dynamo. She has been magnanimous and generous in bringing dance to a wide audience but can be tough and merciless in her demands for precision. In Kim Bears, a 1986 alumna of the University of

---

[14] Ibid., p. 21.

[15] Horwitz, Caril and Stockstad, Kim. "Voices/Interview with Nancy Hauser," *Contact Quarterly*. Winter 1989, Vol. XIV, No. 1, p. 34.

the Arts and 1993 recipient of a Bessie Performance Award, she found a bold dancer, a woman ready to assume the opportunities that existed at Philadanco. Brown sensed a commitment, energy and professionalism that matched her own, conditions necessary to the formation and development of a mentoring relationship. Not only did Brown coach Bears as a performer, but she also invited her to observe in the office and, eventually, to assume duties related to the management of the school and company.

"Kim has a belief in the company and wants to be here when success happens. I am her mentor. I oversaw her development from student to professional; from company member to assistant artistic director. I nurtured her and encouraged her, but she is free to leave or do other things with her career and she would not be deserting me. I want her committed to the craft and not to me personally. She must be responsible for her own professionalism, growth and career."[16]

Kim Bears: "I latched onto her. Something connected. She was Mom. Joan teaches and directs in a strict and disciplined manner, yet she allows me to find my own way. She has great confidence in me, occasionally chewing me out but always encouraging me to go on and do more. Her teaching is honest and very human, setting high standards that I strive to reach. She is always behind me, sending me cards, believing in me, thanking me. I am fortunate she is my mom."[17]

Mother-Son Mentoring Pairs

Mother-son mentoring pairs are most common in the areas of dance in which women have been originators and/or principal investigators. Most men in the modern/post-modern dance world were mentored by women. Jose Limon's mentor was Doris Humphrey. Initially, he was a dancer in her company. Later, when he formed his own group, she served as his guide and he named her artistic director. In writing about his female mentors, Limon said:

"In Doris Humphrey I found a master who knew that every dancer, being an individual, was an instrument distinct and unique from any other, and that in consequence this dancer must ultimately find his own dance, as she had found hers. I was instructed, stimulated, trained, criticized, encouraged to look for and find my own dance.... I view myself as a disciple and follower of Isadora Duncan and of the American impetus as exemplified

---

[16] Personal interview, February 10, 1992.

[17] Personal interview, March 29, 1992.

by Doris Humphrey and Martha Graham, and by their vision of the dance as an art capable of the sublimity (sic) of tragedy and the Dionysian ecstasies."[18]

Numerous other men, if not obviously mentored, were strongly influenced by women. Both Merce Cunningham and Paul Taylor began their careers in Martha Graham's company and started their own choreographic explorations while dancing with her. The aesthetics of Alwin Nikolais, Murray Louis and Don Redlich were all shaped by the work of Hanya Holm. Katherine Dunham mentored Talley Beatty. Helmut Fricke-Gottschild, former co-director of Zero Moving Company in Philadelphia, received his dance education from Mary Wigman in Germany:

"Mary Wigman was my teacher and, being one of a group of her more rebellious students, I sought to break away from much she tried to teach us (which she both disliked and respected). Mary Wigman was a parental figure (though fortunately not one of those teachers who keep mothering and cuddling their pupils) whom one loves and against whom one rebels but whose heritage has entered one's blood and will, sooner or later, be discovered and appreciated. For me, it was later."[19]

Mark Taylor, artistic director of the Pittsburgh Dance Alloy, acknowledges his debt to female mentors: "All my teachers and most of the people with whom I have worked have been women. I feel that I have a strong respect for how women have contributed to this field and how women can be role models for men in general. My major performing experience before I started my own work was with Roz Newman. In a sense, she was my choreographic mentor. Bessie Schoenberg was influential beyond the short time I was a member of one of her first workshops for professional choreographers at Dance Theatre Workshop. Later, during rehearsals or at a premiere, I could hear her words. What I learned from her affects my own work as well as the way I look at the work of others."[20]

Father-Daughter Mentoring Pairs

Father-daughter mentoring pairs, the rule in most professional fields, are less prevalent in dance. However, they do exist frequently in classical ballet and rhythm tap. Barbara Weisberger, founder and former artistic director

---

[18] Cohen, Selma Jeanne. *The Modern Dance: Seven Statements of Belief.* Middletown: Wesleyan Univ. Press 1966, p. 23.

[19] Written statement provided by the artist, May, 1993.

[20] Personal interview, March, 1993.

of the Pennsylvania Ballet, credits George Balanchine for giving her the opportunity and support to begin a ballet company in Philadelphia.

"The seeds of the Pennsylvania Ballet were sown in 1960 at Lincoln Kirstein's home when George Balanchine assembled a group of people. 'There are so many great dancers,' he said, 'and not nearly enough companies to employ them.' Mr. Balanchine patted me on the head and said, 'Well, Barbara, you must do this in Philadelphia.' Mr. B. was much more than my mentor. He gave me my sense of ethics, morality, and a strong conviction about ways of doing things. Mr. Balanchine was loyal to me and showed his love by offering me his ballets free of charge. He then, upon my invitation, came to Philadelphia to stage works and coach the dancers in my newly formed company."[21]

The renowned female tapper Brenda Bufalino reflects on her relationship to her male mentor Honi Coles and to the Copacetics, the black male tap dancers who originated the term 'rhythm tap.' As a small white woman working in a form dominated by black men, Bufalino faced multiple obstacles. "Rhythm tap is a very aggressive form — with cutting contests and trading, there was a great deal of athletic drive necessary to learn flash steps. Then, too, venues weren't there for women. They were told and often believed that it wasn't possible for them to do the kind of work that was required."[22]

Her teachers initially encouraged her; she even danced duet performances with Coles and was the first woman and the only white woman to perform with the Copacetics. However, when she began to develop her own material and form her own company, the American Tap Dance Orchestra, her teachers grew silent. She could have benefited from their perspectives as she approached success, yet their support disappeared. Bufalino choreographed a solo for herself, "Too Tall, Too Small Blues," which she used as a vehicle for dancing, singing, and talking about the complex terrain she negotiates in the field of tap, including the relationships with her father mentors. She proposes a dialogue in movement and words, celebrating the heritage she received from her male mentors and questioning how her contributions will alter tap's future.

When father-daughter pairs appear in modern dance, it is not unusual for the father to have been mentored by a woman. In the 1950's Paul Taylor was a member of Martha Graham's company. Although he began making his own dances while still dancing for her, in his

---

[21] Personal interview, April 17, 1993.

[22] Kilkelly, Ann Gavere, "Brenda Bufalino's Too Small Blues," *Women and Performance*. V. 3, No. 2, #6, 1987/88, pp 69–70.

autobiography, *Private Domain*, Taylor writes about the complexity of his feelings for Graham and her influence on him early in his own choreographic career.

"I've probably mentioned that my feelings for her aren't simple. Love, awe, fascination are spliced to a dimmer view, and, once in a while, stresses tug at my commitment to her. Yet, right now, seeing her stand so monumentally, so alone, I feel nothing but admiration for this small, feisty woman, who, for at least thirty-two years, has been lifting dance to new heights. Besides, her knowing eyes have seen something wonderful in me, and I'm determined to be worthy."[23]

Nearly twenty years later in 1978, Ruth Andrien joined Taylor's company: "I was a soloist in Paul Taylor's company for ten years and consider him my principal mentor. Paul is very attracted to physicality and hence the sexuality of his dancers, both male and female. He does not develop sexual relationships with his dancers, yet sexuality remains very much a part of his choreography. He brings out the passionate feminine element of a male and the athletic strength and physicality of the female. The dancers' relation to each other is not stereotyped by gender. Paul sensed who I was and what I felt as a woman and magically and mysteriously brought out a lot of my strengths.

"Paul assumed the role of a father in his company. He responded to me as my father would have. He saw me simultaneously as child and woman, and even though the duets he choreographed for us were about love — new, old, deep, and lost — the choreographer/man Paul did not relate to me as a lover.

"There is nothing I would not do for him, nor he for me. I found that I was capable of performing incredibly complex movements because I sought his approval and understood that he was able to get that kind of commitment without destroying me or without diminishing my power. For me he is an empowering force, a healing father."[24]

Mentoring relationships shift over time. Initially dancer Karen Bamonte was involved in a father-daughter mentoring relationship which, after fifteen years, evolved into collaboration and peer mentoring. She and her mentor later became co-artistic directors of the Philadelphia-based modern dance group Zero Moving Company (1976–1993). Their situation is noteworthy in part because her mentor, Helmut Fricke-Gottschild, was part of a previously noted mother-son mentoring pair with the German modern

---

[23] Taylor, Paul. *Private Domain*. New York: Random House, 1987, p. 84.

[24] American Dance Guild Conference, panel discussion, June, 1989.

dancer Mary Wigman. For Bamonte, Fricke-Gottschild was an actual mentor, and Wigman, by extension, may be seen as a symbolic one.

"I feel very lucky in my own training and history as a dancer. I worked under, and in cooperation with, Helmut Gottschild, who I think has more woman in him than anybody I know. From the outset his approach to making dances, his technique, his whole demeanor and body countenance were very familiar to me. His teacher, Mary Wigman, gave him a set of concepts, a very generous arena in which the body could move. It was not a specific technique or set of steps, but a series of qualities or houses in which the body might live. We worked from the inside out, which meant that we had to make sense of the material on many different levels. We had to digest it intellectually, feel it in our heart, and understand it with our soul. From that approach to working, it seemed normal for me to go on to make my own dances. There was no boundary between the moment of being a dancer and making a dance."[25]

Enmeshed Mentoring Pairs

Of course, like any dynamic relationship, the mentoring phenomenon can become distorted or confused. Personal development can be limited if the protégée remains too tightly in the shadow of the mentor. If the mentor leaves the relationship prematurely, the protégée can be stranded without her own problem-solving abilities. Enmeshed mentoring pairs are interdependent, entangled in an emotional net.

No relationship begins as enmeshed. At the start the mentor is an idealized role model. Each partner wants to become close without losing his or her sense of self. Difficulties arise when the personal boundaries between mentor and protégée become obscured because both are seeking to fulfill needs which are unmet in other spheres of their lives. Both mentor and protégée are responsible and both pay a toll psychologically. When boundaries which allow independent action are violated, the relationship often falters, the idealization begins to fade and the protégée becomes negatively critical, less dependent and finally, breaks away.[26] The Denishawn Company, formed by Ruth St. Denis and Ted Shawn in 1914, is a notable twentieth century example of a relationship which ultimately destroyed its creation. Ted Shawn first saw St. Denis in Denver while she was on tour. A glamorous and successful star, she became his idealized role model. The two dancers

---

[25] Ibid.

[26] Op.cit. Jeruchim and Shapiro, pp. 86–88.

married a short time later and established one of the first and foremost dancing schools and touring companies in the country. As the name of their company suggests, they were considered as a single unit. Their marriage was a stormy one; two enormous egos were constantly in conflict. When they separated in 1931, the Denishawn company, which had achieved significant success and critical acclaim, dissolved. Shawn established a company of men dancers at Jacob's Pillow and St. Denis maintained the school in New York and continued working as a solo performer.

George Balanchine and Gelsey Kirkland exemplify an enmeshed relationship in the ballet world. Beginning in 1960 she studied at his School of American Ballet and, at the age of fifteen, he selected her to enter the corps of the New York City Ballet. Kirkland became a soloist at sixteen and a principal dancer at eighteen. Her rise in Balanchine's company was meteoric. On the basis of this information, it would seem that their relationship followed a supportive father-daughter model. However, in her book, *Dancing on My Grave*, Kirkland points to behavioral peculiarities which suggest an unhealthy situation. She quotes Balanchine's demands for excessive thinness on the part of female dancers: "'Must see the bones.' ...Mr. B did not seem to consider beauty a quality that must develop from within the artist; rather he was concerned with outward signs such as body weight. His emphasis was responsible in part for setting the style that has led to some of the current extremes in American ballet. I allowed him to use me to that end by trusting his advice. He did not merely say, 'Eat less.' He said repeatedly, 'Eat nothing.'"[27]

She also writes of his adherence to a policy of submissiveness on the part of all company members. "Contrary opinions threaten the integrity of the company. Balanchine solved these problems by forbidding dissent. That was his privilege, but he abused that privilege to the point of discouraging even the most innocent question. He often invited those who did not approve of the way he ran his theatre to leave. The problem was, there seemed to be no place to go. ...The problem I have experienced in the ballet world is that free discussion has been inhibited by idol worship and prejudice, by the pressures for success, by the fears of failure within the profession of dance. ..."The difficulty with Balanchine... was that he did not think women were capable of engaging him in ideas, or that Americans were capable of understanding his Russian homeland. We hurt each other in many ways."[28]

---

[27] Kirkland, Gelsey. *Dancing on My Grave*. New York: Doubleday, 1986, p. 57.

[28] Ibid., p. 72.

Life Mentors

A life mentor is someone who sees a person through many stages and passages, never losing interest in his/her development. Some mentors work independently, while others are associated with organizations that facilitate passing on history and technical knowledge through their structures. The Dance Notation Bureau is such an organization and is one in which women have successfully used networking skills to develop and continue the mission. Muriel Topaz, director of the Dance Notation Bureau from 1979 to 1985, has mentored many students. Leslie Rotman, certified notator for 10 years and now director of re-staging at the bureau, describes the time-honored tradition of learning the profession from an older, more experienced woman. She completed her formal studies under Topaz, after which came the time for hands-on learning in the form of an apprenticeship. An apprenticeship is not done in isolation. As an educational process an apprenticeship works because it is within the context of a relationship whereby the mentor and the protégée identify with each other and share values. The protégée wants to learn and the mentor enjoys teaching such a willing student.

"When I finished notator training, Mickey (Muriel) hired me on a free-lance basis to do a very difficult Murray Louis project. I had to notate it from his company and then teach it to the Hamburg ballet. It was trial by fire. I felt terrified by the size of the project but Mickey pushed me beyond what I thought I could do and I did it. She gave me a chance and I owe my career to her. I not only admire her professionally, but use this unusually talented person as my personal example. If I face a sticky problem, I ask, 'What would Mickey do?' Now, I'm 40 and we respect each other as colleagues and we are both Fellows of the International Council of Kinetography Laban.[29]

Ann Hutchinson Guest, Helen Priest Rogers, Eve Gentry and Janey Price founded the Dance Notation Bureau in 1940. From the outset, students studying at the bureau were given opportunities to grow and to try projects of interest. Current executive director Ilene Fox continues the mentoring model she experienced with teacher/mentor Topaz, whose investment has paid off; both Rotman and Fox have taken on positions of administrative and artistic responsibility and continue the work of the bureau. Were it not for this kind of mentoring, the bureau would not exist.

Becoming a life mentor is the last step in the mentoring cycle. It requires that a woman see herself in the role of mentor, that she get a sense of satisfaction from developing others and feel rewarded when counseling,

---

[29] Phone interview and written statement, 1993.

nurturing and promoting others. Above all, a life mentor honestly and accurately understands her unique place in society and in her work. She has a vision for the future, realized in part through her relationship with her protégées.

Like Topaz, Bella Lewitzky easily assumed the role of life mentor to many, personifying the qualities that define good mentorship. In Lewitzky's own development, she recalls modern dance pioneer Lester Horton and his life-long influence on her dance career: "The apprenticeship I had with Lester happened when I was quite young. I was in my teens and I thought everyone learned technique, learned to dance and to perform in this fashion. What I didn't realize was that this man was building a technique directly on my body. I had no prior experience that would have prepared me to make a judgment about how I was learning. Because the technique was built on me, it felt extremely comfortable. Then he made ballets for me and I thought that was the way everybody grew in the world of dance. I didn't know it was extraordinary.

"Lester never said, 'Bella, I'm developing you.' We never had that kind of dialogue. He created approximately fifteen ballets for me which I took as a matter of course. I became Lester's tool, his physical voice, both for a technique and for his repertory. At the end of the fifteenth year of working with him I could extend what he would start because I knew where he would want to go.

"Eventually, as our relationship evolved, he asked me to coach. His training program was quite wonderful. Lester taught choreography to anyone who ever went through that school or was in his company. We had technique classes, partnering, composition, as well as art, current events, mask-making, costuming, lighting, set design and music." Interactions outside the professional arena typify a life-mentoring relationship. Horton taught Lewitzky more than just professional dance: "I learned from Lester how to make Christmas cards and how to cook. Lester was an extremely inventive man. The studio was always abuzz with artists or actors who would come to visit."[30]

Bella Lewitzky is also the biological mother of dancer/choreographer/teacher Nora Reynolds. The apprenticeship Lewitzky experienced with Horton affected the way she mentored her own daughter. "If ever a mother had a hands-off relationship with her daughter, this is the one. She grew up around art but I tried meticulously to let her make her own decision about dancing. I didn't make her life simpler by using my influence. She is an exquisite dancer, a beautiful teacher, and is developing into a very

---

[30] Personal interview, September, 1991.

interesting choreographer. This year I have taken a piece of her choreography into my repertoire. Isn't that wonderful? Both of us were so excited."[31]

Nora Reynolds, former member of the Lar Lubovitch and Bella Lewitzky dance companies and currently an independent choreographer on the dance faculty of University of New Mexico, speaks about her mother as her mentor. "When you consider our two personalities, I'm very much like my mother. There is and was a loving sense of where the boundaries are. I look back at photos of her teaching me as a little girl. She may have been a hands-off mother, but there I was in a leotard.

"I was encouraged to find dance on my own. When I went to North Carolina School of the Arts I had some excellent teachers, but the training wasn't as good as Bella's. When I joined Bella's company I learned how to be an expressive dancer, physically and musically capable. She teaches the subtle information inherent in each movement. At this point in my career, I like her to see my work and I send her videos when she can't see live performances. She gives excellent critiques, telling me why something works or why it doesn't even though our taste is different. I feel she helps me develop my choreographic ideas. She is gutsy, brave and a dynamic role model."[32]

Joan Myers Brown considers Katherine Dunham her life mentor. "Katherine Dunham was the inspiration for much of what I do now and how I do it. Dunham made it possible for me to conceive of Philadanco. During the 1930's she toured sixty countries with an unsubsidized company. I stay in touch with her regularly, going to St. Louis for advice, sitting by her side to learn her managerial and political skills. I also bring Ms. Dunham to my dancers in Philadelphia to benefit from her wisdom and give them a connection to history."[33]

Symbolic Mentors

The influence of symbolic mentorship is felt in all areas of the dance world: administration, choreography, education, performance and scholarship. Unlike other types of mentoring relationships, symbolic mentors do not engage in daily contact with protégés or even necessarily know them personally. Symbolic mentors provide motivation and inspiration through

---

[31] Ibid.

[32] Phone interview, May 17, 1993.

[33] Personal interview, January, 1993.

the example of their lives. Dance matriarchs have served as symbolic mentors for generations.

Anna Pavlova was a nineteenth century symbol of female perfection. Pavlova's work as the director and choreographer of a ballet company continues to be a significant positive force although perceptions of her physicality and performance technique have been modified in response to contemporary ballet standards. Margot Fonteyn is legendary for her ability to develop sensitively interpreted roles. An impressive technician, she embodied the courtly grace and dignity upon which ballet tradition rests. After her retirement from the stage, she embarked on a career as a writer and created a new image for herself as a spokesperson for dance. In both her book *The Magic of Dance* and the accompanying video, she was transformed from a stage personality into a popular ambassador for dance worldwide. Agnes de Mille, with her fiercely American pioneering spirit, challenged the boundaries of ballet and incorporated a broader vocabulary, drawing from American social and modern dance and creating a new genre of theater dance. The roles she created in *Rodeo, Fall River Legend* and the landmark musical *Oklahoma!* defined women as self-actualized. Contemporary female choreographers have seen her as a symbolic mentor as they continue their own investigations of women's roles.

Isadora Duncan was a significant symbolic mentor to Ellen Forman (1945–1990), a Philadelphia dancer and choreographer. Forman devoted her professional life to studying all aspects of Duncan's work and life. "Duncan combined intellect and emotion in her choreography, writing and life. The dichotomy between these two in our culture is my own struggle. Duncan has inspired me to pursue my own work involving dance, writing and teaching. What kind of intellectual education are we giving our dancers? Regrettably, young students often do not have much of an intellectual life. Duncan understood the importance of forging links among dance, other arts and the intellect. I follow her example."[34]

Since their life spans didn't overlap, Forman never had the opportunity to meet Duncan. Some women are more fortunate. Judith Jamison was inspired by encountering Pearl Primus, who became one of her symbolic mentors. "When I was ten years old I attended a lecture/demonstration at the University of Pennsylvania given by Pearl Primus. She talked about her own work as well as her commitment to African dance and culture. Pearl Primus, Katherine Dunham, and the American ballerina Janet Collins all had a great deal of influence on how I thought about myself as a

---

[34] American Dance Guild Conference, panel discussion, June, 1989.

Black woman artist. They influenced me to have enough gall to go forth and do whatever I wanted to do. These very strong women talked about history, Africa, and the power of women. They were continuing traditions which provided the links for me between history and the future."[35]

Thousands of young students all over the world are profoundly touched by the work, words, and wisdom of female dance pioneers who they now know only through films, books, and their studio experiences with their own teachers. The movement vocabulary some pioneers developed in response to the capabilities of female bodies became central to choreographic visions in their time. The scholarship and administrative skills of other women established models of excellence which have been inspirational to succeeding generations. Today, these older generations of artists serve as symbolic mentors to students as they develop their own careers in dance.

---

[35] American Dance Guild Conference, Keynote Address, June, 1989.

PART II

MATRIARCHS

Matriarchs, pioneers, and history-making iconoclasts who influenced the course of twentieth century dance have been instrumental not only in passing on dance traditions but also in serving as personal repositories for this often unpreserved art form. "Matriarchs" spotlights three artists and their work from three different and distinct styles of dance. Each artist seized the opportunities available to her in her time, and in doing so, forged a path that allowed women who followed greater freedom. "A Portrait of Catherine and Dorothie Littlefield," written by Ann Barzel, draws on her personal knowledge of these two visionary ballet leaders. The Littlefield Ballet and its dancers provided the basis for George Balanchine's first company and school in New York. The Littlefields were early models in the United States of independent female choreographers, company directors and performers. One of the leading pioneers in dance in Argentina is featured in an interview with Stephanie Reinhardt, "Renate Schottelius: Dance at the Bottom of the World in Argentina." This South American matriarch's renown as a teacher helped to ignite legions of dancers and to develop modern dance in her country. Bella Lewitzky was the first woman to create and sustain a modern dance company on the West Coast of the United States. In "Making My Way in Dance," she reveals the artistic environment that nurtured her and shaped her far-reaching and inspirational career.

A PORTRAIT OF CATHERINE AND DOROTHIE LITTLEFIELD
Ann Barzel

The Littlefields of Philadelphia were a force in the world of American ballet in the 1930s and 1940s, an era marked by a ferment of dance ideas, and the recognition that dance was taking a place in the cultural life of the nation. The Littlefields were active. They were pioneers. They made waves.

They were a family, united in their involvement in dance, and, as they often declared, they were stage-struck. The father, James Littlefield (Big Jim), although not directly involved, was interested in the ballet activities of his wife and his brood. His business as a film distributor put him into the theater world. His wife Caroline, maiden name Doebele, known as Mommie to scores of dancers, trained as a concert pianist, including a stint at the Paris Conservatory. She had enough dance training and dance experience to conduct a dance school. The Littlefield children were Catherine, Jimmy, Dorothie and Carl. Jimmy had a career as the conductor of a popular orchestra and he wrote popular music. Catherine was the director of the company known as the Littlefield Ballet or the Philadelphia Ballet, of which she was also leading dancer and principal choreographer. Dorothie was ballet mistress of the company and a principal dancer. Carl, an athlete, was drawn into dance, one can say, inevitably.

Caroline Littlefield had been brought up in a religious environment. Her husband James introduced her to the wonder world of theater. At first it was from the audience, but when the Philadelphia Civic Opera Company recruited supernumeraries and extras from among the subscribers, she was soon behind the footlights and "walking on" in the opera ballets. The ballet master was Romulus Carpenter, whose European training was along traditional lines. Caroline studied with Carpenter, and, although she started too late to achieve virtuosity, she received a basic training. She danced in the opera ballet, eventually attaining solos, including the role of the Spanish doll in *Fairy Doll*.

Caroline Littlefield's dance school, which trained dancers for the company, started accidentally. It grew out of the recreational classes that were part of the social program of a women's club. A professional ballet master could not be secured so Mrs. Littlefield was the teacher. Among the youngsters who were trained in the school was her daughter Catherine.

When the Philadelphia Junior League presented a musical revue *Why Not*, Caroline Littlefield directed the dances and teen-age Catherine danced. Florenz Ziegfeld, Jr., who had lent costumes for the show, came to see how they were used. He found pretty young Catherine talented and engaged her to be one of six little girls in *Sally*, starring Marilyn Miller on Broadway.

That was in December, 1922. While in New York, to hone her classical technique Catherine studied with Russian ballet master Ivan Tarasoff. After *Sally* she danced in several Broadway shows — *Annie Dear*, *Kid Boots*, *Louis XIV*, and for fourteen weeks in the Roxy Theater (a film-cum-stage-show theater) as soloist in an elaborate production of Ravel's *La Valse*.

Meanwhile, Caroline Littlefield was having success with opera ballet. Having proved herself in a production of *Aida*, she was invited to take charge of the ballet of the Philadelphia Civic Opera, and later of an Italian company with a larger repertoire. She realized it was more than she could handle and Catherine was drafted to help. The latter, while still in New York, prepared for this type of theater dance by studying with Luigi Albertieri, concentrating on the choreography of the opera ballets at La Scala in Milan, with which Albertieri had been connected. Then she went to Europe and studied with Leo Staats, director of the ballets in the Paris Opera. In Paris Catherine also studied with former Imperial Russian ballerina Lubov Egorova, to whom she returned several times in the following years for further study. At this time she also made the acquaintance of the Paris Opera Ballet's leading ballerina Lucienne Lamballe, who became a close friend.

The Littlefields entered the world of dance through opera ballet, and it was the foundation of what became the Littlefield Ballet. Catherine came to it with respect for the medium, and a will to make the dance episodes in the operas theatrically exciting. She was very much a novice when she created her first choreography for an opera ballet. In an interview she told how she tried to cover up her lack of inspiration by directing the same combination of steps to be performed in different directions, hoping the movements looked different from a new angle. In due time, with Mommie at the piano urging and criticizing, Catherine developed beyond this primitive choreographic device. She soon got the drift, not only of putting together academic steps, but of originating movements and plotting designs.

In addition to her duties as choreographer, Catherine was the leading dancer. The ballet group consisted of the advanced students in Caroline Littlefield's school. They become experienced performers and branched out from opera ballet and took on engagements for social organizations.

James Littlefield had died, and financial affairs were precarious in the Depression era. The school became important as the family's chief source of livelihood. It outgrew its location on Locust Street and moved to 1815

Ludlow, an address familiar to many dancers for the next decades. Catherine taught and Mommie was accompanist, but from her place at the piano her quick eye caught all that went on, and she sometimes called directions and made corrections. Professional dancers such as William Dollar, Douglas Coudy, and Jack Potteiger came to the classes and took part in performances.

By the later 1920s the Littlefields were identified with opera ballet and Catherine and her group were invited to be the ballet for the prestigious Philadelphia Grand Opera, which was affiliated with the Curtis Institute of Music. The list of benefactors included the wealthy Curtis Boks and Leidys. Catherine was an ornament of the opera. A poster for the 1931 season announced the opera *Carmen* would be graced by "Catherine Littlefield, première danseuse." Younger sister Dorothie, who had been studying in Paris with Volinine, Preobrajenska and Egorova, came home and joined the group.

During the 1931–32 season the opera ballet was entrusted to present Ravel's *L'Heure Espagnole,* and Catherine's choreography was praised. In 1932 the Philadelphia Grand Opera gave the young ballet director a most special assignment — to create the choreography for *H.P.,* a spectacular ballet conceived by Mexican artists Carlos Chavez and Diego Rivera. Chavez composed the music, Rivera designed the settings and costumes, and the two artists collaborated on the libretto, which spotlighted the socioeconomic situation of the Western Hemisphere.

The ballet aimed to show that the natural assets, the fruit and fish of the tropical south, when combined with the machinery and enterprise of the north, would result in a richer life for everybody. *H.P.* or horse-power, symbolized Man the powerful who, "in his plenitude of intellect and physical power" would bring about the synthesis of the gifts of the north and south.[1]

---

[1] The role of H.P. or Man required a heroic male dancer, and for this Catherine brought from Paris tall and brawny Alexis Dolinoff, who had danced in the last seasons of the Diaghilev Ballet and with the Ida Rubinstein and Pavlova companies.

The ballet was in four elaborately costumed scenes. Scene I introduced HP/Man in the rhythmic format of the Machine Age. Dolinoff in this role was abetted by an energetic ensemble in syncopated movement. Scene II depicted a cargo ship at sea, symbol of commerce between north and south. The dances were gymnastic, based on setting-up exercises by sailors showing off acrobatic skills. In contrast to their vigor was the languor of the tropics as seductive and sensual mermaids and sirens boarded the ship. Dorothie Littlefield led a band of guitar-twanging senoritas who, as described in the program note, danced a hot-blooded tango "swept by pleasures of syncopated dance." A school of superhuman-sized fish accompanied the mermaids and senoritas, their bulky costumes a choreographic problem.

In Scene III the ship was at dock in a harbor, loaded with "a plenitude of the South's fruits for the North." The "fruits in abundance," dressed in gaudy papier-mâché costumes, tried to cavort in a space crowded with swaying palm trees and "natives selling wares."

The event, presented on March 31, 1932 in Philadelphia's Metropolitan Auditorium, commanded wide attention. In spite of bad weather, a Pullman car of New Yorkers came to Philadelphia. It was front-page news in the New York *Times*. There was also a music review plus an article by the recently established dance critic John Martin, in which he commended Catherine Littlefield for her efforts. He commented that in an era of revived dance art, this event garnered more attention than Stravinsky's *Apollo*, given its premiere within the same time frame. Martin did mention the imbalance prescribed by the libretto, which set one male dancer, HP, to compete with 114 musical instruments. Catherine Littlefield, an ex-Ziegfeld girl, and Dolinoff, an unknown ballet dancer, were no match publicity-wise for fair-haired idol Leopold Stokowski and international celebrities Rivera and Chavez.

The ballet *H.P.* was never repeated and the distinguished collaboration had been forgotten by dance history. Bruised but unbeaten, Catherine Littlefield and her group went on to more amenable kinds of dance. Due to the Depression the Philadelphia Grand Opera ceased to exist. Catherine realized that she had a group of trained dancers, whom she wanted to keep together and to keep dancing even if there was no opera to pay regular salaries. She developed a repertoire of one-act ballets and divertissements, and for the next three years she sought and found engagements to keep the dancers busy. They presented programs for schools, musical societies, political meetings and, most profitably, as the "live show" or "prologue" preceding motion pictures in the Fox, Earle, Stanley and Mastbaum Theaters.

Although the music contained dance themes, the costumes were more interesting as art than functional for dance. Catherine did manage to set the tree-costumed dancers swaying to a section the composer marked "Zandunga." The composer's direction at one point was, "Enter three Pineapples." There was little the choreographer could do for the three enormously costumed fruits, but let them waddle and join the Bananas for a dance.

Scene IV was the City of Industry. Against a backdrop of skyscrapers, HP (Dolinoff) directed workers and machines. He urged them to more effort in the cliché of the era, a "machine dance." Graphically costumed dancers represented among other machines a Ventilator and a Gas Pump. Dorothie, as a Flapper, led the "dance of the age of the automobile." The libretto by Diego Rivera mentioned the expected "revolt against the despotism of machinery." Capitalism, represented by a Stock-Ticker, was panic-stricken as revolting workers opened a safe labeled "Natural Resources" from which tumbled "Gold, Silver, Iron, Fruit." In the peaceful finale, workers went back to simple activities, men and raw materials blending for the common good to the rhythm of H.P.

The orchestra played during the scene changes and it was clear the music was the important element. Inexperienced Catherine Littlefield was swamped by impossibilities. She followed directions and made no demands, although it is recorded that at the dress rehearsal, faced with the myriad problems, at one point she simply knocked her head against a drum.

The dancers were developing. Caroline Littlefield encouraged several of the young men to go to Paris during the summer's lull to polish their technique. William Dollar, who was brought to Philadelphia by Mordkin, found his way to the Littlefield school and had been recruited for performances. He told of a summer in the early 1930s in Paris. "Mommie lent us the money for the trip, to be paid back from our salaries during the following season. In Paris she rented a large apartment where we all stayed. There was a piano and a large room to practice what we had learned at each lesson. We took classes with Volinine, Preobrajenska, Egorova. After every class we had to write notes on the lesson — the combinations, the barre work, the corrections. Mommie also saw to it that we went to concerts, dance events and art galleries."

Early in 1934 George Balanchine, who had been enticed to America by Lincoln Kirstein and Edward Warburg, conferred with Catherine and Dorothie Littlefield, whom he had met in Paris. He was aware of their involvement in ballet and the respect they commanded in French dance circles. He surmised that the Littlefield school, administered by such knowledgeable and able artists, would be producing dancers with secure foundations in the art. He told the Littlefield sisters the big plans, including the financial backing there was for an American Ballet, and that he was seeking well-trained dancers for the company. He had found young dancers in the Paris schools of Preobrajenska and Kshesinska, who became the stars of the popular new Ballets Russes de Monte Carlo, and he expected to find young talents in Philadelphia to be his American stars.

Dorothie brought a group of Littlefield students to New York to audition for Balanchine. Six chosen girls were given scholarships and sustenance stipends. They were the foundation of the School of American Ballet, established first in Hartford, Connecticut, and moved later to a studio on Madison Avenue in New York.

The Philadelphia dancers whom Balanchine accepted were Holly Howard, Heidi Vossler, Hortense Kharklinch, Helen Leitch, Joan McCracken and Audrey Girard. They figured prominently in Balanchine's early American performances. They were outstanding in the new school's advanced class and impressed the romper- and tunic-clad outlanders with their sophisticated European-style classroom attire. Soon sleek black tights were de rigueur for even the most naive students.

The Philadelphia scholarship students danced leading roles in Balanchine's first New York season, the 1935 American Ballet that played in the Adelphi Theater. (Joan McCracken had left the Balanchine-directed school. She danced with the Littlefield Ballet for several years, then had a distinguished career in Broadway musicals.)

Dorothie Littlefield maintained a strong Balanchine connection for many years. She taught often at the School of American Ballet and one of her protégées was Patricia Wilde. She reported that Balanchine told her that at auditions, when a girl was pretty and could dance, he knew she was from the Littlefield school in Philadelphia.

Tracing the Littlefield-Balanchine relations has diverted the Littlefield story from its main road. With the debacle of the Balanchine-Kirstein-Warburg American Ballet of 1935, Catherine thought it tragic to abandon the idea of a full-scale American ballet just when classical ballet was making headway with the successes of the Ballets Russes de Monte Carlo. She still had an active group of well-trained and experienced dancers and she decided, with them, to enter the classical ballet arena. With financial and deeply loyal backing by wealthy husband Philip Leidy, in late 1935 Catherine Littlefield announced the formal organization of the Littlefield Ballet. The nucleus of the personnel was the group that had been with her in the Philadelphia Opera. Alexis Dolinoff was designated the premier danseur and well-known Edward Caton was engaged as a principal. (He also choreographed a couple of ballets.) The contingent of male soloists listed Thomas Canon, who had trained in the Littlefield School, augmented by seasons in Paris. There were also experienced dancers Douglas Coudy and Jack Potteiger, who had danced in the 1935 New York season of Balanchine's American Ballet.

Although the new company assigned no titles, Catherine was the artistic director, the resident choreographer and the première danseuse. Dorothie was a principal and ballet mistress. Both Littlefields conducted rehearsals and gave classes. Mommie on the sidelines was chief consultant and advisor. Among the leading young ladies were Joan McCracken, Karen Conrad and Miriam Golden.

Catherine, aware of the importance of virile male dancers, always had an eye out for possible recruits, especially at athletic events. A champion boxer, a football player and a dock worker were soon signed up. Carl, the youngest Littlefield, had avoided ballet. He was athletic, especially successful at swimming and diving. The arched feet developed in diving helped his line as a classicist when, impressed by the respect garnered by the ballet company, he joined up. He worked hard to catch up and was soon in the corps de ballet. He moved through the ranks and became a first-rate classical dancer and fine partner, especially for Catherine. To avoid the appearance of a Littlefield-dominated enterprise, he was listed as Carl Cleighton during the first seasons.

The company, known during the first months of its existence as the Littlefield Ballet, after much consideration decided to be the Philadelphia Ballet. The announcement as published in a program stated: "After mature consideration in response to numerous suggestions and requests of our interested friends, the Littlefield Ballet Co., which was placed on a permanently organized basis this fall, has determined to continue its activities henceforward under the name The Philadelphia Ballet Company. In so doing, the company is fully cognizant of the great responsibility which the use of the name 'Philadelphia' entails. Under the personal direction of Catherine Littlefield and her corps of assistants, your company will strive to continue to present to the dance and music public of Philadelphia the best in the classical and modern-classical dance. New ballets will be produced from time to time with music specially written for dance, and it is hoped in the very near future, among other things, to present what the management of your company sincerely believes to be true American Ballet. The aim of your company will be to give performances not only in large but small auditoriums at popular prices, in order to develop in all sections of the city and its vicinity a ballet-conscious public. In contemplation for the coming spring is a presentation of the full ballet 'Daphnis and Chloe' by Maurice Ravel, in three acts, and the American ballet previously referred to, for which music is now being written."

After this announcement, the building of a repertoire was begun. A number of the divertissements the opera ballet group had been dancing were retained. Among the items were *Tarantella* (Massenet), *Norwegian Dance* (Grieg), *Bartered Bride Suite* (Smetana), *Mazurka* (Glinka), and a suite of dances from *The Nutcracker*. Catherine began to choreograph new one-act ballets. The first program consisted of *Soirée Galante* (Chopin), *Minstrels* (Debussy) and a divertissement of several solo and group dances. For the next three seasons (1936–37, 1937–38, 1938–39) this embryo ballet director created an impressive repertoire.[2]

---

[2] Following is a list of the major works choreographed between 1936–1939: *Soirée Galante* (Chopin) was a suite of classical dances in romantic style; Nocturne, Valse, Mazurka, Grand Adagio, Valse Brilliante. Unlike *Les Sylphides*, instead of one male dancer, there were sixteen. *Minstrels* (Debussy) was a flirtation. The cast consisted of a young girl, her two friends and their fiancées, a spinster chaperone and a wandering minstrel. The costumes were by S. Pinto.

 The Fairy Doll was Catherine's version of that Pavlova favorite *Puppenfee* to music by Josef Bayer. The set was a Viennese doll shop and the characters included Spanish, French, Japanese, Tyrolean, Porcelain, Harlequin and Columbine dolls, a mischievous Jack-in-the-Box and the magic Fairy Doll. Catherine usually danced the Fairy Doll.

 Bolero, to the popular Ravel music, was in the expected pseudo-Spanish style. A pair of dancers, usually Dorothie and Dolinoff, were the central figures, and, as the music increased in volume, additional groups of dancers were introduced. The costumes included long trains reminiscent of the Spanish *bata*.

Although Catherine was prolific, from the beginning she sought guest choreographers and encouraged the choreographic efforts of company members. Dolinoff, Caton and Potteiger contributed ballets, and, notably, there was guest choreographer Lazar Galpern. Galpern had studied ballet in Russia, and was linked with avant-garde circles in Moscow. As a modern

---

Fête Champetre with music by Grêtry, Lully and Rameau had an 18th century setting, the Petit Trianon. The action included games and a masquerade in the spirit of Marie Antoinette. The Queen, masquerading as a milk-maid, had a couple of real milk-maids on hand to confuse her lover. The ballet included a pastorale, a picnic and a game of blindman's bluff. There was an Eros who shot arrows at the wrong lovers and a series of Watteau-like tableaux and tongue-in-cheek humor. Catherine usually danced the Queen, Dolinoff, a Chevalier, Dorothie a milk-maid, and Edward Caton a gardener.

Viennese Waltz, to Johann Strauss music, was in three scenes. In the first scene outside a café, girl ballet students flirted with uniformed Hussars. One girl and a Hussar were particularly attracted to one another, first love. Scene Two was an audition in which the girl was chosen for the Royal Opera. Scene Three was "years later" in the palace of the archduke. The girl, now a star, notices her Hussar of the first scene among the guards. She decides her career is more important and she does not acknowledge him — "love is a broken dream." The ballet school scene was not only Catherine's way of displaying her well-trained dancers, but evidence of her deep love of danse d'école.

Parable in Blue, to music by Martin Gabowitz, was a nod to contemporary mores. The setting was a penthouse party to which came three uninvited guests — Fate, Fortune and Sorrow. They altered the destinies of guests. Fate brought two lovers together. Fortune led a boy to be tempted with riches by the hostess. Sorrow brought the entire party to reality.

Poème, to Ravel's *Pavane Pour un Enfant Défunte*, had a romantic scenario with a sad ending. Caton was a poet whose Inspiration, Joan McCracken, was killed by Executioner Dolinoff. Mournful Men and Maidens in Black were the ensemble.

The Snow Queen was created to serve those revenue blessings, children's matinees. The commissioned score was composed by Murray Cutter, who conducted the premiere. The ballet was based on the Hans Christian Andersen fairy tale about the boy Kay who became naughty and wayward when a splinter entered his eye. He runs off with the imperious Snow Queen and various unsavory characters. Rescued by playmate Gerda, when the splinter falls from his eye he sees again his good friends. The role of the boy Kay was first danced by Karen Conrad; later Dorothie was beguiling in the role.

The Rising Sun was a pièce d'occasion, a ballet history of Old Philadelphia choreographed by Catherine Littlefield in December 1937 to mark the 150th anniversary of the ratification of the Pennsylvania Constitution. In pageant format, among the historic happenings depicted were the arrival of William Penn and a Tory ball. The then Mayor S. Davis Wilson and prominent city and state politicos were present.

Let the Righteous Be Glad was choreographed by Catherine and Dorothie to spirituals arranged by Jeno Donath. This was in the 1930s and the dancers in black-face, performing seriously, were not considered offensive. There was not a whisper of parody. Catherine, with her customary thinking-big, included an African jungle scene and an Arab slave market. This was a serious essay, a statement that Blacks were in America and making contributions.

Bach Classical Suite had some of Catherine's most inventive choreography. It was a plotless piece in five parts.

dancer and choreographer he was the dance director in Germany's Dusseldorf Theater, where he staged many ballets. He was brought to America for the opening of Radio City Music Hall, but was considered a misfit and let go. Catherine had seen him in *The Romance of a People*, a Jewish pageant in Philadelphia, and invited him to the Littlefield studio. The classical ballerina and the modern dancer became friends. When the formation of the Littlefield Ballet was announced, Galpern came to Catherine with ideas for her company. She listened and accepted him as a choreographer. In an interview he praised her artistic liberalism. "This was a most courageous move. I was a modern dancer. Artists were usually limited in outlook. Miss Littlefield as a dancer and a choreographer has an amazing breadth of mind."

With a varied repertoire the Philadelphia Ballet was presented in many venues. Its mentors knew that to make an impact, the dancers must dance often. The company had high visibility, appearing at such contrasting spots as the proscenium stage of the Academy of Music and the makeshift performing space of a ballroom of the Bellevue Stratford Hotel. There were also appearances at the State Teachers College in West Chester, at Haverford Township High School, at the Theater of Plays and Players and many, many more. Presenters or sponsors were the Women's Republican Club, the Pennsylvania Athletic Club, the Episcopalian Club, the Rotary Club, the Youth Recitals of the YMCA, Manufacturers and Bankers Club, *et al.* These are enumerated to make one realize the studied campaign to make a wide public aware of the presence of the Philadelphia Ballet. Catherine and the company were getting recognition. Catherine was awarded the Pennsylvania Arts and Sciences gold medal in recognition of her creative work in developing a distinctive American arts organization.

Sometimes the company danced to a lone piano played by Florence Weber, and there were special occasions with the Philadelphia Symphony. A special occasion with a full orchestra conducted by Saul Caston was the premiere of the ballet to Ravel's *Daphnis and Chloe*, which Catherine considered her best work. The myth of the beleaguered shepherd lovers was in three scenes. Catherine danced the role of Chloe. Greek dancer Iolas Coutsoudis danced the first performances of Daphnis. Edward Caton was the rival Dorcon and Dolinoff the pirate Braxis. A choreographed combat between Caton and Dolinoff was a popular scene.

In July of 1936, though not yet in existence one year, the Philadelphia Ballet took its two Ravel ballets, *Daphnis and Chloe* and *Bolero*, to New York's Lewisohn Stadium for Manhattan's critical audience. The ballet drew a crowd of 10,000 the first night. John Martin wrote in the New York *Times*, "To Catherine Littlefield must go great credit for the way in which she has whipped the young company into shape and the generally workmanlike character of its performance… *Daphnis et Chloe* is perhaps not the best choice for the New York premiere for it is a definitely dated work of the scarf-and-garland period. Miss Littlefield has not attempted to disguise this quality, but has utilized it frankly for what it is worth. Her choreography is crystal clear…The evening as a whole made an excellent impression and pointed the fact that not all of the important American dance world lies east of the Hudson."

The director of the Philadelphia Ballet always thought big. Her next venture was a full-length classic, *The Sleeping Beauty* to the great Tschaikovsky score. Catherine, in her studies with Egorova in Paris, had learned the Petipa choreography of the third act grand pas de deux and also the Bluebird pas de deux. Blithely she originated her own versions of the rest of the three acts. At the memorable premiere, Catherine danced the role of Princess Aurora, partnered by Alexis Dolinoff. The Bluebird episode was danced by Edward Caton and Marian Ross. Dorothie was the Rainbow Fairy (the re-christened Lilac Fairy), and a half-dozen Philadelphians destined to make dance history were the gift-bearing fairies. They were Karen Conrad, Joan McCracken, Miriam Golden, Dania Krupska, June Graham and Dorothie Littlefield. Lazar Galpern was the ceremonial Catalabutte and Caton (like Enrico Cecchetti, the Bluebird of the St. Petersburg premiere) doubled as the wicked fairy, Carabosse.

The premiere on February 11, 1937 was in the Academy of Music. Boris Goldovsky conducted the Curtis Symphony and the company of the usual 60 dancers had been augmented to a cast of 100. Balletomanes came from California as well as nearby New York. Audiences and critics were ecstatic. The Mordkin Ballet had staged a version of *The Sleeping Beauty* in Waterbury, Connecticut sans orchestra. This was the first American full-scale production. In the New York *Times* John Martin wrote, "That a ballet which has nothing fresher to tell than an old fairy tale… should prove so consistently interesting speaks well for Miss Littlefield and her spirited organization… she finds in the Princess Aurora role one admirably suited to her. Her daintiness of manner, her clean cut technique with its finely balanced pointes and brilliant beats and her general leanings toward the classic in style, have everything to work with." In July the Philadelphia Ballet presented this large-scale *Sleeping Beauty* in New York's Lewisohn Stadium; Alexander Smallens conducted the orchestra.

In the months between the February premiere of the classic and the New York presentation Catherine was very busy adding two American theme ballets, *Barn Dance* and *Terminal*, to the repertoire, for the company had been invited to dance in Paris as representative of American art in the 1937 Exposition of Arts and Technocracy in Modern Life.

Barn Dance, which became the company's signature ballet, had a score by Louis Gottschalk and John Powell, arranged by David Guion. The scenery and costumes were by S. Pinto. (There were two Pintos, A. and S., designing for the Philadelphia Ballet.) As its title explicitly states, this was a rural festival. The time was the mid or late 19th century, the place somewhere in the land. The material was American folk dance plus natural gestures expanded for the theater and dressed up with touches of classical ballet. The several scenes or episodes were: Preparation, Dances by groups of adults and children, Arrival of guests, Breakdown dance for one couple, Scandal — the Light Lady and City Slicker, Repentance, Rejoicing.

In *Barn Dance* the dancers let go and danced with the high spirits and the high energy that came to epitomize American ballet. The stage exploded with energy. Every dancer was an individual — a child, a deacon, a mother, a farmer, a farmhand. There were two outsiders, the Light Lady and the City Slicker. The Lady was a renegade daughter of the community. But after upsetting her compatriots, she repented her shocking ways and was taken back into the fold. Dorothie Littlefield and Tom Cannon always danced these roles.

Terminal, to a commissioned score by Herbert Kingsley, actually was in the works before the European tour was contracted. Catherine first approached then *Dance Magazine* editor Paul Milton with the idea in January of 1936, and he recommended composer Kingsley, who had provided suitable scores for several modern dancers. Catherine, who always acted immediately on suggestions, met Kingsley within days, recited the scenario about a railroad station with a stream of travelers coming and going. Kingsley liked the idea and agreed to compose the score to her specifications, in spite of the fact that he was on the point of leaving for a tour with Alfred Lunt and Lynn Fontanne in *Idiot's Delight*. He took on the commission and wrote the score as the play toured. He received from Catherine notes on tempo and texture of music for each scene. Coming in piecemeal, the needs of each part clearly described, the music fit. It was not classical. It was tuneful theater music with a surface gleam of jazz.

Terminal had its premiere in Paris and remained a popular item in the company repertoire. The set by A. Pinto was a railroad station, not unlike the cavernous Grand Central in New York. Resident in the terminal were porters, bootblacks and a newsboy. As each train came in, it disgorged a different group of passengers. From the Commuters Special came bustling businessmen, stenographers, office workers with brief cases. The train from Reno brought a bevy of brash ladies who performed the Dance of the Divorcees. Dialogue was a humorous dance by the Spinster, who asked a zillion questions of a beleaguered Information Clerk. The Dixie Limited brought families of African Americans from the South. (The 1990s would find the stereotypes of the Black family offensive, but in 1937 it was accepted in the spirit of the intended good-natured fun.) From the Train from the West (Las Vegas) stepped the Crooner, and a glamorous movie star, ready to be interviewed and pose for publicity, came on the Hollywood Special. The Honeymoon Express brought cooing couples.

Catherine, as the newsworthy cinema queen, displayed her great talent for comedy as she complied to the ridiculous requests of the photographers — posing with mixing bowl as a homebody, and in the swimsuit as the athletic all-American girl. Dorothie was a hyperactive Newsboy, with an ever higher grand jeté.

In the broad repertoire there were many roles, and the company developed dancers of individuality. The company that started with eighteen dancers kept adding personnel, and numbered sixty dancers through most of its life. There was stability in the retention and development of most of the original eighteen. More were added from the Littlefield school. Some dancers, particularly males, were accepted from the not very large pool of professionals who applied wherever there was work. And there was Catherine's addiction to athletic events for the purpose of discovering and recruiting likely males. Incidentally, the director-choreographer was "Catherine" to everyone, never "Miss Littlefield." And Caroline was "Mommie" to all. She accepted the name completely, even signed most letters "Mommie."

The technical level of the ladies in the Philadelphia Ballet ranged from good to excellent. The training that continued after acceptance in the company stressed correct placement, turnout and neat foot work. Not all these virtues were universal, but were present in decent degree. This company had no misfits to be hidden in the back row. Some of the gentlemen barely made it as classical dancers, but all had virile strength. If some lacked the niceties of well-pointed feet, all had good jumps and turns. They looked more like all-American boys than stereotypes of the ballet-prince. Very important, there was a company style, unaffected self-presentation, and exuberance. Frequent performances bred unselfconsciousness and this was especially true when performing the American-theme works in which much of the choreographic material was derived from familiar movements.

Catherine Littlefield, the première danseuse (prima ballerina was a title not yet in common use), as a product of much European training had a great regard for the formal danse d'école. She was not a virtuoso, but her dancing had purity and neatness. Of medium height, slim and with the dimensions of the ideal classical ballet body, she presented the proper image of the classical ballerina. Added to those gifts was her glamorous blonde beauty and a sense of authority.

Dorothie was a virtuoso, even when measured by the heightened standards of the 1990s. Her technique was polished to meticulous precision. She had perfect placement and turnout, well-arched feet that were never slack. Her extensions were fantastic and contributed to her fine line. And there was her high, smooth jump and brilliant batterie. Add to all these a sparkling personality. Even her dark eyes seemed to be dancing.

As mentioned, the company had a number of first-rate male dancers and there were talented young ladies such as Karen Conrad, Joan McCracken and Miriam Golden, who gave indications of the distinguished careers they had later with Ballet Theatre and on Broadway.

These were the dancers and the repertoire of the Philadelphia Ballet which was invited to Paris to represent America at the international exposition. The root of the idea for the company to dance abroad came from an idle remark made by Philip Leidy when in Paris on vacation. Dining with his wife and friends he remarked in a mood of clairvoyance, "Soon the Philadelphia Ballet will be dancing in Paris." Catherine perked up. As usual she followed through. In a subsequent conversation with Nadja, the Parisian correspondent for the *American Dancer* Magazine, Nadja advised the Philadelphian to talk to Paris-based impresario Arnold Meckel. Characteristically, Catherine, a doer, followed through. She came to see Meckel with a bundle of press clippings of her company's performances. He was impressed and came to Philadelphia to take a look, and he was further impressed. The result was that Meckel arranged for the Philadelphia Ballet to dance in Paris, Brussels, Deauville, and London. The repertoire could not include the large-scale *Sleeping Beauty*, but at the insistence of the impresario the two American theme ballets, *Barn Dance* and *Terminal*, were taken to Europe. There were also *Daphnis and Chloe, Bach Classical Suite, Aubade, Fairy Doll, Bolero, Viennese Waltz, Parable in Blue* and *Moment Romantique*. The last named was a Chopin piece, a remake of the earlier *Soirée Galante*. When the company was in Paris, the great choreographer Michel Fokine came to watch a rehearsal of the last named ballet, probably to check on whether it encroached on his *Les Sylphides*. He soon realized it didn't, and he left.

On May 14, 1937 sixty dancers, thirty-eight women and twenty-two men, boarded the *Ile de France* heading for Paris. A great crowd of well-wishers saw them off. There had been much publicity about the Philadelphia dancers going to Paris. One paper characterized the trip "In Isadora Duncan's footsteps." The company arrived in Paris at 11:30 P.M. and were greeted by manager Arnold Meckel, by veteran ballerina-teacher Lubov Egorova, by Paris Opera Ballet première danseuse Lucienne Lamballe and by many dignitaries. There were flowers and headlines. The arrival of an American ballet company was big news. One French paper headlined, "Hello, Catherine Littlefield." Photographs of the dancers graced front pages.

The Philadelphia Ballet danced in the Théâtre des Champs Elysées with the Paris Symphony for accompaniment. Members of the Garde Républicaine in red and silver uniforms stood at attention in the foyer and outside the theater. Inside were French premier Léon Blum and American Ambassador William Bullitt. The first number was *Barn Dance* (*"La Grange"* in Paris). It was greeted with cheers. Also danced were *Terminal* and *Moment Romantique*. The final bows were greeted with flowers and more flowers. The President of France sent champagne.

At subsequent performances the company danced *Daphnis and Chloe*, which was especially successful, the score played beautifully by the Paris Symphony. Composer Poulenc played the piano when *Aubade*, set to his music, was danced. The French adored *Terminal*; its satiric humor was to their taste. The reviews during the entire engagement were ecstatically laudatory. They appeared in the many French papers — *L'Echo de Paris*, *Le Petit Parisien*, *Excelsior*, *La Vie Parisienne*, *Paris Midi*, *L'Art Musical*, *Le Matin*, and, of course, the Paris edition of the New York *Herald-Tribune*. The French noted the specifically American elements in their style, "pleine de bonne volonté" or good natured. "Toutes les graces d'une éclate jeunesse," the graces of fresh youthfulness. There were frequent references to the good looks of "les jolies Américains." The newspaper *Figaro* published a tribute to the Philadelphia Ballet by Lucienne Lamballe of the Paris Opera Ballet. Critics mentioned "their synchronized movements... their humor... their accomplishment of difficult steps." Leading critic Jean Laurent commented on the American elements in the choreography and wrote of the exuberant youth of the dancers, "vibrant, refreshing to the viewer."

Distinguished critic Emile Vuillermoz wrote that the Philadelphians "have traditions of European ballet, but with American imprint." He found *Terminal* "exceptional... and in *Barn Dance*, a subject animated by remarkable vigor, spirit, virtuosity." Georges Auric in *Paris Soir* wrote, "Let us gladly acknowledge the great success of Catherine Littlefield's *Barn Dance*. This is simplicity itself and excellently designed." Not all reviews were positive. There was a negative voice which found "music hall elements" in *Barn Dance*. And there was the sour note of a dissenter who queried, "Why bring Americans when the Paris Opera has such a magnificent ballet?" The engagement was sold out. Audiences were made up of the expected ballet enthusiasts and the American compatriots living in or touring France. Many Frenchmen, intrigued by the publicity, came to see, and stayed to applaud.

Leaving Paris, the Philadelphia Ballet traveled first class by train for a week's engagement in Brussels. Performances were in the Royal Galleries Theatre. King Léopold in dress uniform attended on the second night, his first public appearance since the death of Queen Astrid. He was delighted with the first number, *Barn Dance*, applauded loudly and asked to meet Catherine and Dorothie. The Americans had been instructed in the protocol of curtsies. However, Catherine, costumed in tight slacks for the next ballet, *Terminal*, couldn't bend to the proper "low." She extended her hand and American style shook hands with the King of the Belgians.

The next stop, London, was approached with trepidation. The London public was known to be discriminating, and prejudiced in favor of Russian ballet. Their own company, the Sadler's Wells, was dancing in the home theater, and Ballets Russes de Monte Carlo was in the Royal Opera House at Covent Garden. The Philadelphia Ballet opened, not without misgivings, in the Hippodrome, a venue for popular offerings. As they say, the rest is history. The English adored the Philadelphians. In *Barn Dance* they found traces of their own folk dances. They appreciated the good dancing in *Moment Romantique* and enjoyed the humor of *Terminal*. London did not see *Daphnis and Chloe* because the Hippodrome's orchestra pit could not accommodate the 85 musicians required to do justice to the Ravel score. Famous dancers Irina Baronova, Alicia Markova, Léonide Massine, David Lichine, Tatiana Riaboushinska attended performances and came backstage to offer congratulations. Lady Astor brought a party of Englishmen to enjoy American ballet.

Arnold Haskell, England's leading dance critic, at first was a formidable roadblock. He had announced that the kindest thing he could do for these upstarts was to ignore them and spare them the harsh criticism they would deserve. Catherine prevailed on him to attend a rehearsal and he was overwhelmed. He climbed on the bandwagon and joined the cheering. He wrote paeans in newspapers and periodicals. Haskell devoted a chapter to the Philadelphia Ballet in his book *Dancing Around the World*. Among other things he wrote, "I missed them in America on purpose, having not sufficient faith to make the one-hour journey to Philadelphia from New York... Fokine, Massine, and Balanchine have been working for considerable periods in America, but it has taken an American woman to produce the first important work for American dancers to find favor both in Paris and London. The Russians have performed in America, taught in America and made money in America; the whole inspiration has come from them, but the Americans are showing the first tangible results. Catherine Littlefield is a very remarkable woman... instead of buying up some of the names discovered by Diaghilev, she has decided to discover for herself... she is a choreographer of very great promise — musical and essentially theatrical.... Her *Barn Dance* is a little masterpiece... Catherine is a dancer of charm, intelligence and strong personality... Dorothie Littlefield's virtuosity is appreciated." One racy London newspaper apprised the public in this headline, "Whoops, M'Dear: Football Players and Boxers Comprise a Ballet Company That Expects to Startle England"

The company was described as "Ballet from the wide-open spaces." Where the American press usually referred to the Philadelphia choreographer as "glamorous Catherine Littlefield," the English press emphasized another facet and dubbed her "the world's wittiest ballerina." Her outspoken style was compared to that of Ninette de Valois and praised for sensible ideas.

There were some reservations . . . "*Moment Romantique* is Americanized *Les Sylphides*" . . . The Choreography of *Terminal* descends to musical comedy". The smart magazines, *The Bystander* and the *London Sketch*, had spreads of photographs and, back in America, the press noted the European success of the Philadelphia Ballet.

Paul Longone, manager of the Chicago Civic Opera, saw the Philadelphia Ballet in Brussels and was charmed. When he learned that Catherine Littlefield had been directing and dancing in opera ballet for many seasons, he approached her on the possibilities of directing the ballet for the Chicago opera. She said it was possible if her company was hired along with herself. Longone agreed to the condition. The deal was that the company, as well as appearing in dance episodes in operas, would on the opera's off nights have the use of the Civic Opera House for all-ballet programs.

This arrangement was viewed with alarm in Chicago, where a more or less stable group of dancers had served in opera ballets under various ballet masters. The opera season was short and most of the Chicago dancers had other means of livelihood — the Federal Theater Project, teaching, etc. Some, on hearing of the new plans, were off to New York's Metropolitan Opera Ballet. But there were a few agitators, who in the name of civic loyalty made noises. Catherine met this problem head on. She held an audition and hired several Chicagoans. Her strategy of joining the opposition was disarming. She cooperated with Chicago organizations, gave free lectures for the Chicago Dance Council, taught classes for the Chicago Association of Dancing Masters, charmed all and won legions of admirers.

As usual Catherine had excellent relations with the press. She gave interviews airing her views on the qualifications of American dancers for classical ballet and on the importance of athletic male dancers. A frequent quote was "America is destined to produce the finest dancing the world has yet seen... Those with vision see a splendid future. Our aim is not only to present good ballet, but to provide good entertainment."

The company, reduced to 45 dancers, was now designated the Littlefield Ballet. The dancers caught the contagion of Catherine's adventurous attitude and went at the opera ballets with enthusiasm. The opera company presented many works that 1938 season — *La Traviata, Aida, Othello, Martha, Turandot, Tristan and Isolde, Tosca, Manon*. Catherine's past experiences with opera in Philadelphia served her well. She was familiar with the scores and could sing or hum the ballet music when an accompanist was not available. She knew thoroughly the stories of the operas, the atmosphere and how the dance episode fit the general scheme. Her dances suited the period and had theatrical substance. She did not treat the opera ballets as a minor chore of her Chicago season, and appeared personally in many of the operas.

An example of her wholehearted cooperation was her full company in the dances for *Aida*. She led the triumphal scene in minimal costume, her body covered with gold paint from headpiece to toeshoe. The dance perked up the opera, and the audience. As for the dancers, they took pride in being effective; it didn't matter that it took hours to clean up, and that paint clung to hair, eyebrows, fingernails for days. Catherine Littlefield not only took opera ballet seriously, she really liked it. She accepted the limitations of the opera stage as a challenge to her ingenuity and resourcefulness. She was not content to bring her dancers on stage for short sequences while the continuity of the drama stopped, then to shoo them off when the singing recommenced. Her dancers were on stage often, when not dancing, taking part in the action, adding color to the stage picture.

The Littlefield dancers danced wholeheartedly in the opera ballets, but it was in the seven all-ballet programs of their own repertoire that they gave their maximum. They were received with enthusiasm. Although the large Civic Opera House (3,600 seats) was not ever a sellout, there were audiences of a respectable size. The public was impressed with the technical ability of the company, particularly the brilliant dancing of Dorothie, who garnered a personal following. The repertoire had been increased by two more American-theme ballets — *Ladies' Better Dresses* and *Café Society*. The full-scale *Sleeping Beauty* was not taken on tour, but, in the manner of the Diaghlev Ballet, the third act was presented as *Aurora's Wedding*.

Ladies' Better Dresses, to a commissioned score by Herbert Kingsley and settings and costumes by Joy Michael, was one of what Catherine termed her "cartoons of American life." It satirized the fashion industry as it followed the evolution of a dress design, from its creation to its emergence as a popular item in department store bargain basements. This humorous ballet prepared the public for the premiere of one more American ballet, *Café Society*. There was much hoopla for this lavish joke. A score was commissioned from famous jazz composer Ferde Grofé, who conducted the premiere. The unimaginative costumes were by Carl Shaffer. The design for the set did not get program credit, at least not in the program for the world premiere which took place in Chicago's Civic Opera House on November 13, 1938. The piece was in the ballet-cartoon genre in which Catherine on several occasions successfully lampooned the social scene. The title, *Café Society*, identifies the era, late 1930s, early 1940s. The scene was the Cafe Too Too Too (222 on the entrance awning) and everything was too much, from the gentleman who was too drunk to the Debutante who was too bored and the Columnist who was too nosy. There was also a Pugilist and his Manager, a pair of sightseeing Newlyweds, Collegeboy Stags, a Party-Thrower, Society dames with paid escorts and visiting nobility — all contributing to the confusion. The ballet was a simple cartoon rather than the sharp criticism it could have been. The national press took notice of the lively goings-on in the ballet world. *Life* Magazine sent photographers for a multiple-page spread.

A good part of the Littlefield Ballet repertoire was danced that seven weeks in Chicago. *Barn Dance, Moment Romantique* and *Bach Classical Suite* were most popular. The Chicago press appreciated the company in both the operas and in the all-ballet repertoire. Leading critic Eugene Stinson wrote in the *Daily News*, "The town's new pet, the Littlefield Ballet, has proved a singularly refreshing addition to the opera season. The largest of American dance companies, it has also the largest repertoire and an enviable lot of scenery and costumes. But its most striking asset is its sprightliness... the freshness of ideas... the real brilliance of its dancing." Usually acerbic Claudia Cassidy of the Chicago *Tribune* wrote, "The Littlefield Ballet has been an ornament to the opera stage, both by its fresh costuming and its willingness to help out in any capacity from ballerinas to shield-bearers."

In the late summer of 1939 the Littlefield Ballet danced in the Hollywood Bowl, drawing a reported 40,000 people to see the company dance in *Aida* the first night. A similar crowd came to see the dancers in their own repertoire the following night.

The Littlefield Ballet returned to Chicago in the fall of 1939, again for seven weeks of opera ballet and twice a week all-ballet program. During this season there was an extracurricular opera ballet created and performed at the request of impresario Harry Zelzer. Catherine choreographed dances for the Polish opera *Halka*, danced in the Civic Opera House on December 11. It says something of the stamina and discipline of the dancers, for not only did they have to learn the ballet in a short time, but it was performed on a Sunday evening after a matinee performance of three demanding works of their usual repertoire, presented for a series in the Auditorium Theater.

In the summer of 1940 there was employment for the Littlefield dancers, and for many more dancers at New York's 1940 World's Fair. Catherine was engaged to create the dances for a major spectacle, *American*

Jubilee, a celebration of American history, presented in an outdoor theater seating 7,000. This musical kaleidoscope was produced by Albert Johnson. The staging was by Leon Leonidoff, the music by Oscar Hammerstein and Arthur Schwartz. Lucinda Ballard designed the costumes. Among the characters depicted were George Washington, Jenny Lind, Lillian Russell, P. T. Barnum, Abraham Lincoln, Theodore Roosevelt and a company of Rough Riders. These and scores of anonymous people of various eras were played by a number of well-known actors, singers, comedians, dancers. Props included a real carriage of the Lincoln era. For the five numbers she choreographed Catherine used one hundred dancers. Paul Haakon, the top male dance star of the day, was the featured dance soloist. The show was presented three or four times daily, seven days a week. In addition to the entire Littlefield Ballet many free-lance dancers were hired for *American Jubilee*. Some of the well-known ones were Michael Kidd, Zachary Solov, Jerome Andrews, Dodie Goodman.

In the fall of 1940 the Chicago Civic Opera engaged Ballet Theatre on similar terms to that under which the Littlefield company had danced in 1938 and 1939. Ballet Theatre presented programs of its own repertoire twice a week and had a brilliant season. However, the opera ballets were neglected and the Littlefield Ballet was re-engaged for the 1941 opera season. This time the opera was under the new management of Fortune Gallo, Pavlova's former manager. He took pride in having an exceptional ballet troupe with his opera company and the Littlefield Ballet was featured in the announcements and advertisements. The opera season listed *The Masked Ball*, *Carmen*, *Faust*, *Daughter of the Regiment*, *Othello*, *Barber of Seville* and *Tosca*, with opera greats Lily Pons, Lawrence Tibbett, Grace Moore, Elizabeth Rethberg, Gladys Swarthout and Giovani Martinelli. The ballet director was given equal recognition with these stars. The brochure announcing the season stated, "The glamorous Littlefield Ballet, which was so favorably received here during the 1938 and 1939 seasons, returns this year... Catherine Littlefield is the directress and prima ballerina."

The opera ballets were as fresh as ever. The company, though smaller than in past seasons, danced with the usual verve, led by the three Littlefields — Catherine, Dorothie and Carl. It was noteworthy that botched musical cues, mishaps that happen often in the world of opera ballet, never occurred. Critics still mentioned the excellent costuming, because the Littlefields brought their own and did not dance in the grimy garb too often dug out of old opera trunks.

In the first half of 1941 the Littlefield Ballet toured the United States. It was seen in 42 different cities, traveling 8,000 miles in 16 states and Canada. Statistics quoted in a trade paper stated 114,595 saw the company.

Chicago was included in this tour, and in a season that also scheduled Ballets Russes de Monte Carlo, Col. de Basil's Original Ballets Russes and Ballet Theatre, the Littlefield Ballet drew sold out houses.

It was during the 1941 engagement that on December 7 Pearl Harbor was bombed. It had a very sobering effect on Catherine, who was concerned and keenly aware of world events. When war was declared, most of her male dancers volunteered and joined various branches of the United States military forces. Carl Littlefield was accepted in the Air Force. (Eventually he attained the rank of Lieutenant, and flew a bomber christened "The Ballerina." In the basket painted on the plane's side, a rose was added for every successful foray.) Catherine had always trumpeted the importance of the male dancer in ballet, and when the Littlefield Ballet lost most of its male dancers, the company was "temporarily" disbanded.

For a number of years Catherine had been receiving requests for her choreographic talents for enterprises outside her company. She had taken a few, and now, to fill the time "before the boys came back" (and she expected it would be soon and she would reorganize the Littlefield Ballet), she took on assignments in ice shows, Broadway musicals, television. Dorothie, whose talents for teaching had been utilized there before, taught at the Balanchine-directed School of American Ballet.

Ice Shows

For the next decade Catherine was involved with ice shows and Broadway shows. She had one half-hearted involvement with the ballet world, when in 1944 she was invited to stage *Barn Dance* for Ballet Theatre. In spite of the fact that Dorothie and Tom Cannon were guest artists and danced their original roles at the premiere, the ballet looked all wrong. The great dancers of Ballet Theatre seemed dull. They danced correctly, but lacked the high energy, the joy in dancing that was the Littlefield style. They lacked the rollicking way of dancing. The ballet was soon dropped.

Catherine was very busy in the 1940s. She considered her work with the ice shows a stop gap until she could resume her real life work, developing American ballet, the dancing in the language of the classical *danse d'école* with an American accent. However, she was intrinsically honest and did not short-change the commercial project. She approached each show with her characteristic enthusiasm and inventiveness. She was interested in the possibilities of ice-dancing and viewed each skater with appreciation for his ability. Always bursting with ideas, with her quick intelligence she researched the ways of moving on skates and made attractive, theatrically effective numbers, even artistic ones.

She used the precision and speed innate to ice skating and added ballet's harmonious line. Within the strictures of the medium, she introduced ballet-based movements and without inhibiting the necessary use of the arms in the act of skating, she devised positions and movements that minimized the usual flailing. Most of all she was imaginative and clever in making the most of the medium and its trained performers. Before she plunged into creating the huge arena shows for which she became famous, she had made numbers for the Leonidoff-produced ice shows in New York's Center Theater. For *It Happened on Ice*, her first ice show, she choreographed a ballroom dance with couples in white-tie and evening gowns gliding romantically. Chases are de rigueur on ice, and with her sense of humor she had a poodle chasing a lamp-post. Witches on broomsticks are a cliché, but Catherine had a bevy of housewives sweeping by on broomsticks. And there was a touch of classical ballet in *The Legend of the Lake*, a version of *Swan Lake* to the Tschaikovsky music. Critic Walter Terry quipped, "*Swan Lake* is about to freeze over." With *Hats Off on Ice* and *Stars on Ice* at the Center Theater Catherine increased her knowledge of the medium. In fact she learned the difference between ice skating and ice dancing, even the rules of figure skating. Then for almost a decade, 1942 to 1951, she staged and choreographed a large-scale annual *Hollywood on Ice*, arena shows starring Sonia Henie.

Catherine's last ice show was *Hollywood Ice Revue* of 1951. She died shortly after the show opened and after her death Dorothie choreographed and staged the annual *Hollywood Ice Revues* through 1953. After Dorothie's passing in 1953, Carl Littlefield was recruited for the 1954 *Hollywood Ice Revue* to stage numbers and to design the lighting, a theater art at which he was adept. All the *Hollywood Ice Revues* were rehearsed in Chicago, and Mommie (Caroline Littlefield) came to Chicago to help Carl with the music. Choreographing, especially a large-scale show, was too big a task for one completely new to the medium and Carl had a hard time. He never did another ice show and that was the end of Littlefields in the world of ice dancing.

Musicals

Catherine Littlefield's initiation into professional dance had been in a Ziegfeld musical, and throughout her career, to some degree she was involved in musicals. In fact, there were elements of musical theater in her ballets such as *Terminal* and *Cafe Society*. An inauspicious assignment was to make the dances for a Broadway show *Hold On to Your Hats*. It was a vehicle for Al Jolson with a weak story about the Wild West. This was before dance-integrated musicals in which the dances contributed to the plot. In the Jolson show numbers were inserted for no more reason than to liven proceedings. As dance director Catherine had to make dances for a bevy of half-trained chorus girls, and a half dozen tall and haughty show girls. She solved the problem of dealing with the chorus girls, who could not keep together, by giving each a different thing to do.

A more grateful project was making dances for Lubov Rostova, an ex-Ballets Russes dancer featured in a musical titled *Crazy with the Heat*. Rostova was very chic and beautiful and for her Catherine arranged French-flavored miniature ballets. One of the last Broadway shows Catherine was involved with was *Follow the Girls*, into which she was inveigled because she admired the star dancer Irina Baronova. The producers did not want miniature ballets; all the choreographer was to do was set "routines". These the ballerina performed with charm.

Dorothie and Carl, too, had flings in musicals. Dorothie was a featured dancer in *Vagabond King* and principal dancer and also ballet mistress for the Balanchine choreographed dances in *Song of Norway*, a musical based on the life of composer, Edvard Grieg. Carl was in the ensemble of *Song of Norway* then toured in a long-running production of *Oklahoma!*, in which he danced in the Agnes de Mille ballets.

Catherine Littlefield died of cancer in 1951 at the age of 46, when she was in Chicago, putting the finishing touches to her last show. She had received a number of awards during her busy life and there has been a posthumous honor. In the National Museum of Dance in Saratoga Springs, New York, she is included as a major artist among the greats who contributed to dance in America. Dorothie had a heart attack and died in Chicago in 1953 at the age of 36. During her last days she was teaching, choreographing ice shows, and working with a junior ballet. Carl gave up dancing and died in 1966 after a long illness. Mommie died in New Jersey in 1966.

The action-packed years of the short-lived Catherine and Dorothie have ended, and the amazing Littlefield Ballet, which existed for less than a decade, is no more.[3] But the story has not ended. The Littlefields made waves, and the ripples go on and on.

---

[3] Catherine Littlefield was born in Philadelphia in 1905. She married Philip Leidy in 1933 and divorced him in 1947. In 1948 she married Sterling Noel, an editor of the New York *Journal American*. In 1949 she developed cancer and after a number of operations died on November 18, 1951. Services were held in Philadelphia and the burial was in Chilton Hill Cemetery. A sidelight on her relations with Philip Leidy include the fact that he was very interested in Catherine's ballet activities, and when performances were not in Philadelphia she called him after every performance to discuss how things went. Although they were divorced and there was a new husband on the sidelines, Catherine turned to Philip Leidy when she became ill. They communicated daily and it was Leidy who took over at the funeral. Philip Leidy died in 1964.

Dorothie Littlefield married Bill Lane circa 1940. He was an athlete — football, basketball and baseball at Bucknell College. The marriage was short-lived and a couple of years later Dorothie married Harper Flaherty, an ice skater, later a businessman. They had one child, Catherine Flaherty, in 1951. Dorothy died in Chicago in 1953. Carl Littlefield married Lois Girardeau, a dancer. They had two daughters, Catherine and Leslie, and a son, Jason. Carl died in 1966.

RENATE SCHOTTELIUS: DANCE AT THE BOTTOM OF THE WORLD IN ARGENTINA
Stephanie Reinhart

Argentina has one of the longest histories in modern dance of any country in Latin America and one of the closest connections with the modern dance movement in the United States and Europe. One of the motivating impulses for the development of a modern dance movement in Argentina in the 1940s (not unlike the Argentine literary trends of "Florida" and "Boedo" which preceded it) was the urge to create new movement expressions of universal themes which transcend cultural boundaries. Resembling its northern progenitor in the United States, Argentine modern dance pioneers rejected restrictions of classical ballet while welcoming modern dance innovations issuing from Europe and the United States.

The emergence of Argentine modern dance in the pioneer period is a complicated story and reflects the paradoxical nature of Argentine identity. As a country on the periphery located in the extreme southern cone of Latin America, Argentina has had a difficult time in acquiring a national consciousness because of the preponderance of European immigrants. It is a country which has tended to view itself as separate and distinct from the rest of Latin America. Isolated geographically, it seems a most unlikely place for a major modern dance movement to have taken root.

This movement clearly resembles the origins of North American modern dance to the extent that Argentine women provided the inspiration and propelled the movement. It was an expression of yearnings to launch an Argentine dance culture in which the pioneers could express their individuality and be released from the restrictions of the past. They, too, did what modern dancers from the United States and Europe have done — draw on their own expression and creativity.

During a three-month Fulbright research grant in the fall of 1993, I had the opportunity to interview many of the pioneers of modern dance in Argentina, focusing on the period of the 1940s and 1950s. During this process I conducted several interviews with modern dance pioneer Renate Schottelius, who has a long, distinguished and influential career as a modern dancer/choreographer and teacher. She is currently Artistic Advisor to the Ballet Contemporaneo Teatro Municipal General San Martín. What follows is an edited composite of our dialogue in interviews on October 4 and 25, 1993.

SR: What was your first experience in modern dance?

RS: I loved dance and my parents were not against it. On the contrary they moved to Berlin so I could study dance. In 1928–29 when I was eight years old I entered the children's ballet school at the Municipal Opera of Berlin. We had ballet and modern every day, acrobatics two times a week and rehearsals. I was good at all three of them but I always liked modern dance better perhaps because I wanted to choreograph. My teachers were Wigman-trained, including Ruth Abramowitz. I saw Wigman, Palucca, Schoop, Kreutzberg, and the Jooss Ballet. Modern dance was in vogue in 1929. When "Petroushka" was presented at the opera, it was more modern than balletic.

SR: How did you come to Argentina?

RS: I had to leave Germany; I am half Jewish. I couldn't have had the career I wanted in Germany. In 1936, at the age of 16, I came alone to Buenos Aires, Argentina. We were a very small family: my parents, myself and my grandmother. An Argentinean uncle had enough money to invite only one of us over. My grandmother felt nothing could happen to her since she was not Jewish. My parents did not want to be separated. My mother was Jewish and my father was persecuted because he was against the Nazis. Although it was a hard decision for my parents, I was chosen to come. I was excited; I didn't understand that I might not see my parents again. As it turned out, my father died at the age of 49 in Colombia, but I was able to bring my mother to Buenos Aires in 1941, where she lived with me for twenty years.

SR: What dance did you find when you came here?

RS: There was no modern dance whatsoever. I went into the Conservatorio Nacional (which is now the Escuela Nacional de Danza) and took some ballet classes in the evening. In 1936–37, a German who came from Hellerau, Annelene Michiels, taught Dalcroze-based eurythmic studies and gymnastics for women. She also had a small performing group.

There was also another German woman, very much involved with the Nazi German colony here, named Fasel. She taught rhythmic gymnastics. She was a Nazi so I didn't study with her.

Margarita Wallman, originally a student of Wigman, came to Buenos Aires during World War II and was the principal choreographer of the Teatro Colón. She was a contemporary of Hanya Holm. She did a lot of classical work and also taught modern dance. Paulina Ossona was a student of Margarita Wallman's. Wallman had a small modern dance group that performed in the Teatro Odeón. She was a very important lady in dance and later on in opera; she choreographed operas in La Scala for many, many years. She wrote a book: *Balcony of Dance* (in Spanish). She stayed in Buenos Aires for many years, but eventually returned to Europe.

SR: I understand that there were people coming from abroad who brought this new dance. There was one group that came and left including the Sakaroffs and Ines Pissaro. Then there was another group, under Miriam Winslow, who stayed.

RS: First in 1939, the Jooss group came and performed all their great works, including *The Green Table*. Sometime between 1939 and 1941, Clotilde and Alexander Sakaroff settled here. She was German and he was Russian. They were called 'the poets of the dance' and were beautiful together. While they were familiar with Wigman and may have seen Isadora, they created their own training methods. He was a painter and designed all the costumes. Their work, which they danced barefoot, was inspired by composers like Debussy and Ravel. They had no school, but their influence was widely felt. When I asked them to come see a rehearsal of mine, Alexander gave me such valuable and intense criticism. They started to give final performances in Argentina when the war was about to end and ultimately went to Italy in 1948. I remember Ines Pissaro vaguely. [Ed. note: She came to Argentina in 1939 for the first time.] She came from Chile. I think she was a member of Ballet Nacional de Chile, where Uthoff and five other members of the Jooss Company danced.

   Miriam Winslow came to Buenos Aires for the first time with Foster FitzSimmons on a South American tour in 1941. Her performances were among our first contacts with U.S. modern dance. She toured Brazil, Chile and other countries in 1941 and offered a 2–3 week course that Cecilia, Paulina, Luisa, Ana Itelman and I all loved. In 1943 she returned and formed a small group of girls. She paid us! This was outstanding. I was the only one who had previous training in modern dance. All the other girls only had classical training. Later Ballet Winslow added six boys. It was at that time she performed without Foster FitzSimmons and decided to stay and continue the group.

SR: What did you think when you saw her work?
RS: We couldn't believe it when we saw her. All of the things we had been reading about — Denishawn, Martha Graham — were there in her dances. She had studied with Denishawn, Wigman, Escudero and Kreutzberg.

SR: What was so appealing about the movement? Was it just so different?
RS: Yes. My early training was in German modern dance, but then I discovered American techniques. In German technique you emphasized

expression; maybe you would turn for two hours or jump for two hours. In American techniques many movements were incorporated into one class.

SR: Why do you think Winslow's work happened to take root and why were you all so eager?

RS: Until Miriam Winslow came there was no teacher specifically committed to modern dance. Winslow trained and formed a company of Argentinean dancers — seven women in the first group — and later added the men to form the bigger company. She was a wealthy woman from Boston and got our salaries from her family. People in the United States thought she didn't have to work. Maybe in a way she had the idea to go to another country and do pioneer work to prove that she could do it on her own. Still, Winslow never learned Spanish. This was a kind of barrier that caused some misunderstanding. The stage manager, who was bilingual, spoke to the dancers and translated.

On tour we traveled with lights, elaborate costumes, scenery and our own equipment. We traveled in the old Denishawn way with everything, which was very good because many of the theaters didn't have such sophisticated equipment.

Hers was the first real resident Argentine company and there was considerable interest by musicians, painters, photographers and other artists in her work. She asked Argentine composers to do music for her ballets — *Scarlet Letter*, *Ceremonial & Incantation* in 1944–45; *Little Women*; *Barn Dance*; *In the Fields*; *Salute to the World* (inspired by Walt Whitman) with music by American Jess Meeker. She created *Negro Spirituals* for the men. This piece had a kind of relation to Tamiris in that it was done at almost the same time.

SR: Tell me where you rehearsed.

RS: We rehearsed in a beautiful studio, a huge studio with a balcony and a little theatre, which doesn't exist anymore. Ekatarina Galanta owned it, and it was built for her after she came with Pavlova to Buenos Aires. Miriam rented that studio and we rehearsed there Monday through Friday. Winslow was the first person who offered a salary and steady work. The schedule was the company class from 10–12:30 or 1:00 and then rehearsals from 2:00–5 or 6. At first, she was the only teacher; later I taught as well.

SR: What were classes like?

RS: We would start standing up or stretching; then we had floor work, diagonal and center work with jumps and turns. She was a beautiful teacher and gave her all to the teaching. Looking back, teaching was her strong point. Her choreography was important because nothing else existed at that time.

SR: How much performing did you do?

RS: We performed regularly in Buenos Aires, doing both matinee and evening performances at the Teatro Odeón and at Politeama Theater for two weeks at a time. Then we went on tour to different places in the interior where people up to this day remember we were there. Winslow had an agent who booked the company in Rosario, Cordoba, Mendoza, Tucumán, Salta, Jujuy, Mar del Plata, and Montevideo, Uruguay. Houses were full and the audiences loved us. Critical response was positive, we always played in the best theatres with live music. The company was very well promoted. Wherever we went we had enormous posters. A full year contract meant that we didn't have to work at other jobs. It was like a fairy tale. I could give up my dreadful secretarial job. We were around 22 people in the company.

SR: What finally happened to Ballet Winslow?

RS: In 1947 Winslow wanted to take us to Europe. It was a very expensive proposition and although Winslow had money for passage, food and hotel, she did not have enough to guarantee the salaries demanded by the male dancers. At this point, too, the Kniaseff Ballet Company was formed and wooed the men away. So unfortunately, this was the end of the career of Miriam Winslow, who was still a beautiful dancer. She just collapsed. She went back to the States and visited Argentina afterward, but that was the end of her dance career.

SR: Did any of the people in the group teach outside classes at that time or were they basically totally involved in the company?

RS: We were totally involved. I taught very little at that point. I don't know about the others. One who stayed only the first year was Ana Itelman, who came from an English family in Chile. After one year with Winslow, Ana went to the U.S. and studied with Holm, Nikolais and Limon. When she first returned to Argentina, she gave two or three beautiful and experimental concerts. For example, her piece *Disco Virgin* had only the sound of the needle on a phonograph. [Ed. note — Itelman developed into another important teacher of modern dance in Argentina.]

After the collapse of Ballet Winslow everyone went back to teaching. Luisa Grimberg, Cecilia Ingenieros and Paulina Ossona formed their own groups. We all started to do our own work. It was tragic that the company stopped, but we just struggled on. Through the work of Ballet Winslow, modern dance had become very popular and people wanted to study modern dance. Most of our pupils really wanted to become modern dancers.

SR: When did you first go to the U.S.?
RS: In 1953–54 I went to the U.S. to study with Graham, Holm, Horst, Humphrey and Limon. I starved that year, but it was beautiful. At the American Dance Festival in Connecticut I saw *The Moor's Pavane*. I'm sure I could not have choreographed the way I did afterward without having seen this work and without the classes that I took that year. After my return I resumed teaching and choreographing at Escuela Nacional, at the Teatro Colón and in La Plata and I had my own academy.

SR: When did you form your own group?
RS: In the 1950s I had a group of pupils who also took composition with me. They wanted to form a small performing group and asked me to supervise them, and I did, and I gave them my studio (which was my home) so they could work. At first I had no connection except for seeing the dances which they composed. This was called "Grupo Experimental de Danza Contemporanea." Later they asked me to choreograph. I joined them and reset some of Miriam Winslow's works, such as *Saludo* and *Negro Spirituals*. We toured Argentina, Brazil and Uruguay. In some places they had never seen modern dance. Either we arranged the tours ourselves or sometimes the National Association of Culture assisted us, but the financial situation was very different from that of Ballet Winslow. We worked for nothing. I did the managing and we split the money once we had engagements. It was a cooperative. I got two 'points' and they got one. I lived on my teaching, but the dancers couldn't live on what we made. The tours were not frequent, maybe only twice a year.

SR: Where did you perform in Buenos Aires?
RS: In Teatros Astral, El Nacional, Presidente Alvear and finally at the Colón. Usually only one performance unless we had a commission. We rehearsed all year round more or less. When we finally went to the Colón in 1956 it was as "Renate Schottelius and Grupo de Danza Contemporanea"; the name had changed. We were the first modern Argentine company to perform at the Colón and our performances were sold out. These performances were arranged by my impresario Conciertos Gerard; he handled all my activities and performances and took 10% of all performance revenue. No films were made of the group. We were much too poor. There is one excerpt of me which was made when I went to the U.S. but the speed can't be reproduced.

SR: What became of this company?
RS: When we went to Brazil, we were still Grupo Experimental. The original group did only their choreography and many times it was group choreography. When the name changed to Renate Schottelius and Grupo de

Danza Contemporanea in 1956, it was only my choreography and Miriam Winslow's. That company lasted until 1962.

SR: Can you tell me something about Amigos de la Danza, which I understand was a very important organization in the 1960's.
RS: In 1961 Amigos de la Danza was founded by a group of choreographers, critics and people interested in dance including: Ekatharina Galanta, Tamara Gregorieva and Roberto Giachero, classical; Amalia Lozano, neo-classical; myself, Renate Schottelius, modern; Fernando Emery and Ines Malinow, both critics. With the help of the municipal director of culture who gave us the Teatro San Martín once a month, we managed to make an important contribution to the artistic life of the city. In particular, we wanted young people to have a chance to do their own choreography. Such important choreographers as Oscar Araiz, Susana Zimmerman and Lia Labarone all got their first opportunity at Amigos. The association lasted ten years. The fantastic thing was that we always had classical and modern on each program.

The University of Fine Arts in La Plata opened up a dance department in which Maria Ruanova headed the classic dance and I directed the modern. This was during Peron's time. I taught technique, composition and movement for actors. People came to me in La Plata and asked me to join the party of Peron. I declined and gave up the job because of that. I said I had left Germany to be free and refused to join.

SR: A search for an American identity permeates literature and modern dance in North America. Are there similar concerns among Argentinean artists or has your aesthetic developed in response to other factors?
RS: This search, which I know has been very important in the States, is not so important here. You do find writers grappling with these questions and certainly composers like Ginastera and Piazzolla have brought recognition to Argentina through their musical compositions. In the first generation, sometimes choreographers wanted to do 'our thing'; then we would incorporate tangos or other folklore elements into the modern idiom. However, you cannot compare the urge of North American people to get to their own roots with what happened here. We did not have a movement with people like Humphrey, Graham or Weidman. People might have used Garcia Lorca or Neruda as inspiration, not as a rebellion against what preceded. Now, some companies such as Nucleodanza are more conscious of presenting themes particular to Argentina but I see these themes as more universal — oppression of people, problems of non-communication — and not just Argentinean.

MAKING MY WAY IN DANCE
Bella Lewitzky

I was born into a European family who held the arts to be a vital and integral part of life and so it was natural that I singled out the arts for a career. I have retained to this day the same feelings of wonder and discovery that the arts always provided for me. Here lies information, imagination and a deep form of communication. Here it is possible to experience inner and outer truths simultaneously. Process and product in the fine arts tend to be unpredictable, difficult to analyze, individualistic, unresponsive to formulas and without finite answers. Much of what society values is accountable, is responsive to analysis and formulas. This difference leads many to view the arts with mistrust and to cloud them in mystery. Yet how persistent and lasting is the value of the arts. Through art personal human history is revealed to us and touches us.

We feel something of the quality of persons who lived in the caves of Southern France through their wall paintings; we know and share Goya's agonies over the atrocities of war in a time which was not ours. We still learn from the penetrating wisdom in the beauty of Shakespeare. I was reminded of the value of this kind of role the arts play as I fell heir to one of the rare tickets to the Tutankhamun exhibit and found that in order to utilize this ticket I had to arrive there at midnight — kind of a witching hour. As I stood there waiting in line, I thought, this is a most remarkable experience — here is an exhibit so popular, so in demand that its viewing has been booked throughout the day and the evening. As I stepped into the exhibit I realized that part of its attraction was the illusion that we could step back in time to the 18th dynasty of King Tutankhamun, a remarkable act.

Future eras will know us via our art works. Even though the arts have intangible qualities, there shines through a common function and purpose. The arts serve society as reflectors, critics, moralists, perceivers, recorders and, in the hands of genius, forecasters, no small task, and an essential one for society whether or not it can be weighed or measured. Albert Camus summed it up: "We have art in order not to die of life."

Amongst the arts I was irresistibly drawn to the most victimized of them all, dance. If common opinion held that the arts were frivolous, wasteful, certainly not worthy of serious consideration as a profession, then dance was the basest. It was clearly a pursuit for non-intellectuals, silly, vapid, sensual and somehow immoral.

During all of the time that I apprenticed and grew in my chosen field, I railed and winced at the misconceptions leveled at the art form I love, that is, if the omissions were not so great that it was not even mentioned. I began to learn how to champion dance. I began to put into words the intuitive knowledge I was gaining about this art form. I began to realize that what one loves deserves defense. I became a fighter, I learned to shed my fear of confrontation. I had a wonderful teacher, dance itself. As I grew to be a strong technician, performer, teacher and choreographer I was able to penetrate deeper and deeper into the substance of dance. There lay all the ammunition I needed. I discovered the limitless world of the body/mind. We record impressions and facts from our first movement. We have a store of body/mind information. We learn about space with our first gesture of reaching out. We know about time, through heartbeat and breath. We know about weight and its transference with our first step. We know about gravity with our first jump. We know about balance and the marvels of coordination. We experience the manufacturing of energy. We know that emotions and ideas have shapes and form. We are capable of taking the unknown and bending it into forms which permit us to cope with it. We discover paths to learning, all of this in dance.

I can still recall my general state of mourning in the final moments of the Federal Theatre and my anger and shame at how badly dance was used to help deal the death blow. The Federal Theatre existed during the Depression, when the Federal Theatre Project under the Works Projects Administration gave an opportunity to artists to earn a livelihood and still practice their profession. It created a renaissance of American theatre. Some things came out of it which still remain — Orson Welles' marvelous theatre, the Theatre of the Living Newspaper, and dance was a part of that. As it grew in popularity, it gained a lot of opponents as well as some proponents. One aspect after another of Federal Theatre began to be removed, failed to be supported in spite of international pleas. Congress decided it was indeed frivolous, empty, could not be quantified, and therefore was of doubtful value. In one of these congressional hearings, a man who was a congressman from Iowa, arose and danced up and down the aisle of Congress in mockery of ballet and stated, "Here is where our money goes." That act left me with a burning anger over his poor use of the art form I had learned to respect.

My anger and shame have long ago been replaced by a secure knowledge of what I value. My road as a practitioner of concert dance has always been exciting and fun, although as a profession it has some pronounced peculiarities. If one defines profession as a method for earning a living, one is in immediate trouble. When I began, concert dance was something one had to afford rather than a means to earn a living. One could teach, wait tables, be a secretary in order to afford dancing. There were paying jobs in dance, in the movies, clubs, in musicals and operas.

The quality of work left much to be desired. In the commercial media, a woman dancer was generally viewed as a sex object in motion. In opera, dance occurred only if the libretto called for a ball or a bacchanal. Important choreography and choreographers made inroads to help alter this image, but it's still an uphill battle and these few people are exceptions rather than the rule. In the past even small jobs were few and far between. Many years ago I was called to address a high school career day on dance and what the career might offer young students headed into a professional life. I contacted the four or five unions which cover dance; I wish I had never done that. Much to my dismay I found that dancers were virtually unemployable in those days. In the film extras' union, about a thousand dancers were registered at that time, of which 10% earned any living at all. The same was true in AGMA, the guild which covers musical artists. They told me they didn't even keep a record of the dancers, since there were so few. It was equally true of Actors Equity, the union which handles musicals. All of this forced me to look for things other than employment in talking with young people about reasons for selecting a career in dance. Happily, that has changed considerably today, but security is still not the prime consideration in selecting this career. That drawback is adequately compensated for by the reward of the consuming, totally absorbing and creative practice of concert dance. Things are changing; there has been a remarkable growth in dance. Employment opportunities exist today not only in dance but in supporting and related fields.

The dance profession has always been more open to women than most. It is now and has been common to find important women artists in dance. This has created some interesting experiences for us. There was a time when my company had a staff as follows. I was the artistic director and choreographer, a woman. As I stepped onto the stage I confronted an all-male crew. Now, they were willing to tolerate me. They felt it somehow indispensable that I was going to be around and they would deal with me even if I was of the 'wrong' sex. Then I presented our company manager. She was a woman. When finally they asked, "May we speak to your sound technician?" I brought forward another woman and all hope disappeared for the crew at that point. It happened that we were totally staffed by women because these women were competent, not simply because they were women. It was a very interesting set up on that stage as the male crew said things like, "Would the women mind removing their purses from the footlights?" I doubt that this scene would occur today. Today we find female dancers, choreographers, technicians, and designers in dance.

American modern dance is identified with women, beginning with the originators, Martha Graham, Doris Humphrey, Hanya Holm, and Helen Tamiris. The second and third generations include many women choreographers and artistic directors. There are also women producers and founders of major national and international companies.

There are numerous other women who have been important to the field. Dame Ninette de Valois was the founder of the Royal Ballet. Madame Marie Rambert introduced Anthony Tudor, Agnes de Mille, Sir Frederick Ashton and others to the field of dance and gave them an experimental place in which to work. The Countess de Rothschild established the two major companies in Israel, Bat Sheva and Bat Dor. Barbara Morgan's name is legendary in the field of dance photography; she received a National Endowment for the Arts grant to categorize and preserve her dance photographs. Theatre in this nation owes a great debt to lighting designer Jean Rosenthal, who began as a designer for Martha Graham. My own lighting designer, Darlene Neel, has been another contributor, along with numerous female set and costume designers, composers and accompanists, stage managers and stage technicians. Today when I walk onto the stage the crew is no longer all male; there are always several women. There are women writers, and critics, historians, researchers, notators, film makers, teachers, publicists, managers, and booking agents.

Our nation is beginning to realize that to better the quality of life we must cultivate the arts. President Kennedy gave voice to this when he stated, "The life of the arts, far from being an interruption, a distraction in the life of a nation, is very close to the center of a nation's purpose and is a test of the quality of a nation's civilization." Congressmen Brademas and Thompson and Senator Pell proposed a White House Conference on the arts and humanities. The Congress approved and President Carter signed this act. This placed concerns for the arts and humanities in public view and into public consciousness. The conference marked a huge step towards national recognition of the arts and humanities, alongside agriculture, commerce, labor, health, welfare and defense.

I have seen many changes for the better in the course of my career. There are several attributes I have found of great importance in pursuing a life in dance. They are commitment, passion, the capacity to rebound from adversities and the power to dream.

An earlier version of this essay was written as a commencement address for Scripps College in 1978.

PART III

MENTORING

The chapters in Part Three investigate the contributions of numerous female mentors to furthering the development of twentieth century tap, jazz dance, dance education and administration. Cheryl Willis' "African American Rhythm Tappers" uncovers a few previously unheralded mentors and performers in tap. In "Mentors of American Jazz Dance," Judy Austin chronicles the many contributors in this style whose public reputations as performers obscured their more subtle contributions to jazz teaching and choreography. "Body Wisdom" is Gay Cheney's personal, imaginative recollection of her mentors' methods of linking the body, mind and spirit in movement and comments on how she has extended those methods in her own teaching. Linda Caruso Haviland's "Women in Dance in Higher Education" outlines the present status and past contributions to the establishment and growth of dance education programs at colleges and universities.

AFRICAN AMERICAN RHYTHM TAPPERS
Cheryl M. Willis

The joyful music and dance of the Swing Era (1935–1950) served as an antidote for many Americans during the Great Depression. The musical sound of "swing," upbeat, happy, and energizing, swept the country. Dance halls opened in which crowds of thousands were challenged nightly with the physically demanding Lindy Hop. Nightclubs and theatres featured singers, dancers, and comedians accompanied by the swing sound of the Big Bands. The movie industry lured the public from the reality of hard times into a world of glamour and fantasy. Many large theatre owners capitalized on a combined presentation of film, live entertainment, and the Big Band sound.

Tap dance with its many approaches to rhythm became a popular dance form of the era. Fred Astaire, Gene Kelly, Ann Miller, and Eleanor Powell were considered leaders in the field. Despite the racially segregated disposition of the times, several African American men such as Bill "Bojangles" Robinson, the Nicholas Brothers and Sammy Davis Jr., were also recognized for their unique styles of tap. Dance research has not chronicled the presence of African American women who tap danced, yet their role spans over one hundred years in show business. In the peak years of tap dance in the United States (1935–1950), African American women performed as chorus girls, song and dance teams, and tap dance teams. A few entered the competitive dance style known as rhythm tap, a traditionally male-dominated dance form. These women were pioneers who broke traditional roles and gender constraints. Several women from the Philadelphia and New York areas performed rhythm tap professionally and were a vital part of the tap dance milieu during the Swing Era.

Rhythm tap parallels the swinging rhythms of jazz music which became popular during the Swing Era. Rhythm Tap is characterized by intricate rhythmic motifs, polyrhythms, multiple meters, and elements of swing defined as off beat phrasing and suspension of the beat. For example, a rhythmic phrase may have several simultaneous rhythms with the accent off the beat or in a delayed response to the beat, which produces the swing feel. Structured and collective improvisations (two or more dancers contributing improvised rhythms within the structure) are components of the rhythm. The movement of the dance is quick, yet subtle. Weight is balanced on the entire foot as the dancer moves easily between heel, toe, ball and side of the foot. Rhythm tap moves in a horizontal plane with weight shifts initiating from the pelvis. Arms and torso respond to the shifting of weight.

Although the dance may be choreographed, it continues to be dependent on the creative individuality of the dancer, who may vary it as she is inspired to do. Rhythm tap requires technical control contrasted by elements of surprise, consisting of facial expressions, gestures, humorous verbal comments, pauses in the rhythm, or acrobatic stunts known as Flash (the execution of flips, splits, spins, and leaps). The audience contributes to the dance through vocal and rhythmic expressions. This give and take between the audience and dancer creates a cooperative feeling which encourages the dancer and continues a reciprocal exchange of energy.

In the African American community, tap dance "challenges," friendly competitive contests in street corner dancing, were generally reserved for men. The development of tap dance as a male-dominated form is shaped by history. Steps danced from the early 1800s, which evolved into several styles of tap dance, were nurtured and presented in the male cast of Minstrelsy. Women did not appear in the performance of tap dance until the 1890s.

The gender roles of the dominant culture seem to be another factor in the development of tap dance as a male dominated form. In many public arenas, women were dependent and non-competitive. Additionally, a restrictive sense of etiquette governed dress, manners, social gatherings, and entertainment. Despite restrictions, however, African American women were more successsful than African American men in their ability to support a family, maintain a job, gain self-dignity, and move between the two separate worlds of "black and white." In their struggle for acceptability, these women adhered to standards of behavior which disparaged street dancing and other overt public exhibition for women. Those who chose to dance rhythm tap were often unwelcome in this male domain.

By the 1930s women began to accept the "challenges" of Rhythm Tap not only on neighborhood street corners but also on the professional stage. Although they competed against the male dancers for jobs and recognition, a separate set of standards was imposed on women. Edith "Baby" Edwards of Philadelphia, who learned to dance from her brother "Harry Carey" Edwards, performed with a male partner in a team known as "Spic and Span." She recalled that she was often criticized by male dancers, who told her that she should dance softer. "Hard tap dancing," which referred to virility, strength, energy, and a cool attitude, and included difficult rhythms, turns, and other acrobatic stunts, was a standard expected of male dancers.

(Edwards 1990a) Mildred "Candi" Thorpe, in addressing the double standard that women faced, explained that it was more acceptable for a woman to dance softly and to portray feminine or sexy qualities. Yet, this style of dance for a woman was not considered on a par with the male's "hard dancing style." Paradoxically, males were able to display both "hard dancing" and dainty and classical movement. "Coles and Atkins" demonstrated this in their signature routine of a slow soft shoe. (Thorpe 1990)

The male dancers expected a woman's dance to display her femininity by moving in a feminine manner, wearing frilly costumes, and exposing her legs and midriff. However, the women rhythm tappers challenged these conventions. Many chose costumes from the popular male fashion of the times, which included tuxedos, Eton jackets[1] or zoot suits,[2] and the oxford style of shoes worn by the male dancers. Thorpe, who performed in a man's suit, explained her choice of costume. "We didn't show any part of our body but our face… they could see and liked what they'd see. You didn't have to expose your body if you had something to offer." (Thorpe 1990)

The Dancers

Born in 1923, Edith "Baby" Edwards, as she is still called by many entertainers, began her performing career in amateur contests when she was three years old. She was later cast on "The Horn and Hardart Children's Hour," a weekly radio broadcast featuring American children. (Edwards 1990b) In 1939 Edwards auditioned and was cast in Erik Charell's Broadway musical *Swingin' a Dream* at the Centre Theatre. In 1941, Willie "Span" Joseph formed a partnership with Edwards. "Spic and Span," as the team was known, performed on a platform that was approximately two feet high and wide and about four feet in length. The top of the platform rested on the wooden initials "S.S.," which faced the audience. Edwards sang a Blues solo, followed by "challenge dancing" to a more upbeat tune. For the finale, Edwards did a spectacular sliding split across the floor and returned to a standing position while her partner did a straddle jump off the platform and over her head. (Edwards 1990b) The team performed nationally and internationally for more than twenty years, during which time they were featured in clubs and

---

[1] An Eton jacket is a short black jacket with long sleeves, wide lapels, and an open front.

[2] The term zoot suit was coined by Harold C. Fox, a clothier and bandleader. This flashy suit of extreme cut consisted of a thigh-length jacket with wide padded shoulders and peg pants with narrow cuffs.

theatres throughout the United States, toured Europe with the USO shows and appeared on several television shows in the 1950's. (Edwards 1990)

Mildred "Candi" Thorpe was born in Philadelphia in 1919. Thorpe learned to dance by attending shows and asking the performers for instruction at the end. As a young girl she was one of the few who competed against male dancers in "challenge dancing" and received positive acknowledgement for her ability. In the mid-1930's she began her professional career in Tally's Minstrels, a troupe of eight African American tap dancers who performed songs and dance in "blackface" on a carnival circuit. According to Thorpe, while in Hopkinsville, Kentucky, the owners of the carnival embezzled the money, which left the troupe and the carnival stranded. She then returned to Philadelphia and performed in small clubs until she teamed up with Jewel Welch. (Thorpe 1990)

Like Candi Thorpe, Jewel "Pepper" Welch of Philadelphia, born in 1922, learned to dance with the boys on the street corners of Philadelphia, competing with them and performing rhythm tap and flash. (Welch 1990) When she was ten years old, she entered a bar on a dare from her friends and performed her debut with a three-piece jazz band. She measured her success by the amount of money thrown on the floor by the audience. This was a common childhood experience recounted by many African American tap dancers. Welch was soon competing in amateur and kiddie hour contests in Philadelphia's Nixon Grand Theatre. (Welch 1989)

In 1939 Welch and Thorpe formed the team "Candi and Pepper." Their break into show business came with a booking at Harlem's Apollo Theatre. Welch was featured performing flash, challenged by Thorpe who was known for her improvisational ability. Thorpe explained that through this style she was able to express herself in rhythm and add a slide, a wing,[3] or a trench[4] according to how she felt while dancing. (Thorpe 1990) "Candi

---

[3] There are many variations of the wing but the basic technique is a side shuffle on the supporting foot or simultaneously on two feet. The feet are in a parallel position and remain in this position as one foot or both feet are brushed out to the side and quickly brushed inward and the dancer lands in the starting position. There are three sounds in this step: brush out, brush in, and step.

[4] Through the Trenches or Pulling Trenches: This is one of the earliest flash steps, which made its appearance on the entertainment stage in 1914 by African-American Toots Davis. One version of this step is executed as the dancer stands on the right foot and springs upward to the outside edge of the foot. The dancer pulls this foot backward in an arc pathway. Then the dancer steps on the left foot and reverses the movement. The body is on a forty-five-degree angle and the arms reach for the floor in opposition to the foot. The step travels from side to side. (Edwards 1990)

and Pepper" toured the East Coast and the Midwest for several years and were featured with the big bands of Louis Armstrong, Fats Waller and Erskine Hawkins. In the early 1940's, Thorpe retired from show business. Welch subsequently formed a partnership with Edwina Evelyn. (Welch 1988)

Born in 1922, Edwina "Salt" Evelyn had enjoyed tap dance as a popular form of recreation in her New York neighborhood. Although she had opportunities to attend dancing school, Evelyn claimed that the real "dancing school was right out there on the street, doing the dance and challenging each other..." Evelyn began a semi-professional career as a young girl as she performed with Annie Ree Gilliam[5] and Anne Baxter.[6] (Evelyn 1990) In 1944 Evelyn joined in a partnership with Jewel "Pepper" Welch. "Salt and Pepper" had a fifteen-minute musical arrangement during which rhythm, flash, vernacular dance, and comedy routines were performed. Although both dancers performed rhythm and flash, Evelyn was featured as the rhythm dancer while Welch performed daring feats of flash. Intricate footwork was complemented by spins, slides, splits, jumps, flips, and a version of "Kazotskys."[7] (Welch 1989) The pair performed together until 1954 as "Salt and Pepper" and were featured in theatre, nightclub, and USO shows throughout the United States and Canada. (Evelyn 1990)

Born in 1916, Ludie Jones of New York was inspired to tap dance when a family friend taught Jones the tap charleston which focused on making rhythms with the feet. Jones later auditioned and won a place in the chorus of Lew Leslie's *Blackbirds*[8] of 1934 in London, England. (Jones 1990a) On her return to the United States, Ludie Jones, Peggy Wharton, and Marion Worthy Warner who were also in the show formed a team called the "Lang

---

[5] Together this team won an amateur contest at New York's RKO Regent Theatre. Annie Ree Gilliam married and became Ann Shelton. She and her husband had one daughter and moved to Cleveland, Ohio. According to Evelyn, Gilliam was one of the first women trolley conductors in Cleveland.

[6] The team of Edwina Evelyn and Anne was known as "Edwina and Anne." This team was featured several times at Harlem's Apollo Theatre. (*Variety* 11 March 1942)

[7] Kazotsky is a Russian dance step which starts from a squat with the arms folded on chest. The dancer kicks out one leg, as it returns the other is extended outward. This is repeated in a series. (Stearns 1968, 248)

[8] *Blackbirds* opened in 1926 and continued to be produced in Europe and in clubs and theatres in the United States. *Blackbirds of 1928* popularized the Stair Dance which was performed by Bill Bojangles Robinson, the first African-American to perform the Stair Dance on Broadway. (Stearns and Stearns 1968, 155)

Sisters" who worked the RKO and Loew's circuits and were featured with the Big Bands of Fats Waller, Louis Armstrong, and Louie Russell. Jones formed another group in 1941 with Sylvia Warner and Geraldine Ball called "The Three Poms." The trio was featured as the opening act for the Cab Calloway Band and performed a high speed routine lasting six minutes that employed three styles of dance: Warner, from Canada, performed a fast showy "buck and wing" dance;[9] Geraldine Ball did acrobatics; Ludie Jones was the rhythm dancer. The act concluded with a challenge step, "through the trenches," and a final flip by Ball. Traveling with Cab Calloway's Band, "The Three Poms" performed in theatres, clubs, and USO shows throughout North America, Europe, and the Orient. The trio remained together until the early 1950's. (Jones 1990a)

Little is known of Louise Madison's personal life, yet she is renowned. Charles "Honi" Coles, who was a personal friend, spoke about her status: "She wasn't just a woman dancer. She surpassed all tap dancers." (Coles 1990) Coles learned his first "five tap wing"[10] from Madison. (Coles 1990) Madison performed in *Blackbirds*,[11] which premiered on 25 December 1933 at the Apollo Theatre and ran for a year. She was featured in the musical number "Tappin' the Barrel"[12] and was chosen for the London production in 1934. Madison performed in club and theatre circuits throughout the 1930's and 1940's. Philadelphian LaVaughn Robinson, recipient of the 1990 National Heritage Award for his lifetime contributions to tap, performed with Madison at Harlem's Apollo Theatre in the late 1940s. He confirmed her legendary status: "Louise Madison was one of the greatest women tap dancers. She danced like a man, was a terror.

---

[9] According to Stearns the Buck was similar to a Time Step and the Wing was a simple hop with one foot flung out to the side. The wing of the Buck Dance was more of a tap step than a Flash or air step. (Stearns 1968, 191) "Buck and Wing" and "Pigeon Wing" both relate to dance steps that flap the arms and legs resembling wings. The wing movement of the legs later evolved to a side shuffle step action on one or two feet, which resembles a wing as the leg goes away from and back under the body. (Emery 1988, 89–98)

[10] One version of a Five Tap Wing is to execute two side shuffles before landing on the supporting foot or feet. Another version is to begin the wing in a squatted position, push off the feet and execute the wing by syncopating the feet. Land on the two feet simultaneously in a squatted position.

[11] *Blackbirds* was a musical production featuring African American performers which was produced by Lew Leslie.

[12] *Blackbirds 1933–1934* Playbill File. New York Public Library System: Schomberg Center for Research in Black Culture, Harlem, New York.

She was tougher than any man, and wore white tails and top hat... even the men went to her to learn steps." (Robinson 1988)

Edwards, Evelyn, Jones, Madison, Thorpe, and Welch represent some of the best African American women tappers from the Philadelphia/New York area performing between 1930 and 1950. These pioneers are not often credited in written dance history accounts, but their contribution is significant: not only did they enter the masculine tradition of tap dance which valued competition, personal style, and intricate swinging rhythms but they challenged the standards of femininity within the dance world.

As unofficial American cultural ambassadors, Germaine Ingram and LaVaughn Robinson have been sent all over the world by the National Council for the Traditional Arts. While Ingram is continuing her partnership with mentor Robinson, she has recently begun an apprenticeship with Edith "Baby Edwards" Hunt. With Edith Hunt as a female mentor, she wants her work to express a fuller range of emotion, color and texture. She sees her work with Edith Hunt as an opportunity to capture and preserve the distinctive style of this celebrated tap dancer and to extend the heritage begun by other women pioneers in rhythm tap: Edwina Evelyn, Ludie Jones, Louise Madison, Mildred Thorpe, and Jewel Welch.

This article was supported in part by a grant from the Commonwealth of Pennsylvania Council on the Arts.

Interviews

Brown, James. Interview with author. Boulder, Colorado, 20 June 1990.

Coles, Charles. Telephone interview with author. September 1990.

Edwards Hunt, Edith. Interview with author. West Philadelphia, Pennsylvania, 18 July 1990.

Edwards Hunt, Edith. Interview with author. West Philadelphia, Pennsylvania, 3 October 1990.

Evelyn, Edwina. Interview with author. Greenwich Village, New York, 26 April 1990.

Fambro, Isabelle. Interview with author. Philadelphia, Pennsylvania, 14 August 1990.

Jones, Ludie. Interview with author. Harlem, New York, 20 July 1990.

Jones, Ludie. Interview with author. Harlem, New York, 24 September 1990.

Robinson, LaVaughn. Interview with author. Philadelphia, Pennsylvania, 14 September 1988.

Thorpe, Mildred. Interview with author. Elwood, New Jersey, 18 November 1990.

Welch, Jewel. Interview with author. Philadelphia, Pennsylvania, 1 March 1989.
Welch, Jewel. Interview with author. Philadelphia, Pennsylvania, 15 July 1990.

Bibliography

Apollo Reopens 1985: The Legend. Apollo Manuscript File. New York Public Library. Schomberg Center for Research in Black Culture, Harlem, New York.
Davis, Angela. *Women, Race & Class*. New York: Random House, 1981.
Dixon-Stowell, Brenda. "You've Taken My Blues and Gone: A Seminar on Black Dance in White America." *Dance Research Journal*, 16/2 Fall 1984.
Emery, Lynne Fauley. *Black Dance from 1619 to Today*. Princeton: A Dance Horizons Book, 1988.
Fox, Ted. *Showtime at the Apollo*. New York: Holt, Rinehart and Winston, 1983.
Frank, Rusty. *Tap: The Greatest Tap Dance Stars and Their Stories, 1900–1955*. New York: William Morrow and Company, Inc., 1990.
Franklin, John H. and Alfred A. Moss. *From Slavery to Freedom: A History of Negro Americans*. New York: Alfred A. Knopf, 1988.
Giddings, Paula. *When and Where I Enter: The Impact of Black Women on Race and Sex in America*. New York: Bantam Books, 1984.
Haskins, Jim. *The Cotton Club*. New York: Random House, 1977.
Lewis, David L. *When Harlem Was in Vogue*. New York: Vintage Books, 1982.
Schiffman, Jack. *Harlem Heyday: Pictorial History of Modern Black Show Business and the Apollo Theatre*. New York: Prometheus Books, 1984.
Schiffman, Jack. *Uptown: The Story of Harlem's Apollo Theatre*. New York: Cowles Book Company, Inc., 1971.
Stearns, Marshall, and Jean Stearns. *Jazz Dance: The Story of American Vernacular Dance*. New York: Schirmer Books, 1968.
Stearns, Marshall W. *The Story of Jazz*. New York: Oxford University Press, 1958.
Willis, Cheryl. "Tap Dance: Memories and Issues of African-American Women Who Performed Between 1930 and 1950." Ed.D. dissertation, Temple University, 1991.
Woll, Allen. *Black Musical Theatre: From Coontown to Dreamgirls*. Baton Rouge: Louisiana State University Press, 1989.

MENTORS OF AMERICAN JAZZ DANCE
Judy Austin

As jazz dancers, choreographers and teachers, we are beginning to establish a tradition that includes the history of the art form. We have heard about the "father" of jazz choreography, Jack Cole. Many of us have been lucky to study with the "fathers" of jazz technique: Matt Mattox, Luigi, and Gus Giordano. These men helped give birth and raise jazz dance through its adolescence into its current state of budding maturity. We now witness, with some regularity, jazz in a concert setting, as well as on the theater stage, in television and in film. Yet one aspect of its history seems to be missing. Every child with a father also has a mother, equally responsible for the conception, birth and nurturing process. Who are the "mothers" of jazz dance?

Early History

As early as 1923, Albertina Rasch formed a ballet/theater troupe and school in New York that performed a style she called "symphonic jazz." Sometimes performed on pointe, her choreography nonetheless had an emphasis on irregular rhythms and contained angular movements. Rasch went on to choreograph shows for Florenz Ziegfeld from 1927 to 1931, as well as the *MGM Colortone Novelties* from 1929 to 1933.

Katherine Dunham co-choreographed *Cabin in the Sky* with George Balanchine in 1940, introducing to the Broadway stage elements which are at the foundation of the development of jazz dance. Often considered a modern dancer and choreographer, Dunham combined Afro-Caribbean and modern dance techniques into a hybrid, with the percussiveness, rhythm, and orientation to the floor which we now consider integral to the form of jazz dance.

In the 1940s, it was nearly impossible for a woman to choreograph on Broadway. Peter Davison writes of Agnes de Mille, who was the first woman to break through the male-dominated field of Broadway choreography with her "dream ballets" in *Oklahoma!* (1942) and *Carousel* (1945), "...she has always known that to succeed as a woman... she had to do more, speak more clearly, and fight harder than men of equal stature."[1] For a black woman such as Dunham it was even harder. De Mille, in her own book, *Portrait Gallery*, describes some of the hardships Dunham and her company of dancers suffered as they began to tour in a concert dance venue alongside established white companies. Dunham paved the way for other black companies with jazz dance in their repertories, such as the Alvin Ailey American Dance Theatre and the Joseph Holmes Chicago Dance Theater.

The '50s: Broadway

The 1950s, which witnessed the blossoming adolescence of jazz dance, introduced an abundance of women to the field. Often the silent collaborators (Broadway's earliest photo of Gwen Verdon is captioned "Jack Cole and Dancer"), they were nevertheless instrumental in the creation of what we now call jazz dance. In the public eye, there were two groups of women rising to success in jazz dance: female dancers who were "molded" into stars by male choreographers or partners, and female assistants to well-known male choreographers.

Often unheralded, women teachers were making their impact on the field through their students. Luigi has said, "It's not that men are more important to the evolution of jazz dance, it's just that there were fewer of them."[2] Fewer of them, but in higher powered positions. We must remember that this was the era of woman-as-housewife as seen on *Father Knows Best*, when it was difficult for women to rise to the top of any field on their own merits.

Jack Cole liked his women dancers to have what Gus Giordano calls a "pixie look" — short hair, small breasts and hips—in short, a boyish appearance.[3] In *Unsung Genius*, by Glenn Lonely, Francine Ames recalls a time in class when Cole claimed that women shouldn't need to wear bras, but should learn to control their muscles instead.[4]

Verdon was able to capture the precision of Cole's isolated choreography, yet we can argue against the idea that she was "created" by Cole. The daughter of a dancer, Verdon studied ballet with Ernest Belcher (Marge Champion's father) and could, as we shall see, master many styles of dance and many people's choreography. Verdon first saw Jack Cole in a

---

[1] De Mille, Agnes. *Portrait Gallery*. Boston: Houghton Mifflin Co., 1990, jacket notes.

[2] Personal communication, Luigi, January 19, 1992.

[3] Personal communication, Giordano, March 5, 1992.

[4] Lonely, Glen. *Unsung Genius*. New York: Franklin Watts, 1984, p. 132.

nightclub act when she was eighteen. "Being a ballerina was what I had in mind," she says, "but what Jack did seemed like complete movement, and I saw there was more to dance than pointe shoes."[5] She began studying with him — he taught four-hour classes that consisted of a ballet barre, a floor warm-up and work on choreography for his nightclub act.

After performing for and assisting Jack Cole, Verdon returned to Broadway in 1953 to dance the lead in *Can-Can*, choreographed by Michael Kidd. Kidd's choreography was very athletic, she recalls, but easy for her because she had also been a tumbler and an acrobat. "I'd done jump splits and one-armed walk-overs all my life!"[6] Verdon began her association with Bob Fosse in 1957, in *Damn Yankees!* She claims that although Fosse's choreography was very balletic, she did not master it until the second time she worked with him, in *New Girl in Town* (1958). "In "The Pony Ballet," I learned to dance on a straight leg even in high-heeled shoes!" she laughs.[7]

According to Verdon, Fosse was greatly influenced by Agnes de Mille's theatrical innovation of using dancers as characters within the plot, instead of what de Mille called "animated wallpaper."[8] Fosse demanded acting through dance, and was both the director and the choreographer in *Redhead* (1959), in which Verdon starred. Frank Ashton, of the *World-Telegram and Sun*, wrote in 1959, "(Verdon) is a rocketing, endearing success."[9] She went on to star in Fosse's *Sweet Charity* (1966), and *Chicago* (1975). "Bob used every possible movement the body could make as dance," Verdon says, "not just a sequence of battements, pliés and port de bras."[10] Called the "ultimate Fosse dancer," Verdon was obviously a meticulous dancer with impeccable technique and sensitivities to choreography, capable of doing almost anything. Although she says, "I never did what I considered jazz — I never studied so-called jazz technique,"[11] Verdon has played a tremendous role in the development of what we call jazz dance today. She symbolizes the "dancer as character" element we find in most jazz choreography, where the

---

[5] Personal communication, Gwen Verdon, February 19, 1992.

[6] Ibid.

[7] Ibid.

[8] Ibid.

[9] Steven Suskin. *Opening Night on Broadway: A Critical Quotebook of the Golden Era of the Musical Theater, Oklahoma! (1943) to Fiddler on the Roof (1964)*. New York: Schirmer Books, 1990, p. 184.

[10] Personal communication, Gwen Verdon, February 19, 1992.

[11] Ibid.

dancer needs to act *through* the given choreography in order to further the dramatic intent of the work.

Verdon is still active in the dance field today, carrying on the tradition and legacy of both Cole and Fosse, as well as her own contributions to dance. She has taught theatre dance in the U.S. and China, and serves as both chairperson and administrator of the scholarship fund set up in Fosse's name. She has helped to restage Cole's works for the American Dancemachine, and in 1991 set Fosse's "Percussion Four" from *Dancin'* on the Hubbard Street Dance Company, a world-renowned Chicago-based company. Lee Theodore, director of American Dancemachine, once said, "Within (Verdon's) body exists the art of Jack Cole, Bob Fosse, and Michael Kidd, all of whom have created works on her. She is a fabulous, fabulous teacher!"[12]

Carol Haney was also considered the epitome of the Cole dancer. She too became a success due to her own abilities. After owning her own studio in New Bedford at the age of fifteen, she served as assistant to both Jack Cole and Gene Kelly while they were on staff at the Metro Goldwyn Mayer studios, and returned to New York with Bob Fosse in 1954 to become an overnight star in *Pajama Game*. Walter Kerr, in his review of the show in the *New York Herald Tribune*, said, "…she makes "Steam Heat" hotter than even its doting composers could have hoped for."[13] This performance was to be a turning point in the development of jazz dance, responsible, according to Gus Giordano, for the "street look" and association with popular culture that jazz dance has today.[14] Haney had directorial aspirations but, despite her successful work as a choreographer in Broadway shows such as *Flower Drum Song* (1958) and *Funny Girl* (1964), found it difficult to break into Broadway as a director, such as Jack Cole, Bob Fosse, Gene Kelly, Gower Champion, and Jerome Robbins had done. She turned to industrial productions for her directing outlet. In an interview with Edwina Hazard in 1964 she said, "For a woman, this position [of director/choreographer] is extremely difficult to achieve on Broadway."[15] Her industrials, especially the annual Oldsmobile Show, helped encourage the use of dancers in industry, and bring jazz dance to commercial success. Her untimely death of a respiratory ailment at the age of 40 (just after the 10-year anniversary of *Pajama Game*) robbed the jazz dance field of an incredible talent. However, according to Barbara Cohen-

---

[12] Gruen, John. *People Who Dance*. Princeton: Princeton Book Co., 1988, p. 118.

[13] Op. cit., Suskin, p. 178.

[14] Personal communication, Gus Giordano, March 5, 1992.

[15] Hazard, Edwina. "The Product is the Star." *Dance Magazine*, December 1962, p. 44.

Stratyner in *The Biographical Dictionary of Dance*, "Haney's personal style, with choice of isolated angular movements or soft extensions was picked up by other dancers and choreographers and survives her."[16]

Chita Rivera exploded into the public eye in 1957 as the character of Anita in *West Side Story*, choreographed by Jerome Robbins. She personified all those characteristics we now define as jazz: angularity, irregular and Latin-influenced rhythms, dynamism, percussiveness, street moves, "hot" and "cool" styles, technical prowess, and dramatic interpretation. Many jazz dancers and choreographers can recall watching her performance and the impact it had on their career choices. Her arrival onto the dance scene marks the arrival of jazz dance into young adulthood.

Rivera left her scholarship at the School of American Ballet in 1962 to work with Robbins, and later worked with Michael Kidd, Gower Champion, and Bob Fosse. In an interview with Arlene Croce, Fosse called both Verdon and Rivera "ideal dancers — in other words, ideal instruments..."[17] He also acknowledged their creativity and intelligence, admitting that they often had choreographic input into the numbers he was creating. "...they're valuable, as well, for their judgments and opinions," he continued.[18] Rivera still impresses audiences today in her dancing solo nightclub act, after a debilitating car accident several years ago which shattered her left leg. She credits her remarkable strength and recovery to her solid ballet and jazz technique. In an interview with Marian Horosko in 1991, Rivera said, "To me, the best life is one that is a life of dance, not a life with dance in it as a career."[19] Rivera has helped to legitimize jazz dance as an art form worthy of dedicating a life to.

West Side Story also brought us Lee Becker Theodore, who played the original role of Anybodys. In 1962, after the run of the show, she formed her own small company, the Jazz Ballet Theatre, in which she trained dancer/choreographers. In an interview with John Gruen, Theodore said, "I had the idea that America needed a serious jazz company. Essentially, what I did was to cover the spectrum of old jazz, new jazz, contemporary jazz and, at the heart of it all, improvisational jazz."[20] She spent four months "training" dancers to choreograph, including Michael Bennett, Eliot Feld, Alan Johnson,

---

[16] Cohen-Stratyner, Barbara. *The Biographical Dictionary of Dance.* New York: Schirmer Books, 1982, p. 342.

[17] Kislan, Richard. *Hoofing on Broadway.* Englewood Cliffs, New Jersey: Prentice-Hall Press, 1987, p. 108.

[18] Ibid.

[19] Horosko, Marion. "Chita: Better Than Ever," *Dance Magazine.* September 1991, p. 65.

[20] Op. cit., Gruen, p. 114.

Jay Norman, and Jaime Rogers. Theodore's largest contribution to jazz dance came later in the formation of the American Dancemachine in 1978, a school, research center and performance company dedicated to the reconstruction and preservation of American theatre dance. The repertory included works by Agnes de Mille, Jack Cole, Bob Fosse, and Onna White. Since Theodore's death in 1987, that company has yet to revive.

Television

Other venues in which women were helping to create jazz dance began to flourish in the 1950s as well. As prime time television developed, variety shows usually included dance sequences, and June Taylor was instrumental in the conception and execution of dance on television.

Taylor was born in Chicago, where she began studying dance at age ten. At thirteen, she made her professional debut in a George White production and at seventeen left Chicago to perform in London with the Ted Lewis Band. After her return to the United States, she collapsed from tuberculosis during a performance. She was hospitalized for two years, after which she walked out to the dismay of the doctors, who claimed she would live only three more months. Although Taylor recovered to return to the dance studio, she realized she would never regain enough strength to resume her performing career. It was then she turned her focus to teaching and choreography.

Taylor's first troupe, consisting of three friends and her sister Marilyn, opened for band leader Ted Weems in Chicago in 1942. They were an instant success, and within a year had grown to six dancers and received offers from around the country. Taylor chose to go to New York to work with Duke Ellington, who wrote "Take the A Train" as an opening number for the group. She stayed with Ellington for a year, forming six other groups which toured the U.S. In 1948, Taylor began her now-famous association with television, choreographing for the "Toastettes" on Ed Sullivan's *The Toast of the Town*. She choreographed for Sullivan for one and a half years, then joined Jackie Gleason on the *Cavalcade of Stars* from 1952–70. It was there that she changed the name of the group to "The June Taylor Dancers" and earned the reputation as "the lady who owns Saturday night."[21] According to Taylor, "In 1952 'The June Taylor Dancers' increased to 16. We started overhead camera work at the beginning of the Jack Cole era and the move toward modern jazz dance."[22] The group grew to 32 well-matched female dancers

---

[21] Ibid., p. 866.

[22] Personal communication, June Taylor, April 17, 1992.

doing precision jazz in a line which usually culminated in a circle formation shot from an aerial view. In 1954 Taylor received an Emmy Award for television excellence. It may also be noted that she was the first television choreographer to include a black dancer in her line in 1963, something the Radio City Music Hall Rockettes would not do until 1988.

June Taylor was also instrumental in the training of dancers. She began teaching children while she was only twelve years old herself, in exchange for dance lessons during the Depression. Later she founded the June Taylor School in New York City, where her faculty and students included such teachers and choreographers as Michael Bennett, Jaime Rogers, Richard Thomas, Karel Schook, Matt Mattox, Luigi, Arthur Mitchell, and Donald McKayle. She closed the school in 1964 when *The Jackie Gleason Show* moved to Florida, where she still lives. She has since served as director-choreographer of the Miami Dolphin Cheerleaders, and in February of 1992 produced and directed the much-acclaimed UNICEF benefit, "A Tribute to the World's Children," which starred Audrey Hepburn, Liza Minnelli, and 450 children of diverse ethnic backgrounds. Taylor was honored for her contribution to the field of dance at the Capezio Awards in 1991.

Film

Maggie Banks is often overlooked in the history of jazz dance. Banks was well-known and certainly well depended upon as an assistant choreographer in films and television. At a time when men dominated the choreography of film, Banks was usually hired by 20th Century Fox as the assistant choreographer before her superior was hired. Her knowledge of jazz was solid, and she was often called upon to choreograph sequences or give the dancers the "style" of the choreography. She served as assistant to Jack Cole, Gene Kelly, Charles O'Curran, Hermes Pan, Nick Castle, and Jerome Robbins, for whom she worked on *West Side Story* in 1962. Part of Banks's contribution to jazz in film and television was her knowledge of the camera. She not only knew what angle and lens to use during filming, but often helped to cut, splice and edit dance sequences as well.

In films of the 1950s we began to see the Gene Kelly classics, and were introduced to his female partners, all technically proficient dancers. Cyd Charisse, who had danced for the Ballets Russes de Monte Carlo in 1939, was considered by some to be the best-trained dancer to turn to jazz dance. She is most famous for her sultry number with Kelly in *Singing in the Rain*. This number helped establish the stereotype of sexuality often looked for in a female jazz dancer, furthered in the 70's by Donna McKechnie and Ann Reinking: long legs, well-developed bust, a mysterious demeanor and versatile technique.

Las Vegas Revues

Juliet Prowse reigns as queen of the Las Vegas revue, another venue giving rise to jazz dance in the 1950s. Like Charisse, Prowse had been a professional ballet dancer in South Africa before turning to jazz dance. She worked for Jack Cole in London, and originally came to the United States at the suggestion of Hermes Pan to portray the lead can-can dancer in the film version of *Can-Can*. Prowse has become the prototype of the Vegas female star — a sensual dancer with long legs, high extensions, and charming personality, always surrounded by jazz-dancing men who lift her, turn her, and compete for her attentions.

Teaching Centers

With the so-called "arrival" of jazz dance, jazz began to be taught as a separate technique in more studios across the United States, and in metropolitan centers world-wide such as Paris, London, and Milan. In the late '50s and early '60s other jazz dance concert companies like Theodore's began to form.

Luigi, who had begun teaching his technique in 1951 at the Rainbow Studios in Hollywood, moved to New York in 1956, and by 1957 had an established reputation as a jazz teacher for Broadway dancers. He trained many women who have gone on to teach jazz, such as Eva Von Gencsy, Liz Williamson, and Lynn Simonson. Gus Giordano founded his studio in Evanston, Illinois in 1955 and in 1962 formed his jazz dance company, influencing women teachers such as Lea Darwin, Patty Obey, Meribeth Kisner and Susan Quinn. It should be noted, however, that most teachers at this time were women, and in smaller cities and rural areas, jazz teachers such as Beverly Fletcher (Michael Bennett's teacher) and Patsy Swayze (now known as Patrick's mother) continued to train up-coming performers and choreographers.

The '60s: Choreographers

Dance in the '60s suffered from lack of production, especially on Broadway and in film, as the popular culture focused on individuality and the sexual revolution. It was that focus that gave rise to the possibility for more and more women to impact the field of jazz dance.

Margo Sappington seems to best represent the woman jazz choreographer emerging in this era. She started as a ballet dancer with the Joffrey Ballet, and after an injury left to pursue a Broadway career. Luigi says, "When I first saw Margo she was a pure artistic ballet and modern dancer. Next thing I know she's choreographing *Oh Calcutta!*"[23] The show, most famous for its daring nude pas de deux, opened in 1968 and ran for decades.

Sappington has pursued her choreography career, and is now considered one of the leading jazz choreographers of our time. Her works are very kinetic, often filling the stage in a frenzy of undulating torsos and expansive leaps. "Cobras in the Moonlight," choreographed for the Hubbard Street Dance Company in 1986, is a haunting piece about the male and female energies existing within a woman. "Step Out of Love," created for HSDC in 1987, depicts five women dealing with thwarted relationships in harsh movements that verge on self-punishment, only once coalescing into an ensemble passage. Sappington has choreographed pieces for Les Ballet Jazz de Montreal, Netherlands Dance Theater, the Joffrey Ballet, Houston Ballet, Pennsylvania Ballet and the Central Ballet of China in Beijing. She also choreographs for the Broadway stage and music videos, and has taught at the American College Dance Festival Association's choreography school in Austin for a number of years. Gwen Verdon calls her works, "wild and wonderful things, which you must be a trained dancer to do."[24]

Lynne Taylor-Corbett is another choreographer of note to emerge in the 1960s. She was a member of the Alvin Ailey American Dance Theater, and performed in Michael Bennett's *Promises, Promises*, among others. She helped to found the Theatre Dance Collection, for whom she choreographed for several years before becoming well-known in the 1970s. She has choreographed for ballet, jazz and modern dance companies as well as television and film. Her jazz works can be seen in the repertories of the Hubbard Street Dance Company, Les Ballets Jazz de Montreal, and The Atlanta Ballet Company, as well as in the film *Footloose* (Paramount, 1984). Taylor-Corbett has a unique ability to choreograph for the subtle qualities of each individual dancer she is working with — both physically and emotionally. Especially memorable are her male-female duets, such as "Diary" (1982) and "Go, Said Max!" (1983) for HSDC, as well as her now-famous "Appearances" (1983) for the Atlanta Ballet, which explores the gender roles of men and women.

Probably the most influential of all women choreographers, Twyla Tharp established her popular theater reputation with the film *Hair* (1979).

---

[23] Personal communication, Luigi, January 10, 1992.

[24] Personal communication, Verdon, February 19, 1992.

Tharp studied ballet with Richard Thomas and Barbara Fallis, modern with Martha Graham, Paul Taylor, Merce Cunningham, Alwin Nikolais, and Erick Hawkins, and jazz with Luigi. Although often considered a modern/ballet choreographer, Tharp's work defies categorization. Dance critic Joseph Mazo makes a good argument for Tharp's inclusion in the history of jazz dance, for several of her works are set to jazz music although they do not use the codified jazz dance vocabulary. Nevertheless, they interpret the spirit of jazz music, as well as capture aspects of social dance, on which jazz was originally based.[25] These works include "Eight Jelly Rolls," (1974) "Sue's Leg," (1976) "Baker's Dozen," (1981) "The Golden Section," (1981) and "Nine Sinatra Songs." (1982) In 1990, Tharp entered into a relationship with the jazz-oriented Hubbard Street Dance Company. Claire Bataille, former principal dancer and assistant artistic director of HSDC, says, "Once you understand Twyla's movement, and can do it intelligently, it's incredibly satisfying."[26]

In 1972 Eva Von Gencsy teamed with Genevieve Saibaing to found Les Ballets Jazz de Montreal. A Hungarian ballerina who had danced with the Royal Winnipeg Ballet and Les Grands Ballets Canadiennes, she studied with Luigi in New York and returned to Montreal to begin teaching jazz classes in his lyrical style. "Jazz was a revelation to me," she said in a 1974 interview, "Although I love ballet, it did not allow me to completely express myself, as jazz did."[27] Les Ballets Jazz is now one of the premiere jazz companies of the world, with works by many women in their repertory, including Sappington and Taylor-Corbett. Although Von Gencsy left the company in 1978, she continues to teach jazz internationally.

The '70s and '80s: Jazz Technique Accepted into the Dance World

The '70s and '80s led to a rise in the teaching of jazz dance technique, as women who had studied with the masters began to teach on their own. Jazz dance had previously infiltrated the convention circuit, but now became part of the serious dance festival as well.

The American Dance Festival in Durham, North Carolina started their jazz program in the early 1980's; Liz Williamson (d. 1995) was their principal teacher. She also taught jazz at each U.S. International Ballet

---

[25] Mazo, Joseph, "Twyla Tharp," *Dance Magazine*. April 1992.

[26] Personal communication, Claire Bataille, May 28, 1992.

[27] Maynard, Olga, "Les Ballets-Jazz: Dance Le Style Québecois," *Dance Magazine*. January 1974, p. 73.

Competition held in Jackson, Mississippi. Williamson studied with Luigi and danced with the Alvin Ailey company before turning her attention to teaching jazz internationally on a full-time basis. Luigi remembers her as a student: "Liz would take class with a smile from ear to ear for the entire hour and a half. I've never seen a dancer so inspired, so happy."[28] She went on to inspire students in many countries, including France, Germany, Belgium, Brazil, and Quebec, Canada. She published a book on the history of jazz from its African origins to the present, and wrote numerous articles on the teaching of jazz dance.

Lynn Simonson, associated with the Jacob's Pillow Dance Festival for many years, was instrumental in the formation of their Jazz Project. A former student of Luigi, Simonson has long been considered a stable and respected teacher in New York for dancers wanting to study a serious jazz technique. In 1984 she founded Dance Space, Inc., with four other teachers, including jazz choreographer Laurie DeVito. The studio specializes in Simonson Technique — her own approach to jazz with roots in modern dance. According to Laura Orley, Educational Programs Coordinator for Jacob's Pillow, "Lynn teaches with a holistic point of view — the premise that all dancers can dance injury-free."[29] She has influenced many dancers and teachers, such as Katiti King and Diane McCarthy, who teach at Dance Space, Inc., and Claire Bataille, who credits Simonson with teaching her to "breathe and move at the same time!"[30]

Jazz-Tap

Another aspect of jazz dance to be mentioned here — a child of the 40's and 50's when jazz music was at its prime — is jazz-tap, wherein dancers create jazz percussion with their feet. Brenda Bufalino, Artistic Director of the American Tap Dance Orchestra, is said to be doing for tap what Jack Cole did for jazz — in essence, she may be called the "mother" of jazz-tap. Bufalino approaches tap as a form of jazz music, composing and arranging the percussion sound as well as choreographing the stage movement. Her work is sophisticated, complex, and primarily rhythmic — based on the syncopations of jazz music. When not touring, Bufalino taught at her studio, Woodpeckers, in New York.

---

[28] Personal communication, Luigi, January 10, 1992.

[29] Personal communication, Laura Orley, April 2, 1992.

[30] Op. cit., Bataille.

Sarah Petronio was the major force in establishing jazz-tap in France. She was a partner of Jimmy Slyde and founded the Paris Tap Dance Company. "Being accepted into the tap world as a woman is difficult," Petronio says. "Being accepted into the jazz music world is harder. Because I am accepted as a musician, I can bring dance to that world as well."[31] Petronio also approaches tap as both jazz music and dance, using a lot of improvisation in her work. She currently lives in Chicago, where she teaches and performs at well-known jazz music clubs.

Lynne Dally and Dianne Walker are also contributing to the field. Dally, artistic director of the Jazz Tap Ensemble, has performed with Gregory Hines, Honi Coles, and Brenda Bufalino, and has received NEA fellowships for her choreography. Walker is co-director of the Leon Collins Dance Studio in Boston, where she passes on the legacy of Leon Collins, Willie Spenser, and Jimmy Slyde, with whom she studied and performed. Walker both performed in and was assistant choreographer of *Black and Blue* on Broadway, and can be seen in the film *Tap!*

Jazz Dance Today: The Second Generation

Not to be overlooked in the evolution of jazz dance are the daughters of jazz-dance pioneers such as Nan Giordano, Liza Gennaro-Evans, and Nicole Fosse. These women, who have experienced the growth of jazz dance along with their own growth into adulthood, are passing on the legacy of their fathers while adding their own indelible mark to the form.

Nan Giordano, who claims to have put more pressure on herself to succeed in dance than her father did, is now the Associate Director of Gus Giordano Jazz Dance Chicago. Like her father, she spends much of her time teaching. "It is hard to break into the big teaching circuit as a woman," she says. "Although I teach the Gus Giordano center-based technique that uses energy and strength, I add my own flavor. I am establishing my own reputation independent of my dad."[32]

Liza Gennaro-Evans, daughter of Peter Gennaro, teaches and choreographs in and around New York City. She has served on the faculty of the Harvard University Summer School and the American Theater Dance Workshop's summer program at Hofstra University. Nicole Fosse, daughter of Bob Fosse, is best remembered for her role as the daughter in *All That*

---

[31] Personal communication, Sarah Petronio, March 30, 1992.

[32] Personal communication, Nan Giordano, March 17, 1992.

Jazz (Fox Pictures, 1979). She continues to perform today. By watching these women come of age within the field of jazz dance, we also witness the second generation of jazz dance itself — proof that it is indeed more than just popular movement, proof of its inherent artistry and classic sustainability.

Jazz Dance Tomorrow

Today we find many women in jazz dance. They still outnumber men as dancers and teachers, and are becoming more and more recognized for their contributions to the field. As choreographers, the numbers appear to be increasing. Nan Giordano, who served as Company Coordinator for the 1992 Jazz Dance World Congress, estimated that 80% of the entries for the choreography competition to be held in conjunction with the Congress were submitted by women. Patty Obey, now based in Holland, was the first woman to teach jazz at the Congress. I (Judy Austin) taught jazz dance at the National American College Dance Festival held at Arizona State University in May 1992, alongside Daniel Nagrin and Billy Siegenfeld. More and more universities are opening up to jazz curricula, thanks to the pioneering work of women in academia such as Jean Sabatine, formerly at Wayne State University in Detroit, who wrote passionately on the need for jazz in the curriculum, and Jo Rowan of Oklahoma City University, which offers, along with The University of the Arts in Philadelphia, one of the only dance majors with a concentration in jazz dance.

Women writers, such as Minda Goodman Kraines and Esther Kan (*Jump into Jazz*), Christy Lane (*All That Jazz and More*), and Janice LaPointe-Crump and Kimberly Staley (*Discovering Jazz Dance*), have written primers for jazz students and teachers which help to legitimatize the form. And television has opened up opportunities for such choreographers as Emmy-award winner Debbie Allen, and video choreographer Paula Abdul, who attempts to incorporate a classic jazz technique into her popular music videos.

Much of the responsibility to pass jazz dance on rests on the shoulders of women. Men are still minorities in the field, and often in the limelight as star dancers or choreographers, leaving the important role of teaching to women. As Claire Bataille says, "Teachers must constantly feed themselves with information. Teachers must teach not only how to dance, but who came before."[33] Both the fathers and the mothers of jazz dance are

---

[33] Op. cit., Bataille.

to be recognized and remembered, in order to nurture this art form to its full maturity.

An earlier version of this article first appeared in *Dance Teacher Now*, July/August, 1992. It is reprinted with permission of the editor, K. C. Patrick.

Bibiliography

Beckford, Ruth. *Katherine Dunham: A Biography*. New York: Marcel Dekker, Inc., 1979.

Chapman, Sarah and Kraus, Richard, *History of the Dance in Art and Education*. Englewood Cliffs, New Jersey: Prentice-Hall Press, 1981.

Cohen-Stratyner, Barbara. *Biographical Dictionary of Dance*. New York: Schirmer Books, 1982.

David, Martin A. "Spotlight on Roving Jazz Teacher Liz Williamson." *Dance Teacher Now*. March, 1987.

De Mille, Agnes. *Portrait Gallery*. Boston: Houghton Mifflin Company, 1990.

DeGroot, John. "Still Kicking." *Sunshine: The Magazine of South Florida*. Oct. 12, 1986.

Emery, Lynne Fauley. *Black Dance from 1619 to Today*. New York: Dance Horizons, 1972.

Feliksdal, Benjamin, "Impressions of Jazz Dance Development." *Ballet International*. July/August, 1986.

Frank, Rusty E. *Tap! The Greatest Tap Dance Stars and Their Stories*. New York: William Morrow and Company, 1990.

Gaiter, Dorothy. "1,2,3, Kick Prejudice" *The Miami Herald*. January 1, 1988.

Giordano, Gus. *Anthology of American Jazz Dance*. Evanston: Orion Publishing House, 1978.

Grubb, Kevin Boyd. *Razzle Dazzle: The Life and Work of Bob Fosse*. New York: St. Martin's Press, 1989.

Gruen, John. "American Dance Machine: The Era of Reconstruction." *Dance Magazine*. February, 1978.

Gruen, John. *People Who Dance: 22 Dancers Tell Their Own Stories*. Princeton, New Jersey: Princeton Book Company, 1988.

Hazard, Edwina. "The Product is the Star." *Dance Magazine*. December, 1962.

Horosko, Marion. "Chita: Better Than Ever." *Dance Magazine*. September, 1991.

Kan, Esther and Kraines, Minda Goodman. *Jump into Jazz*. Palo Alto: Mayfield Publishing Company, 1990.

Kenney, William Howland. "Jazz: Bibliographical Essay." *American Studies International*. April, 1987.

Kislan, Richard. *Hoofing on Broadway*. Englewood Cliffs, New Jersey: Prentice-Hall Press, 1987.

Lane, Christy. *All That Jazz and More: The Complete Book of Jazz Dance*. New York: Leisure Press, 1983.

Lonely, Glenn. *Unsung Genius*. New York: Franklin Watts, 1984.

Maynard, Olga. "Les Ballets-Jazz: Dance Le Style Québecois." *Dance Magazine*. January, 1974.

Mazo, Joseph. "Twyla Tharp." *Dance Magazine*. April, 1992.

Moore, Mike and Williamson, Liz. "That Eclectic, Elusive Dance Called Jazz." *Dance Magazine*. February, 1978.

Petronio, Sarah. "What Is This Thing Called Tap?" *International Tap Association Journal*. Winter, 1990.

Smith, Ernie. "Recollections and Reflections of a Jazz Dance Film Collector." *Dance Research Journal*. Spring, 1983.

Stearns, Jean and Marshall. *Jazz Dance: The Story of American Vernacular Dance*. New York: Schirmer Books, 1968.

Suskin, Steven. *Opening Night on Broadway: A Critical Quotebook of the Golden Era of the Musical Theater, Oklahoma! (1943) to Fiddler on the Roof (1964)*. New York: Schirmer Books, 1990.

Wershing, Susan M. "Note from the Publisher: What Is Jazz Dance?" *Dance Teacher Now*. October, 1990.

Williamson, Liz. "The Jazz Beat." *Dance Magazine*. February and March 1978.

Williamson, Liz. "Jazz Dance — Learning for Teacher and Student." *Dance Magazine*. March, 1978.

BODY WISDOM
Gay Cheney

Body wisdom is an incredible gift and resource to all of us but it's primarily women who tune into its availability, who are willing to quietly listen, to allow the movement to inform us. Unfortunately men are so focused on making things happen, making themselves jump hurdles, pump iron, get one more client for the firm, that there's seldom a one, a special one, willing to put it all aside to see what else is there. Basically, says Mary Whitehouse, "there is the unconscious fear of the body itself, that the emotions are rooted in the body." While women "know dancing as the meaning of the body,"[1] as the manifesting of feeling, men often shy away from both. For her, who creates out of her body, allowing movement to come forth is quite natural, but for him it is usually experienced as submissive, uncomfortable, and definitely not masculine. So this writing is addressed mostly to women and hopefully to the female aspect of us all — brothers as well as sisters.

My main teachers of this way of understanding have been Mary Whitehouse, Maja Schade, Joan Halifax, Deborah Hay, and Janet Adler. You're right — all women! Mary Whitehouse combined her dance training with Mary Wigman and psychoanalytic work with Carl Jung into a pioneering approach to Dance Therapy which she called Movement in Depth. Mary, along with Trudi Schoop and Marion Chace, were among the first of this century to remember the therapeutic nature and power of dance as it had been practiced by primal people. Mary's work became part of the curriculum at UCLA and her private practice in Los Angeles spawned such recognized professionals as Janet Adler and Joan Chodorow. Mary Whitehouse, pioneering dance therapist, began it for me — a whole other way of moving, of sensing the movement, of finding the center of initiation, of understanding with amazement what I as body could bring forth to be learned from and understood.

Sometime soon we need to grapple with our Western language problem which reflects our philosophical dualism: mind-body-spirit as three separate words. Motion and emotion are not so bad. Both are understood as

---

[1] Whitehouse, M. "Physical Movement and Personality." Unpublished paper, p. 11.

body process: e-motion derives from "from motion". We recognize and know this somewhere in our being. But some of our teachers saw things differently. Jose Limon spoke of "the foot." Even "my foot" implies duality: who is the I that possesses a foot? Once I heard Maxine Sheets, dance philosopher and author, suggest we say something like "I extend through the foot" so as to keep our mind-body and our head to toe all part of the same being.

Deborah Hay, dance artist growing out of the hothouse of Judson Church, helped me put this together by teaching cellular consciousness, letting me experience each cell of my material being as intelligent, as full of vitality, as capable of healing itself, as available to my awareness in its own minute individual important sense. How vibrant and electrically alive we are in this conglomerate megalopolis of cellular compounds and structures — intelligent flesh — nerves and muscles, joints and bones. Deborah Hay, child of the 60's, the Judson Church group, those students of Bob Dunn who took traditional dance off into countless dimensions and definitions. While many came back toward center and some left altogether, Deborah continues to pursue her unique and compelling concepts, making dance the special territory of each and every one of us while allowing us to experience the special territory of our own bodies moving with heightened awareness. Susan Foster says of her: "Hay frequently invokes… the idea of a cellular consciousness. She asserts that every cell in the body must participate in each moment of the dance."[2] In Austin, Texas, home of the Large Group Dance, in Seattle, in Vermont, at Omega Institute, wherever she teaches, Deborah's practice involves improvisation in response to mantras, moving and mystical, which take dancers to realms wherein they become conscious of more than they ever knew existed.

I was blessed to study with Maja Schade at the University of Wisconsin. Maja devoted years to studying neuro-muscular states of the moving and relaxed body. Luckily she was available to us as teacher and guide to meditative states years before meditation became a popular practice in this country. A course in relaxation introduced me to the possibility of letting go of control and tension and judgment and simply allowing myself to be. Allowing, simply allowing, allowing and not willing, myself, body, movement; allowing the mysterious and incredible movement story to tell itself. She influenced many dancers and teachers of dance, having herself been close to Harold Kreutzberg and Mary Wigman.

Janet Adler, dance therapist working in Authentic Movement, generated a trust necessary to benefit fully from experience. She sets up a partnership in which the mover's journey is strongly supported, truthfully

---

[2] Foster, Susan. *Reading Dancing*. Berkeley: University of California Press, 1986, p. 9.

and sensitively witnessed so that nothing of possible importance is missed. Janet Adler's moving work with children is captured in the fim *Looking for Me*. Working with "special" children and mainstream adults for years allowed her to refine the ability to "witness" — to observe without judgment, projection or interpretation — just to be present. Currently, she has a private practice in California and occasionally brings her work to groups of students and leaders at places like the Omega and Naropa Institutes.

And Joan Halifax, anthropologist and journey guide, initiated me into the sacred space and alternate reality available through shamanism. Reverence in regard to my (and all of our) relationships to each vital being in the universe extended the realm of who I am and what I know. I could then allow motion to reveal it. Joan Halifax, one time partner of Stan Grof in researching the effects of hallucinogens on the ill and dying, found shamanistic experiences closely related to the alternate realities produced by drugs. Bridging the prophecies and practices of eastern and western mystical traditions, Joan has introduced many of us to the culture and cosmology of Native Americans and the shaman and of Buddhism and the Bodhisattva at Omega and Ojai Institutes, in the canyons of the Southwest and the rainforests of the Amazon.

My Personal Philosophy as Basis for the Work

My personal philosophy arises out of my own life experience and is affirmed by the cosmologies of indigenous people with which I have familiarized myself. Aborigines and Native Americans understand themselves as an interdependent part of the natural world. This year I discovered through a Melanesian student that her people acknowledge this connection as well. Certainly Isadora Duncan returned us from artifice to the natural world. Doris Humphrey's *Water Study* and *Life of the Bee*, Erick Hawkins's *Plains Daybreak* let us know that they worked from a similar premise. More contemporarily, Laura Dean with her overlapping cycles of rhythms and Molissa Fenley riding on currents of generated energy demonstrate these connections at a more abstract level.

I understand that we are made of everything that is and has been in the natural world. That we are the collective sum of all of our ancestors, we have inherited all of their experiences and memories. As we are born of this earth, we are part oil and part coal, part star and part dinosaur skeleton, some beet root and some wolf ear, sweetheart rose and cow dung. Being in relation to the earth, of her energy, we are part butterfly and part tidal wave, part milkweed seed and part thunderbolt. We are, we incorporate (embody) all of it, all of creation. Whether it is our individual emotional history or our collective historical past, our own temporal mood or our part in the phase of the moon, the season of the year, it all lives in us. And it manifests in our movement. We are capable of being entertained by our toes or we can shape shift and experience coyote life in South Dakota. Cellular memory contains all of it. Movement, if allowed, manifests whatever part we are momentarily close to and connected with. Consciousness identifies it for our use, now and in future time. We are, and have access to, all that has been and will be, made available through movement.

So much to know, so little time. How can we, each day, take space and time to know where we are, how we are, how we feel, what all led up to this? What else is there in other beings to know about and learn from, be extended and expanded by, to have some sense of future? Where do we go, by knowing, expanding ourselves as part of the whole universe in relation to slug and salmon, cicada and sequoia; our limitations, our potential; we as finite, we as eternal. We know all of it, we are a storehouse of the memory, of awareness. We are the projection of sorrow, resignation and yet, still hope.

We are of the earth, our mother. We know her support and nurturance, ongoing despite our ridiculous ignorance and misuse of her. Our bodies blend and merge, nurtured by her body, supported, grounded, running with the rivers, held and rocked by the seas. The ocean, womb of the mother, the fluid from which we are born, provides the idea of tides and phases and passions. Oceanic women feelings: gentle and playful, then thoughtful and calm, powerful and dignified, raging and avenging, seductive, longing, sucking us in, sending us scattered, exciting us with her sweeping and rolling and tumbling, supporting us in our floating and resting and going with the current. How well we know the scope of her moods.

Tides and cycles also connect with grandmother moon and the periodicity of women's moontime. From her comes knowledge of rhythm and form — a time to fill: to wax, to rejoice, to act, to shout and to dance; and a time to empty: to wane, to mourn, to listen and to rest. We are on body time; we know and sense and feel it all in our tides and cycles, daily — monthly, empty — full. There is no question that women know their relationship to the earth, sea, and moon.

The Work

Originally this work might have been called movement awareness. Mary called it movement in depth; Janet, authentic movement. I read recently of someone calling it body weather. As it goes beyond the personal for me, I call it body wisdom. It seems to tap into the source of everything we can know.

Mary Whitehouse used to say that it was dancers who had the most problem with movement in depth, that they had been so well trained to move in particular ways, with extended knees and pointed toes, pulled up, tucked under, and so used to consciously directing it to happen that they couldn't release to allow other, more individual, expression and deeply connected, motivated movement to occur. Obviously her experience with dancers had led her to this conclusion, but it was never my experience, nor that of the dancers I have worked with who also have chosen to do this work. I, we, have taken to it like fish finally in water, like we'd been waiting all our lives to do this. We were body-hungry for the truth of it. A self-defined "definitely non-dancer" in my class told me how intimidated she was being around dancers who had all this vocabulary of movement. I tried to make it more accessible to her saying "but this isn't learned dance vocabulary, it's a language we each have access to in our original state." She responded "Well then, it's that their training makes them so articulate, so connected to movement and at home in their bodies," while she, a cerebral person, a Ph.D. in philosophy, was like a stranger in a foreign land. I am sympathetic with this, knowing that from the first time we were told to "sit still" in the first grade, some of us just put our impulses on hold for a while; others froze forever then and there. For dancers, perhaps, feelings are still in a fairly fluid state, available for awakening and tapping into. They often revel in sensations and emotions ready to reveal themselves in movement from the depths, from the primal and unfettered motivation for motion.

My work with Mary, initially guided by some themes I might attach to and focus on, let me understand the significance of simply up and down, left and right, curved and straight. Great metaphors, food for thought. One who walks or paints the straight and narrow, never goes outside the lines, may be direct and overly focused, rigid and uptight. She who follows the curve seems flexible, allowing for alternate routes, exploring the possibilities, open to the process of going, not so driven or goal oriented. And in the extreme she may get totally dizzy and out of control, walking in circles, losing the center of balance.

Mary spoke of a woman she worked with whose husband had recently died. She spent whole sessions rocking back and forth from right to left, left to right and back. Mary didn't coach or interfere, sensing the seriousness of the process, the making of choice, simply waiting. One day it rose to a head: the woman's rocking enlarged and accelerated. She seemed to rock so far to the left that she was about to lose her balance and fall. At the point of giving in to it, she caught herself, stood up, opened her eyes and with feet firmly planted said, "I'm going to live. I'm not going to go after him, I'm going to live!" The hugeness in so simple a theme.

    Mary dealt with levels of space in many different ways, one of the most powerful for me being the exploration of downness, of being in connection with the earth. With Maja Schade, I had practiced releasing my weight to the earth. Now I sensed the Earth as Mother, not only holding and supporting me, but nurturing and nourishing me. It was a group session in which we were guided to press all parts of ourselves, sides, back and front, into the earth, sucking energy, love, whatever we needed from her breast. We fully indulged ourselves in this feast, in this healing. At just the right time (I have learned to sense and see the cues that tell of this readiness to go on), we were cued to find our way to standing. There was no need to direct ourselves to stand but to take as much time as necessary to find the way, the most natural and organic body path to standing, to being in connection with, under the protection of the Father, Father Sky. It had been such a struggle to leave Mother Earth and rise up, at the sound/vision of the Father, I burst into tears heavy laden with the perfection of expectations that the concept seemed to carry with it. I had expected to be so God-like; I had fallen so short.

    We talked, we kept journals, we drew our experiences. It was my beginning, my initial glimpse of what else there was of me that could be accessed through movement of this incredible and wise body that I was in. In the weeks that followed, I worked a lot on upper space, walking on tip toe, reaching up with such yearning. One day in a totally open session, no cues or suggestions necessary from the leader, I was just moving, engrossed in another journey from down to up when I was suddenly conscious of the fact that I had been in relevé on my right foot in perfect balance for 2–3 minutes. (With this self-consciousness, I immediately lost it.) Something I would never have accomplished in a technique class, being instructed to do it. It was the result of a personal, pure and deeply motivated urge to rise that accomplished such a thing. That moment completely changed my sense of what "technique" is and how it might be taught in other than the usual ways, probably not "taught" but arrived at through sincere motivation.

    As I found myself and see my students spending so much time on the floor, close to the earth, I know how much we need it. How difficult it is to stand solidly, firmly and alone on our own two feet. And how important it is to find our own initiation and clear motivation to do it and to take as long as we want and need to do it. How many parents have picked up their children and placed them on their feet wanting them to be there ahead of the other 8-month-olds, the slowest one suggested to be a little dull, less than sharp witted. The slowest one arriving in the most sure and secure position, well grounded and feeling totally supported. I hear that I stood at 7 months. My parents often told this proudly. Some of us have to do it fast, knowing we have to take care of ourselves pretty quickly. Later we have to go back and redo it in our own time, according to our own readiness, for no one else but ourselves.

While I was working with Mary in Los Angeles, I was also choreographing dances as part of my dissertation project at the Univesity of Southern California. Spending long hours alone in the studios, improvising, searching for my own authentic movement with which to choreograph, I actually discovered how many people lived in my body, what a composite I was. For two hours one night, I moved out different personas who each had tones of voices and bits of dialogue to match. My observing part was amazed at the population that unfolded, that I knew about, had seen, experienced and embodied somewhere along the way. Not only human beings but all living beings seemed to be a part of my history or that of my genes, my cells. Working with Mary concurrently, another journey across the earth let me know from what I arose. I discovered that I also knew about many forms of life before my own — single-celled creatures, beings with no arms and legs, beings with many legs, with wings — gauze like or feathered. Too intimately to be accident or casual observation, didn't I know about galloping and rearing, roaring and pouncing and tearing? I knew without a shadow of a doubt that Darwin was right — I knew my full evolutionary heredity. When a study of Native American cosmology twenty years later centered on the understanding of Mitakuye Oyasin, Lakota affirmation of the interrelation of all beings,[3] I understood what that meant. We are all related, so we must honor each and every life on the planet. We, in this present form, are the sum composite of all life forms that have gone before and that currently are.

In one of her Long Dance workshops, Deborah Hay told of being led into a psychic journey, after which the leader was disappointed that Deborah had experienced herself as only a stone. To the contrary, Deborah explained that it was quite wonderful and rich to lie there and feel the rain patting and washing her, and to be warmed and dried by the rays of the sun, tickled by the crossing of an ant, and surrounded by the rich pungence of earth with sweet green tendrils of grass fanning her as blown by the breeze. To be there all night long in the magical light of the full moon was ecstasy! It is in the wisdom of the Native American as well to acknowledge the sacredness of the stone people. They are seen as the oldest beings on earth, therefore those who have witnessed all that has gone before. If we can embody the experience of the stone people, knowing as they do the support of

---

[3] McGaa, Edwin. *Rainbow Tribe*. San Francisco: HarperCollins, 1992, p. 178.

Mother Earth, the warmth of Grandfather Sun, the mystery and magic of Grandmother Moon, how full and wealthy we are.

This year working with graduate students and being in an expanded cosmology myself, we went farther than ever before in the Body Wisdom work. We spoke a lot about weather — acknowledging and honoring our own weather each day, the motion related to it seeming to keep us informed about where and how we were. It was so surprising to see how different we are from day to day, a little frightening, a little insecure-making. So full of endless possibilities. We also needed to acknowledge the effect of the geophysical weather, its influence on our personal climate: the gray days as different from the golden days, and individually, not generalizably, different. Gray being comforting, snug, quieting to some, depressing to others; cold, crispy temperatures causing some to contract and go bear-like into a "cave" to hibernate, enlivening others. Thunder, lightning and slashing rain might one day have frightened us, excited us at other times. Coming when and as it did, it seemed to us like a great gift of the cosmos, magical energy. The lights went out; we moved from rejoicing at the windows into the candlelight ceremony we had already prepared.

Dancing with Joan Halifax at the Omega Institute gave me access to past lives. To the drums of many we danced as I have never known to dance in this life, but I knew exactly how to do it. I left the present space and found myself in a cave with firelight flickering on the walls, dressed in white deerskin, with deer toe rattles at my ankles. On another day, the dancing was sent into abandoned spinning by the vibrations of a huge Korean gong. Gratefully I was received gently by the earth and went into vision which I had not done before nor since. I was a tear of God running down a fine spun silver thread into the clear turquoise sea, where a sunbeam reached me and I became crystal, all facets of my being radiating the sweetest light out into the universe. Knowing myself in this way was so powerful and overwhelming, I cried for a long while afterward. I have spent my life since then trying to understand what I am to do with this knowledge, available to me, to all of us, through movement, spun out of the conscious knowledge of our cells, the wisdom of our body selves.

Ceremony, too. From working with teachers and Native American shamans, I have learned ceremonies. Students and I have intentionally and consciously created ceremonies. But there are ceremonies that simply arise out of the dynamics of time, space, circumstances, the energies of the group coming into singular focus. Half through the semester, knowing the stress and exhaustion of the students, I cued the group (as I sometimes did) in a direction which I thought might provide outlet, solace. Half an hour into it, the release of crying from deep inside one of the women slowly and carefully drew the rest of the group into contact with her. An intuitive laying on of hands helped Lisa to fully feel what was going on in herself, the energy of others acting as conduit for its release and resolve. Once the episode was over, people went back to what they had been moving through. Later, in discussion, we all knew we had been part of a spontaneous healing ceremony called forth by the immediacy of need, the close-knit consciousness of the group.

Groups are so fascinating. Composed of strong individuals, the dynamics constantly shift and change. Relationships occur — some people seem to model significant others for us, having something in common with that person that gives us opportunity to work out issues. At Omega with Janet Adler, I kept trying to move and interact with one of the men, who kept moving out, throwing me away. The more he left me, the more I persisted. Finally one day I went after him with absolute vengeance and tenacity. Even with eyes closed I had found him in the group. Hanging on to him like a giant cat, I could not be shaken loose. And he did shake and try to throw me off. But I clung, held fast. I got hurt over and over again but never gave up. I can remember words coming, "Oh, no buddy. You're not going to get rid of me. You're not going to get away from me this time." Janet was moved by the intensity of it, by my persistence and tenacity, the riding out of all the rejections and attempts to dislodge me. I was like a roughrider on a wild maverick bronco. I emerged the rodeo champion — bruised but be-ribboned. In later discussion, he and I located our connection. I signified his mother, possessive and controlling, from whom he had been trying to emerge; he was my father who was always avoiding intimate contact with me, pushing me from him. We were a perfect match.

My Approach to Teaching the Work

When I first started to teach, my accompanist, much more experienced than me, used to say, "It's amazing. You don't really teach them. You just expect them to do it — and somehow they do!" So I may still bring this attitude with me to Body Wisdom classes and some are carried by it right into the flow of moving. Others aren't. And I have to be careful that, like my father, I don't expect too much of them but find the way to lead them out of their lock up step by step.

How does it happen; how and when do we find it? Do we just push a button and begin? For some of us, yes! Just like that. Once we understand that this other nature exists, we tune into it and begin to move. Other times and for other people this somatic center, this motion source is unavailable, perhaps unbelievable, under so many layers of inhibition and covering up.

It could be terrifying to know and feel what might be revealed to ourselves and to others. So we are careful about it, come to it or go after it slowly, thoughtfully and with infinite patience, awaiting the peeling back layer by layer of the protective skins.

My approach to it probably comes from Mary Whitehouse, who simply suggested, sat still, and quietly supported whatever happened. The sequence of motivation, issues dealt with, comes from years of experience, of discovering what things we need to feel comfortable with and secure about before we can really let go and let it happen. And every group has its own life and energy and ideas and needs that become apparent and guide the progression of events. There are, however, for me, some definite and basic beginnings.

Maja Schade taught me that it all begins with the breath. And that's where I begin after some preliminaries. We start walking through the space of the studio, sometimes a very familiar place but not thoroughly known, checking out the look — the color and texture of the walls, ceiling, floor. We tune into how the walls feel to the shoulders, how the floor boards feel on the soles of the feet, how it is to walk with them and then across them. What it feels like to be in the corners of the room, in the center of the space, walking along the sides, across the diagonals of the space; where it is they are most comfortable; where it feels most dangerous. And where it feels like home. They wind, curl, burrow into that home and really feel it, taste it, know how it is. We start again to move through the room. This time with eyes closed, going by the feel, feel on the soles of the feet, on the skin, of the places which register security and danger. And move through all of the space "seeing" how much we know of where we are; and we return "home." This way we get to know, become familiar with, comfortable in the space we will be working in throughout the experience. It is an in-depth connection with the environment. And sometimes, after we have learned this space, we make the transition to another, carefully and consciously, as practice for transition, change: for leaving home, for leaving school.

Next we move on to the human environment, establishing an initial comfort level with each other. We walk around, past, through, behind each other, feeling vibrations or energies of the others. We consciously look and see each other while moving around and past, checking out hair style, eye color, heights and shoulder widths and hip wiggles. We see eye to eye, we see through or past each other. We make some sort of initial contact — brush, tap, touch, hand shake. (We laugh a lot here, getting over the embarrassment of such intimacy. Just wait!) We see how other people feel, how the movement of individuals feel. We walk behind or beside someone, or facing them, getting the feel of who they are. Later we do a very specific study of someone whom we follow and whose walk and body language we take on, copying exactly in the smallest detail. In walking in the other's shoes, by getting right inside his/her skin, we come to know and understand this other as ourself.

There's much more that will happen between us but here's another small orientation. We make contact between us sideways. We touch shoulders, outsides of arms, or hands. And we feel into each other through this contact so we experience Siamese twin-ness. We get ready, think about it, shift a little to take the first step absolutely together, and keep walking from there absolutely together. We turn the corner together, change direction together, slow down together, speed up together. We feel the same impulse at the same moment to "restyle" the walk, give it more energy up, accelerate it, bend the right knee of it, lift onto the balls of the feet in it. We develop and continue and slow down and come to a stop at the same second on the same foot which is angled in the same direction, taking weight in the same way.

We have made contact. We have established connection. We talk about the experience: how difficult it is to give ourselves up and come into communion with the other; or how easy it is to give up our skin and come into merger with the other. But this is only one of the others, and there is the rest of the world to explore and get to know ourselves in relation to.

We move in relation to basic movement/dance themes. We try out space: moving big through space: moving through big space: moving small. And not just moving but registering how it feels to move huge, to move tiny. And how it feels to move very fast, then very slow. And what is your normal tempo? Where are you comfortable going in time today? Too much rushing around? Relax. Too much to get done? Speed up. And this is just for today. This is where you are today. Tomorrow you may feel like slowing down, the next day may bring energy to tear through it. And how does it feel to you to be taking a full taste of the deliciousness of slow motion and someone else goes racing by? How can you two meet in time, or can you?

We deal with weight, getting into what burdens we carry, our heaviness. The heaviness of carrying another and how we feel about that, depending on how much we already have to carry. And we can transform that weight, and give it up to the earth for awhile and travel light! Fill up with helium and flow. We can shape shift and be anything we choose.

And sometimes we go beyond the usual space-time considerations. We walk through space with closed eyes feeling the attraction to a particular direction. We open eyes and identify how and where we face. We talk about the four directions, identify and give meaning, along with color and animal associated by Native American tribes. These are suggestions, not absolutes. Each person finds her own significance in whatever direction she travels.

We play with the pull of the poles. From where we face, we feel how the magnetic energy of North and South pull and push on us, how we resist, how we follow. We know and feel also the draw of East and West, beginnings and endings of the ongoing cycle, and how we are attracted or repulsed by these. And how it is, in the middle of all these pulls and pressures, to find our own center and move clearly out from there.

Then there is a time when the explorations, the directions, the themes, the cues are dispensed with and one is alone to discover her own motions, follow her own impulses. We lie on the floor letting the earth support us, giving up all thoughts of past and future, in order to be just here, now. To help with this we pay total attention to the breath, that which goes on without our conscious direction. It just keeps happening, regulated by something other than our conscious directing minds. We trust that; we depend on that. We practice watching and allowing that breath simply to be. We see it, feel it, as regular and irregular. There's a deep breath and a sigh. Here's a speeding up as I remember an exam I have next hour, a person I might see as I leave here. We observe that the breathing is all a part of us, reflecting what we sense or feel, accommodating action necessary in relation to that. It is the same central source we go to in order to access movement in depth. We can breathe into, send the inhalations, one by one, into the various parts of the body to awake and enliven, but mostly to take all of it, all of us, into our awareness. We awaken the cells, tuning into their wisdom, their messages, acknowledging the mind in the body and listening for it to speak, in and through us. With the first twitch, shift, adjustment, feeling of necessity to move something somewhere, we sense it as the rising of the wave which we get on and ride as far as it takes us. Then we wait, listen and watch for the next one to begin to gather energy, to build the impulse. Again we simply allow it to happen, letting that wave of energy carry us for as long as it will, following it for as long as we can. We get into the rhythm, the ebb and flow of it, the sensitivity to the currents and streams of the ocean of energy in us, which we acknowledge and allow to carry us.

In the process, we simply allow ourselves to be, suspending all judgment, dismissing all the voices saying: "This is stupid. She's standing up there watching me do this?" The idea is just to be curious and to trust. "Hey, this is surprising. I didn't expect this to happen, I wonder where this will take me." And we're on our way, beginning the journey.

As leader, I establish no goals, no rights and wrongs, only valuing whatever is experienced and encouraging that we have a lot to learn from all of it. We look at it, ponder it, write about it, draw it, and fill in more and more of the empty spaces in our being. While each day provides more openings, we become more adept and sure at filling them. As leader I provide experiences wherein each has developed comfort and security being in the space, being with me and the others, knowing that they are supported by me and the others in their process. They are okay in simply being who they are as honestly as they can be, which is the only thing our body moving selves can give us. Even the attempted lie is obvious — like veneer covering mahogany. We treasure, cherish, respect and totally accept the rich, solid integrity of the flesh beneath. In that atmosphere humans feel safe and free to know themselves and others; in that soil, they have rich nurturance to grow and become.

In Body Wisdom class this fall, we celebrated Rosh Hashanah. My women's ceremonial group had made me aware of it as celebration of the new year and of the symbols attached to it, particularly of the relevance of snakes to women. Ideas come from everywhere for this work if one is open to listening. I took Rosh Hashanah to my class for whatever the idea might embody, renewing, shedding skins, beginning fresh and unburdened. Jewish students were grateful to have moved into a new experience of this holy day; the others of us benefited totally from the rebirth. As from the ceremonial sweat lodge, we reemerged from the Mother, cleansed and new.

Weather, seasons, holidays, relationships, are all things to focus the movement around. Other times movers want and need free time, no cues, no themes, no coaching. Here the witness helps. Helps remind us of what we did, how we were moved, helps us by asking perhaps, what the scratching on the wall was about, how giving my weight totally to Barbara felt. And each person in the group provides another presence to be dealt with, responded to. It seems there are always so many strong and lithe bodies, so many aggressive as well as gentle energies loosed in this work that women provide for each other an ample sampling of the dynamic possibilities of being human.

I am a woman, I am an artist, I am a teacher. I was never a mother to children of my own; I have wanted to know about mothering through my students, and I have been presented with so many of such different kinds, of such different values, of such different histories. They don't all come to Body Wisdom class but Body Wisdom classes have taught me how to come to them — each one of them. I hope to understand each of them in their differentness, their aloneness, their anger, their fear, their joy. I hope to support them, to disperse some fears, to shed some light. They have taught me so much. This work is such a lesson, such a model, for my life, my relationships, it becomes my philosophy. I want to live its values and teachings, proffered daily for as long and as fully as I can. This is the most natural woman's work I know. I celebrate being in this work; connecting with the feminine side of my being. I celebrate being a woman.

Bibiliography

Foster, Susan. *Reading Dancing*. Berkeley: University of California Press, 1986.
McGaa, Edwin. *Rainbow Tribe*. San Francisco: HarperCollins, 1992.
Whitehouse, Mary. "Physical Movement and Personality." Unpublished
    paper.

WOMEN IN DANCE IN HIGHER EDUCATION
Linda Caruso Haviland

The status of women in administrative positions in dance varies over time, within regions of the field, and among institutions. For example, with a few exceptions, it was not until the second and third decades of the twentieth century, through the pioneering work of a handful of women such as Agnes De Mille, Bronislava Nijinska, Ruth Page, Lucia Chase, Marie Rambert, and, later, female directors of regional and smaller urban based companies,[1] that women had access to the direct shaping of the destiny of ballet. On the other hand, college and university programs and the modern dance and educational programs from which they evolved, seemed to demonstrate, from their inception, a more stable history of authority and leadership positions occupied by women. For a variety of well documented reasons, these women were passionately and intellectually committed to the development of new dance in art and education,[2] and for a variety of socio-economic reasons, including the diminishing male status in dance, found the field relatively open, and were, thus, able to establish themselves in these positions.

---

[1] A brief survey of choreographers, maîtres de danse, or opera directors from the 17th through the early 20th century indicates that the place of women was on the stage. André Levinson's *Marie Taglioni* (London: Dance Books, Ltd., 1977) documents the domination of men 'behind the scenes' which was so common. Several books give general accounts of the rise of women choreographers and company directors beginning in the 20th century. These include George Amberg's *Ballet in America* (NY: Duell, Sloan & Pearce, 1949) Lynn Garafola's *Diaghelev's Ballet Russe* (Oxford: Oxford University Press, 1989); John Martin's *Book of the Dance* (NY: Tudor Publishing Co.); Elizabeth Kendall's *Where She Danced* (NY: Alfred Knopf, 1979). See also the biographies and autobiographies of De Mille, De Valois, and others.

[2] Elizabeth Kendall's *Where She Danced* (op cit.), summarizes the innovations in education for children and adults which included the movement exercises of Delsarte, Dalcroze and Laban, and indicates their connection to the work of the early women pioneers in dance. Examples of a particular educational and artistic philosophy can be found in the writings of Isadora Duncan, e.g. "I See America Dancing" in *The Art of the Dance* (NY: Theatre Arts, Inc., 1928) pp. 47–53 and *My Life* (NY: Boni & Liverright, 1927) pp. 174–77, 302–304, 358–59.

But despite the presence of dance programs in colleges and universities since roughly 1916,[3] and despite access to administrative and faculty positions within these programs, women still face significant problems in two related capacities — as women administrators and as dance administators within institutions which in general have been slow to admit women to positions of power and even slower to acknowledge dance as an area of art or scholarship worthy of pursuit and academic credit. Why the hesitation to locate dance near the center of the classic Arts and Humanities curriculum, to recognize its value as both art and academic discipline? Answers to these questions illustrate the intimate connection between social attitudes, including those towards women and bodiedness, and the development of both our artistic and educational institutions.

Clearly, some of the difficulties are engenderd by the fact that dance is an embodied art form in a sense that is all too real for some academics. While all artworks may be physically embodied entities, dance is not contained by stone or pigment but by the living, moving self. Two thousand years of neo-platonic philosophy compounded by Cartesianism and Christianity rendered this body sinful at worst, a hindrance at best, but in any event, certainly not a topic worthy of scholarly inquiry except to reveal its subordinate status to that which was worthy... the mind or soul. It is true that music and visual arts and even dramatic literature have long been topics of inquiry in aesthetics and philosophy; however, these are all forms in which the body has been safely distanced or removed, or text has taken precedence over performance. The categorizing of dance as a bodied art is also inextricably linked to a Western cultural perspective, dominant since the 19th century, that views the major concert dance forms of ballet and modern, as feminine and/or secondary art, in part, at least, because the domain of the culturally associated artist, woman, has also historically been designated as the body.

Ironically, gender typing and negative attitudes towards bodiedness may have assisted the venturing of women into dance and its educational extensions and applications. For example, the consideration of dance as an art in which expression was embodied not in paint or tones but in flesh,

---

[3] Wendy Oliver's "Historic Overview of Dance in Higher Education", *Focus on Dance XII/Dance in Higher Education*. Wendy Oliver, ed. (Reston: American Alliance for Health, Physical Education, and Dance, 1992) pp. 1–4, gives a summary account of the development of dance programs. Richard Kraus and Sarah Chapman (Hilsendager) also present historical background on dance in higher education in several sections of their book, *History of the Dance in Art and Education*, 2nd ed. (Englewood Cliffs, New Jersey: Prentice-Hall, Inc., 1981) (Kraus and Chapman, eds.). See, particularly, pp. 256–258.

usually that of a woman, probably discouraged a fuller particpation by men in its early development as a modern form. This is not to imply that women succeeded in changing the face of dance simply because men declined; on the contrary, they succeeded because they initiated change. This active reponse of women towards negative construals of bodiedness and femaleness was evident in the pioneering work in women's health issues, fashion, education, and in the first wave of feminist political activity, all of which created an essential base from which the new artists could emerge.[4] Isadora Duncan and Ruth St. Denis, for example, were daughters of educated, talented women, who through refusal or failure to accomodate social norms, were located on the margins of middle class respectability, and who turned to elements of this social revolution for inspiration or comfort. The pioneer dancers were true daughters of the female restlessness and revolt that were present in their mothers and in the culture at that time. The strength, intelligence and attitudes toward the natural beauty of the body, women, and art which they inherited were instrumental in creating these new forms of concert dance. That their work sometimes coincidentally illuminated or embodied aesthetic values established as priorities by contemporaneous male artists and intellectuals neither accounts for nor negates the power, beauty, originality, value, or even the 'femaleness' of, say, Loie Fuller's or Isadora Duncan's work, nor does it minimize how fittingly their art addressed various social and aesthetic trends or ruptures in the culture at large. However, the ambivalence which these same men expressed towards acknowledging the very artistry which they revered in these women, suggests a continuing resistance towards disrupting or dismantling those social or aesthetic constructs which were heavily influenced by culturally incorporated mind/ body or male/female dualities.

The identification of dance as bodied and female has been a double edged sword in the university as well an in the art world. Although there were and are genuine impediments to scholarly research generated by the nature of dance and performance, it is the intimate connection of the art form to both women and bodiedness, despite Sparshott's claim, which continues,

---

[4] The amount of information documenting the efforts and accomplishments of women during this period is overwhelming. My students, as part of a course project, compiled a bibliography over 25 pages long on 'Women's Issues and Early Modern Dance', which included Women's Health, Women's Physical Education, Women's Education, Clothing as Fashion or Costume, Political/Social/Economic Issues, Dance, Sister Arts, Images in the Arts, Science and Technology, Indices and Bibliographies, Other Resources. Elizabeth Kendall (op. cit.) provides enough information to provide an adequate understanding of the social and economic context from which the pioneers emerged. See particularly "Prologue" (pp. 2–13); "Health and Beauty" (pp. 17–31); and "Europe and Isadora" (pp. 53–69).

in the opinion of many, to compromise it as an area of serious academic or artistic consideration within an arts and humanities curriculum. However, the designation of dance as a 'female' art, and the commitment which many women made to its development, have also assisted in the creation of programs and in the achievement of leadership roles.

The visibility of women in dance administrative positions within academic institutions has been longstanding. Beginning in the second decade of this century, one finds Margaret H'Doubler, Bird Larson, Gertrude Colby, Thelma Hill, and Mary Shelly just to name a few, as well as others whose work provided important foundations, such as Genevieve Stebbins, whose translation of Delsarte's work was a key element in the development of certain aspects of dance education. Throughout these early decades, dance programs developed in several institutions including University of Wisconsin, Barnard, Bennington, University of Michigan, Smith, Vassar, Wellesley, Adelphi University, NYU, and even at my present locus, Bryn Mawr.[5]

But in these early days, dance in academe was seen primarily as an adjunct. Some institutions valued it because they believed that dance might better prepare the constitutions of women for their 'natural' occupation, childbearing; others were committed to the philosophy that linked healthy body to healthy mind. Although early dance educators were in agreement with the notion that dance was an appropriate avenue to physical well being, many also believed that the avenues of cognition and expression provided by dance were not merely supportive of or supplemental to traditional academic learning, but, in fact, provided viable alternatives for generating, understanding, and expressing important information about ourselves.

However, for the most part, the traditional university had difficulty recognizing this insight. Those disciplines which had evolved and come to comprise the arts and humanities reflected the intellectual (as well as social, political, and economic) priorities of, primarily, white, educated men. It should be no surprise, then, that when dance was admitted within the university at all, it was viewed as contributing to a general good rather than

---

[5] Gertrude Prokosch Kurath, dance and music ethnologist, introduced these new forms of dance during her tenure as the first graduate student in Art History in the mid-twenties. Josephine Petts, as chair of Physical Education through the early forties, continued the tradition by offering courses in body mechanics and natural dancing. She had studied physiology at MIT (it wasn't taught at her women's college, Wellseley), taught at Teachers College, and been trained extensively in Duncan technique, although primarily under the tutelage of Elizabeth, and truly believed that the ideal way to produce physically educated young women was through Duncan dancing. (Personal correspondence)

as a specific area of academic inquiry, and most often found itself housed in Physical Education. Arguments within the discipline itself undermined early efforts to establish its further credibility as art or humanity. Should the university present dance as an opportunity for all to experience and grow more assured in the strength and grace of their movement; should it provide a creative experience, alternative or adjunct to academic discourse; or could it be a place as well which trained dancers and/or scholars for the rigors of the performance and/or academic arenas?

Forty years ago, athough dance had, so to speak, a strong toehold in academe, there were members of the field, who for entirely different reasons joined skeptical academics in questioning the extension of Dance from Physical Education into the humanities. Additional fuel was added to this debate from others inside the discipline who questioned not the appropriateness of a liberal arts program providing professional training, but rather the capability of a college program to adequately prepare a professional dancer. There are still some in our field, who despite the roster of graduated B.A.'s in professional companies, are skeptical that any good dance can come from college programs. Although these administrators and artists were legitmately moved to question the validity of concert dance or dance research because of their commitment to a variety of educational philosophies, the ambivalence generated by these questions often undermined the status of dance within the curriculum of institutions, particularly if they were less philosophically or financially committed to accomodating dance.

Being a woman in a college or university setting generates a whole other set of problems. Women have worked in higher education for over one hundred years and their status as scholars as defined within the traditional academic parameters is accepted, more or less, depending on the particular discipline surveyed. However, their power within the institution is less established. Despite gains made during that period when the courts sanctioned the rectification of misdemeanors generated by discrimination based on race or gender, there are significantly fewer female college presidents, deans, and department chairs.[6] Particularly in positions as departmental chairs, women dance administrators have often preceded their peers in the other academic disciplines.

---

[6] In 1988, in the U.S., the percentage of white women who held the rank of full professor was 9.9%. Black women held only. 6% of full professorships. The percentage of women holding office as college or university president was only 10%, and 1.3% of those were African American. (From a study quoted by Reginald Wilson. "Women of Color in Academic Administration," *Sex Roles*, (v. 21, July '89) pp. 85–97.) See also the *Journal of Social Issues* (v. 41, Winter '85), which devotes the entire issue to sexual discrimination in academe.

Clearly the history of powerful and competent women administrators in dance ensures their continuing consideration for these positions. But its useful to consider the possibility that some piece of this territorial success may have been enabled by default, by a sense that dance, being of women and the body, is not a true academic area and not even one of the higher arts, and does not necessitate the presence of a male to oversee it. Second class fields of study can be governed by second class citizens. This comment is generated less by cynicism than by pragmatism. It is necessary to understand the roots, substance, and extent of one's status in order to change, strengthen, extend, or utilize it.

Such an attitude towards dance may also have been instrumental in giving gay men access to these positions. Unfortunately, as men, gay or straight, began to risk what was initially a social stigma attached to the pursuit of dance, and as institutions began to tolerate and support male incursions into what had been deemed a predominantly 'feminine' province, some tensions, little discussed, but nevertheless, very real, have developed within the dance community. Many women may feel that, despite rampant homophobia in this country, any male candidate, particularly white, will have an advantage in a culture where a predominantly white, male population seems to still control everything from grants to tenure. Statistics and hearsay, merit and prejudice, rational discourse and emotions are quite tangled, but it may be necessary to discuss and address these sensitive issues before they begin to negatively affect the field.

The cultivation of these administrative positions and their concomitant power and status for women, is important and essential to the continuing development of dance in higher education. They have been and continue to be used as a base of power to mainstream dance faculties and curricula into academe. You can't challenge course development, tenure tracking, committee appointments, faculty status, pay scales, budget control, etc. until you figuratively and literally have a chair in which to sit.

The challenge, then, to woman dance administrators is to demonstrate not only that both the academic and the artistic aspects of their field command a legitimate address within the institution but also that they, as women within this field, are as competent artists, educators, and administrators as others in any sector of the institution. The administrator must work to convince the institution that dance, as art and humanity, has a place not at the margins, but at the core of the curriculum. i.e that dance is an acknowledged discipline or field of study with its own set of important, significant, and unique questions arising from a specific topic of inquiry; that it has developed and continues to develop its syntactic structure or unique methodologies required by the conceptual and experiential structures generated by its domain; and that dance provides new and valuable ways of perceiving, making sense of, and expressing the content and structure of human life and thought. Concomitant with this is the need to educate administration and colleagues about the kinds of research dance faculty might undertake, particularly if it is performance or choreography which might be less understood as equivalent to the research and publishing which have long served as models of appropriate and successful academic activity. The administrator must also take every advantage of working with those disciplines with which there is a natural connection. Networking, guest lecturing or demonstrating, team teaching with faculty from disciplines such as ethnology, gender studies, history, philosophy, or physics can engender a better understanding of not only the breadth and depth of dance as a significant and pervasive human behavior but also its integral relationship to the accumulated history of our conceptual paradigms.

The outlook for women administrators in general, and women dance administrators specifically, is hopeful. Our occupation in academe these many years has enabled us to solidify our positions and use these to promote and enable change within our programs and the institutions in which they reside; and our efforts have received an assist from political and philosophical changes which have occured in other areas of the institution as well as in our society in general. These gains achieved by women in academe and the recent questioning of the traditional epistomological paradigms which have long governed the content of and modes of inquiry in traditional academic disciplines have facilitated the increasing legitimization and acknowledgement of dance within higher education.

Bibliography

Acosta, R. Vivian and Carpenter, Linda Jean. "Women in Intercollegiate Sport: A Longitudinal Study, 1977–1990." Brooklyn: Brooklyn College, 1990.

Amberg, George. *Ballet in America.* NY: Duell, Sloan & Pearce, 1949.

Duncan, Isadora. *The Art of the Dance.* NY: Theatre Arts, Inc.,1928. *My Life.* NY: Boni & Liverright, 1927.

Emery, Lynne Fauley. (New chapter by Dr. Brenda Dixon-Stowell.) *Black Dance: From 1619 to Today,* 2nd edition. Princeton: Princeton Book Co., 1988.

Garafola, Lynn. *Diaghelev's Ballet Russe.* Oxford: Oxford University Press, 1989.

Horwitz, Tony. "Young Professors Find Life in Academia Isn't What It Used to Be." *Wall Street Journal*, February 15, 1994.

Jowitt, Deborah. "The Search for Motion." *Time and the Dancing Image.* New York: William Morrow and Co., Inc., 1988.

Kendall, Elizabeth. *Where She Danced*. New York: Alfred Knopf, 1979.

Kermode, Frank. "Poet and Dancer before Diagheleff." *Salmagundi*. #33–34, Spring-Summer, 1976.

Kraus, Richard and Chapman, Sarah (Hilsendager) eds. *History of the Dance in Art and Education*, 2nd ed. Englewood Cliffs, New Jersey: Prentice-Hall, Inc., 1981.

Levinson, André. *Marie Taglioni*. London: Dance Books, Ltd., 1977.

Macdougall, Allan Ross. "Isadora and the Artists" in *Isadora Duncan*. Paul Magriel, ed. NY: Henry Holt & Co., 1947.

Oliver, Wendy, ed. *Focus on Dance XII/Dance in Higher Education*, Reston: American Alliance for Health, Physical Education, and Dance, 1992.

St. Denis, Ruth. *An Unfinished Life*. NY: Harper & Bros., 1939.

Seroff, Victor. *The Real Isadora*. NY: Avon Books, 1971.

Siegel, Marcia. *Shapes of Change*. Boston: Houghton Mifflin, 1979.

Sorell, Walter. *Dance in Its Time*. New York: Columbia University Press, 1981.

Sparshott, Francis. *Off the Ground*. Princeton: Princeton University Press, 1988.

Terry, Walter. *Miss Ruth*. NY: Dodd Mead & Co., 1969.

Wilson, Reginald. "Women of Color in Academic Administration." *Sex Roles*. V. 21, July '89 pp. 85–97.

PART IV

PASSING ON THE HERITAGE

Why do women creators dominate modern dance? Unlike ballet, in which the theoretical and practical foundations were created by men, modern dance was created by women who, through the experience of their own physicality, understood female kinesthetic and imagistic potential. Their self-preservation as dancers, choreographers, educators and writers depended on their ability to re-present themselves through dance. In "Passing on the Heritage," three chapters examine the architecture of women's contributions to modern dance from historical, journalistic and feminist perspectives. "Fire and Ice: Archetypes in American Modern Dance" by Sharon E. Friedler categorizes and puts into historic context the images and dance roles created by women for women during six choreographic generations. Roger Copeland in "Sexual Politics" asks why it is that this is the only major art form in which almost all the creators, the consolidators, the second and third generation innovators have been women. In "Feminist Theory and Contemporary Dance," Ann Cooper Albright explores the interrelatedness in cultural discourse between feminist theory and contemporary choreography, articulating the relationship between physical bodies and social meaning.

FIRE AND ICE: FEMALE ARCHETYPES IN AMERICAN MODERN DANCE
Sharon E. Friedler

American female modern dance choreographers have created thousands of roles for women. Much writing has provided structural analyses of their dances but not of the roles they created for women. The discussion has also ignored important contributions that female mentors have made to the creation of images of women. This essay develops a method for categorizing the roles that women have made for and of each other in the six generations since the beginning of American modern dance at the turn of the twentieth century and points us toward a future direction.

Images of Women

Myths often portray the world as balanced between harmony and discord. The various images of women and men within these myths tend to emphasize positive or negative character traits. In developing a parallel framework for harmonious and discordant images, six categories emerge which can be used to discuss roles female choreographers have made for women in American modern dance.[1]

Harmonious mythic visions of women in 20th century American modern dance generally fall into three types:

1. *goddess/priestess* — representing the enlightened magical world demonstrated in acts of vision and healing;
2. *ancestress/mother/teacher* — symbolizing a continuous thread of physical and spiritual knowledge; and
3. *virgin/wife* — embodying the chaste physical world and affirming cultural norms.

---

[1] Many of the ideas explored in this essay were first framed by the author in a paper presented at the American Dance Guild conference in June, 1989. Although there is no attempt in this essay to gauge whether positive or negative images dominate in the work of female modern dance choreographers as a group, further research in this area would be useful.

These three images of women are mirrored by their counterparts presented in the following discordant mythic visions:

1. *witch/devil/madwoman* — representing the dark magical world and serving as a psychic or spiritual threat;
2. *warrior/martyr* — symbolizing the rational world and posing an intellectual or societal threat; and
3. *temptress/whore* — epitomizing the carnal physical world and implying a physical or sexual threat.

An additional category, the nonmythic, human, female figure evolves from choreographers' shifts away from narrative and toward matters of symbol and structure. This change in orientation, which first appears in the early '60's, is linked to and reflects changes in the American political, social, scientific and technological climates and to changes in dance performance practice. Nonmythic women have also been portrayed by female choreographers as both harmonious and discordant.[2]

Since the inception of modern dance, new choreographic generations have emerged every ten to fifteen years; the ways that women are portrayed changed with each generation. During the first and second generations mythic women are most prevalent. In the third generation, they start to share the stage with nonmythic figures. In the fourth generation the balance shifts; many fourth generation choreographers and dancers present themselves as pedestrian human scale "characters" concerned with doing rather than performing and informing rather than entertaining. The prevalence of non-mythic women continues in subsequent generations.[3]

---

[2] Much redefinition regarding performance practice was initiated by a small group of New York dancer/choreographers who emerged from a composition workshop sponsored by Merce Cunningham and taught by Robert Dunn from 1960–64. These choreographers became known as the Judson Group because their first performances were held at Judson Church in lower Manhattan. The term postmodern dance first began to be used in reference to their work.

[3] Dance historian Judith Lynne Hanna describes the model fourth generation women introduced in the following way: "New guises of women in dance show them as more complex than virgin or whore taking on roles of stature, as human, (rather than supernatural) partners with and physical equals to men, guiltless protagonists rather than pawns of gods and men, antagonists confronting inner fears and thoughts, victims confronting their identity in a social order that resists change, women bonding and exploring romantic encounters with other women, in gender role reversals, or blending as asexual, and as fulfilling multiple roles." Hanna, Judith Lynne. *Dance, Sex, and Gender: Signs of Identity, Dominance, Defiance, and Desire.* Chicago: University of Chicago Press, 1988, p. 202.

First Generation (1900–20's)

Three American women, Isadora Duncan, Loie Fuller and Ruth St. Denis, prepared the climate for what later became known as modern dance and were the primary mentors for the succeeding generation. All three evidenced an independence of mind in their creative processes as well as in their life styles. Elizabeth Kendall points to the breadth of their influence when she writes: "Their dances turned instantly into powerful physical metaphors for what most women in the civilized world deeply wished and feared for themselves: freedom to try out modes of being beyond domestic duty. This effect made Loie, Isadora, and Ruth torchbearers of modernism. Europeans especially acclaimed them because they seemed to be what they danced — independent, eccentric, and unafraid."[4]

Isadora Duncan (1878–1927), 'mother' of modern dance, is the most widely known of the women in the first generation. Historically her revolutionary life style was as significant as were her choreographic contributions. Isadora's images of women are most heavily concentrated in three of the categories mentioned above: virgin, ancestress/mother/teacher and warrior/martyr. Virginal images appear in Isadora's earlier work such as "Chopin Waltzes" in which bounding skips and open arm gestures capture the lightheartedness and innocence of adolescence. Discordant images are prevalent in her later dances such as "Mother Etudes" and "Marche Slave" in which the performer's wide stances and strides emphasize a downward thrust of energy while her clenched fists pound the ground forcefully in frustration.

The second innovator, Loie Fuller (1862–1928), worked in both narrative and non-narrative forms using techniques which led dance historian Sally Banes to call her the foremother of the postmoderns. Banes notes that a number of Fuller's choreographic concerns did not reappear until the 1960s. Among these were an avoidance of virtuosic dance technique, narrative, and the projection of emotion.[5] Her dances did not represent particular women, but were an evocation of the feminine element in nature, as their titles indicate: "Serpentine"; "The Butterfly"; and "Fire Dance". Fuller's imagery did not rest on a complex vocabulary of steps but was achieved through sparse phrases supported by a masterful use of props, costumes and lighting. Many of her images were virginal in their intent; certainly they were dominantly harmonious.

---

[4] Kendall, Elizabeth. "Women Choreographers: A Twentieth Century Phenomenon," *On the Next Wave*. Volume 1 #4, November 1983. BAM Next Wave: Brooklyn, p. 4.

[5] Banes, Sally. *Terpsichore in Sneakers: Post-Modern Dance*. Boston: Houghton Mifflin, 1980, p. 2.

The last of the three, Ruth St. Denis (1877–1968), sought inspiration from other cultures. She reveled in their myths, their movement, their music, and their attire. In the way that a play gives an actress license to explore behavior which she might not exhibit or sanction in daily life, many of St. Denis's roles presented women outside her own experience and that of her audiences. The roles she created for herself in "Nautch" and "Incense" demonstrate her personal preference for the oppositional archetypes of temptress and goddess. The soloist in "Incense," through the use of weighted walks, fluid arm gestures and a penetrating focus, presents a simultaneously mysterious, sensual and spiritual image of a woman engaged in a private yet powerful ritual.

Second Generation (1930–50's)

Two principal choreographers of the second generation, Martha Graham and Doris Humphrey, staged characteristically American revolts against the edicts of their common foremother St. Denis. Gradually, each of these women developed an individual choreographic style which was supported and illuminated by a technique for training dancers. Each also created resonant images of women within particular dramatic contexts.

Choreographically, Graham (1894–1991) began by rejecting the ornate, exotic, and mystically vaulted characters of her mentor, Denishawn. Her early works, such as "Primitive Mysteries" and "Heretic," explored interactions between the individual and the group. As the technique upon which she based her work became more codified and her company more established and more inclusive of both sexes, Graham's choreography turned away from the spare clarity of these early pieces and moved toward full and intricate restatements of classic mythic narratives, with particular attention to Greek heroines. The clear distinction between her mythic heroines and those of St. Denis lay in the way Graham shaped her dances. She molded the action from the emotional reaction of an individual woman, whereas St. Denis often presented more generalized visualizations of literary themes.

In the course of her career Graham dealt with each of the six mythic categories. The character of Medea in her "Cave of the Heart" is a witch/madwoman; the woman in "Errand into the Maze" is a warrior/martyr; Mary Magdalen in "El Penitente" is a temptress/whore; 'she of the ground' in "Dark Meadow" is a goddess/prophetess; the ancestress in "Letter to the World" is a ancestress/mother/teacher; and the bride in "Appalachian Spring" is a virgin/lover/wife.

Medea's role in "Cave of the Heart" and Jocasta's in "Night Journey," Graham's retelling of the Oedipus myth, are two examples of discordant visions that represent a warning and imply a moral from which the observer may benefit. The magnitude of Graham's choreographic contribution to the establishment of mythic females is noted by Deborah Jowitt when she writes: "Before Graham, few defined the female dancer as passion-driven, yet intellectually complex; fated, yet capable of choice. In creating a theatre of the mind where modern women and men jousted with their archetypes for the illumination of contemporary society, she construed herself as both celebrant and priestess, bringing western theatrical dancing as close to ritual as it has ever come."[6]

Widely acclaimed as a performer, appropriately praised as a theorist and teacher, and frequently cited as a mentor, Doris Humphrey's (1895–1958) mark as a choreographer does not have the breadth and depth of Graham's. Her work focuses almost exclusively on two mythic types; the woman as ancestress/mother/teacher and the woman as virgin/lover/wife. The former is clearly seen in the eldress figure of "Shakers" while the latter is evident in the three female figures of "Day on Earth." Although discordant female figures are present, for example the matriarch in "With My Red Fires," the emphasis in Humphrey's mature work is on women of harmony. This is not surprising when one considers her concern for socially relevant and redeeming choreography. Her own words, written about her piece "New Dance Trilogy," speak to her intent: "In almost the entire dance world I had seen nothing but negation. Anyone could tell you what was wrong, but no one seemed to say what was right. It was with this mental conflict that I approached "New Dance" first, determined to open up to the best of my ability the world as it could be and should be: a modern brotherhood of man."[7]

Third Generation (1950–present)

Graham, Humphrey and other members of the second generation distinguished themselves as choreographers, performers, and teachers and did so with almost holy zeal. They were a hard act to follow. As a result, many third generation choreographers have concentrated their efforts on analyzing and integrating the massive excavations of their mentors. Some have built images in the dramatic narrative tradition and have focused on the mythic. Others have moved toward work which arises more directly

---

[6] Jowitt, Deborah. *Time and the Dancing Image*. NY: William Morrow and Co., 1988, p. 233.

[7] Siegel, Marcia. *Days on Earth: The Dance of Doris Humphrey*. New Haven: Yale University Press, 1987, p. 157.

from probing questions about dance structure. By applying movement discoveries generated from structural experiments to narrative contexts, a few have extended the boundaries of that form.

Mary Anthony, Pearl Lang, May O'Donnell, and Anna Sokolow all began their choreographic careers under Graham's mentorship and used the Graham vocabulary to their own ends. The work of Anna Sokolow, born in 1910, is reflective of the urban American experience at midcentury. The female figures of "Rooms" and "Dreams" typify the kind of women one finds throughout Sokolow's work. These women are alone in some desperate circumstances. One appears to relive an intimate affair, another to struggle with suicide, a third trio is caught in an innocent and unattainable daydream. In "Dreams," her meditation on Nazi concentration camps, the women run the gamut from the young and impressionable child to the whore.

Sokolow's women anticipate the nonmythic. Many of the themes she developed during her career exhibit a grim view of humanity and draw heavily from raw emotion. She has said: "You see, for me there's an emotion-motion-emotion cycle in choreographing. I'll feel an emotion — maybe in a piece of music — and I'll feel a movement. I'll give it to the company. Then when they do it, it speaks back to me. It produces an emotion in me. Then I can go on to clarify and build the form and images. To me, emotion and motion are synchronous. Often I don't really know what a dance is about until I'm well into it."[8] As audience members we are invited to draw a direct parallel between the dancers' experiences and our own. If the women depicted in Graham's dances are roused to action by thought, Sokolow's women act and react intuitively. They are human lovers, teachers, madwomen, visionaries, and whores. These characters provide fertile examples for younger choreographers who have seen Sokolow as a mentor and been inspired by the vulnerability and resilience of her characters.

Far from the dance "hub" of New York and in the midst of the West Coast personal growth movement, Anna Halprin, born in 1920, began to broaden the definition of performance and performer. Halprin's early works, called 'happenings', were often riotous collages. Throughout her career she has forged new choreographic performance forms. Acting principally as a director and teacher, Halprin has developed ceremonies in which boundaries between doers and watchers blur; all are participants and all are witnesses. Her rituals involve a community in individual and group process and its participants explore the full spectrum of harmonious/discordant and mythic/nonmythic roles. Halprin's work seems

---

[8] Morris, Kelly and Leslie. "An Interview with Anna Sokolow," *The Drama Review*. No. 45, p. 101.

to suggest that we can gain strength, perspective, and balance in our lives by embracing all of the voices which exist within us.

Her summer workshops in creative process, established in 1959, encouraged this search for new ideas. Through them she served as a mentor to Trisha Brown, Simone Forti, Meredith Monk, and Yvonne Rainer. All of these fourth generation artists acknowledge Halprin's influence on their approaches to dance making. All are strong directors; each has moved away from traditional dance to develop an individual movement style. Writers Barry Laine and Eleanor Rachel Luger suggest that Halprin and Monk have "succeeded in developing movement pieces that rise from and manifest their womanliness. …both are able to bring the audience into their own, personal, female point of view — Halprin by generating creative scores out of her feminine perspective, and Monk by constructing theatre pieces that present women in various aspects of living."[9] Halprin's work in bringing dance closer to daily experience clearly looks forward to that of her successors.

Fourth Generation (1960–present)

As the mythologizing of female characters which is prevalent in the first three generations disappears, new orientations arise. Beginning with the fourth generation, images of women often serve choreographic structure. We are presented with nonmythic human females: bodies moving in space who happen to be women. Often dancers' abilities to present the structure are more significant than their individual gender as they do so. Trisha Brown's early equipment and accumulation pieces, Lucinda Childs' cool and complex geometric pathways, Laura Dean's Sufi-like spinning are dances which focus on the choreographic structure rather than on individual characters.

Both the choreographic and performance styles of Trisha Brown, born in 1936, have had a strong impact on choreographers in succeeding generations. The fluidity, complexity, speed, and slipperiness of Brown's most recent work is characterized by some as more feminine than the linearity of her early pieces such as "Walking on the Wall." However, even in earlier works like "Glacial Decoy" and "Opal Loop" she was building toward the looser use of the spine which is so common in her most recent material, "Foray Forêt" and "Another Story as in falling." While gender is not foregrounded in Brown's work, women and men both emerge as fully present beings. Both sexes exercise their physicality, mental acuity, sensuality,

---

[9] Luger, Eleanor Rachel and Laine, Barry. "When Choreography Becomes Female (Part 2): A Talk with Anna Halprin," *Christopher Street*. December, 1978, p. 66.

and emotional/spiritual knowledge through dance. Through their enactment of Brown's complex structures a variety of nonmythic archetypes are revealed.

The work of Meredith Monk and Senta Driver also presents images of emotionally and physically powerful women. From early dances like "16 Millimeter Earrings" to "Education of the Girlchild" and "Quarry," through more recent works such as "Games," Meredith Monk has developed dance/theatre pieces in which nonmythic women explore a variety of experiences, ages, and relationships among women and between women and men within associative dreamlike structures. Monk has called "Education of the Girlchild" "a humanist piece in that each of the seven women was such a remarkable character that it showed women beings in a positive way."[10] Part of the power of Monk's work comes from its blend of contemporary subject matter with ritual forms. In "Education of the Girlchild," she describes her group as "a heroic matriarchy of ancient women" performing as enlargements of themselves.[11]

Senta Driver, whose company was in existence from 1970 until 1991, celebrated role equality for women and men. In building her dances she asked company members of both sexes to explore and reveal their strength and their vulnerability. Driver pointed to the affinity between her work and that of her symbolic mentors Graham and Humphrey in a 1986 interview: "They had a lot of values we could profitably look back to and resume. Weight. Mass. Size — size for women. There's no flesh anymore… There was a kind of physical and emotional passion, then."[12] Driver's pioneering effort in having women lift men during the 1970's, as well as her emphasis on weighted movement and unisex partnering, all paved the way for many of the ensemble practices which we accept as the norm in the 1990's.

Both Monk and Driver challenged traditional limitations regarding images of dancing women in their work. Monk built works around particular women and the interactions of a wide variety of female archetypes. Her performers use a gender-neutral movement vocabulary. Driver emphasized upper body strength and total body weight/momentum. Women in her choreography also regularly assume assertive roles.

Twyla Tharp, born in 1941 and a major choreographic force in this generation, alternates between works which concentrate on abstract

---

[10] Burt, Ramsey and Briginshaw, Valerie, "Turtle Dreams (Cabaret)," *New Dance*. No. 39, New Year, 1987, p. 12.

[11] Goldberg, Marianne. "Transformative Aspects of Meredith Monk's 'Education of the Girlchild'," *Women and Performance*. V. 1 #1. 1983, p. 20.

[12] Daly, Ann. "Interview with Senta Driver," *Women and Performance*. V. 3, No. 2, #6. 1987/88, p. 95.

structures and those in which characters and stories serve as the motivation for structure. In writing about "As Time Goes By," her 1973 work for the Joffrey Ballet, Tharp points to her awareness of gender representations: "I have always felt that one of the things dance should do — its business being so clearly physical — is challenge the culture's gender stereotypes. Because almost all ballet choreographers have been male, most of the major roles have been written for women. In excluding women from its power center, the ballet world has forfeited the roles for men as kings that women might create. In "As Time Goes By," Larry (Grenier) was the soft one, Bea (Rodriguez) the firm one, yet Larry's vulnerability had everyone longing to support him, while Beatriz's drive was a relief."[13] Images of powerful women continue to figure in Tharp's later work. The complex choreographic structure and rigorous technical demands of Tharp's piece "The Catherine Wheel" revolve around a central heroic female warrior figure (originally danced by Sara Rudner) who exhibits harmonious qualities as she drives the action of this commentary on 'family' life in the chaotic nuclear age. More recently Tharp has created a work for herself and several male dancers entitled "The Men's Piece." This work incorporates romantic and isometric male/female duets in which Tharp claims and celebrates the mother in herself.[14]

Fifth Generation (1970–present)

Fifth generation women come of choreographic age in an atmosphere which is dominated by structural approaches to making dances. In this generation the nonmythic human female remains a vital force. If second generation choreographers created women of grand dimensions in the tradition of the classic Greek theatre, and those in the fourth generation contributed visions dominated by women as technically adept workers, fifth generation choreographers begin with the woman as worker and clothe her in a particular female archetype.

The full archetypal complement begins to reemerge, but this time cast in flesh. Second generation vocabularies and characters presented steely, competent women unassailable and unreachable in body or spirit; a distance was established between observer and performer through dramatic didacticism. In the fifth generation physical and emotional boldness is accessible to the audience through a movement vocabulary drawn from daily life and through spoken text which arises from life experience. If

[13] Tharp, Twyla. *Push Comes to Shove*. NY: Bantam Books. 1992, p. 191.

[14] Tharp, Ibid. pp. 335–41.

second generation choreographers were lecturing to us in a formal and foreign tongue, fifth generation choreographers translate movement language more colloquially in order to engage us in a dialogue. The former asked us to look up to mythic female archetypes, the latter ask us to look at them as human females.

The combination of movement and words begin to address us with directness. In such works as San Francisco-based Margaret Jenkins's "Shore Birds, Atlantic" and Washington D.C. choreographer Liz Lerman's "Docudances I, II, and III" one of the tasks for women and men is to migrate between representing themselves and assuming other personae. While Jenkins's character types may be drawn from literature and are often generalized, Lerman's arise from specific responses to daily events. Her performers confront us with the realities of our social and political systems and comment on them. "Anatomy of an Inside Story," a collaboration between Lerman and her associate artistic director Kim Boyd, is a recent example. Lerman says of this work, "We use many different methods to find the movement for these intense family stories about growing up Black and female in this country. But finally I view the movement as not illustrative of the language at all, rather as a motor that keeps the dancer going. There is no way that Kim could tell the stories without the dancing, and probably no way the audience could hear them either. The dancing is a kind of ever-present witness, soul, or just in-the-present experience for the dancer and audience as she recounts a painful, sometimes glorious, sometimes funny, past."[15] Lerman employs mythic images and archetypes in her multiracial, multigenerational company and uses them to challenge audiences and preconceived notions regarding age, race, and physical ability.

Developing stories and investigating female characters is also a concern of Blondell Cummings, who for a number of years was a member of Meredith Monk's group, The House. In her 1991 duet "Omadele and Giuseppe," a barrage of movement images gathered from a wide variety of vocabularies are added to the audio-taped 'thoughts' of the woman and man in the piece. Simultaneously a questionnaire, to which the audience is asked to respond, is seen in projections and spoken on tape. This rich montage reaches out to us, posing questions about women and also about common prejudices related to race, age, and class. Cummings is extending the dialogue by creating archetypal images of both harmonious (priestess, mother and wife) and discordant (madwoman and warrior) archetypes.[16]

---

[15] Lerman, Liz. "By All Means Possible," *Movement Research Performance Journal*. No. 9, Fall/Winter 1994/95, p. 4.

[16] Postperformance discussion, Bryn Mawr College, February 4, 1993.

Some fifth generation choreographers who began their careers working independently have recently moved on to establish cooperative groups. The mission of the Women's Performance Project, based in Minneapolis and convened by Diane Elliot in 1990, is to explore the healing potential of performance by developing and performing original ritual/dance theatre.[17] Working improvisationally, Elliot and the other members of the group, Susan DeLattre, Margie Fargnoli, Rebecca Frost, and Erika Thorne, employ techniques which range from traditional modern dance and acting to contact improvisation and body-mind centering work. In speaking about the content of their collaborations, Elliot points to a shifting emphasis: "Initially, we were dealing with the effects of abuse, not only sexual and physical, but also the subtler abuses which produce feelings of not having the freedom to be fully physical to express ourselves sexually and otherwise. We are now engaged in another phase of the healing process, letting go and empowerment. Our current work explores our connection with the earth — how we are cut off from it by cultural strictures, racism and fear and hatred of our own bodies."[18] While images of women created by the members of the Women's Performance Project vary, their work generally emphasizes harmony. Groups such as this one hark back to their mentors of the 1960's, collaboratives such as the Grand Union. Interests in cooperative process and in dance which is socially or politically motivated continue to grow in the work of the next generation of women.

Sixth Generation (late 1970's/early 1980's–present)

Sixth generation female choreographers reiterate and extend premises concerning the nonmythic human female which were introduced in the fourth and fifth generations. Women of athletic prowess, conversant in a variety of dance techniques, span a continuum of theatrical forms from ballet, through improvisation, to the evolving and idiosyncratic vocabulary of social dances such as hip-hop. Female warriors reappear in this generation; warriors for whom physical power is as significant as were emotional and intellectual power prior to the fourth generation. This aggressive physicality sometimes gives vent to a darker view of humanity and thus a new interpretation of the witch/madwoman.

Discordant images of both men and women increase. They regularly appear in the work of Karole Armitage, who began her professional career as a ballet dancer and later spent five years in Merce Cunningham's Company.

---

[17] New Dance Lab Report, March, 1993.

[18] Ibid.

While comfortable with ballet vocabulary, she clearly has been influenced by modern and postmodern practices. She positions the ballerina as simultaneously in and out of control by creating off-balance extensions, and challenging jumps and beats. In Armitage's dances the pointe shoe is used aggressively in explorations of sex and violence. Her "Paradise" and "Go Go Ballerina," created in the mid-1980's, dramatically underscore the heroism of her women and their unapologetic use of their partners.

In both the second and the sixth generations, characters and relationships drive structure. However, in contrast to the second generation in which characters are removed from our experience, sixth generation characters and relationships are drawn directly from actual twentieth century daily life. Increasingly, that daily experience includes an acknowledgment of ethnicity. The work of Jawole Willa Jo Zollar and her company Urban Bush Women deals with women's vulnerability in general, and women of color more specifically. The company celebrates the strength of a community of African-American women ("Girlfriends" and "Lipstick"), asks questions about the mutual responsibilities between individuals and communities ("Praise House"), and explores the many roles a woman of color constructs or has constructed about herself in urban, Western society ("Heat").

Even as the incidence of violence in daily life has escalated dramatically during recent years, much dance work reflects cultural tension in its use of physical violence. The choreographic discord which arises in this generation evokes both a psychic and bodily shock in the viewer. Certainly, the intent behind assaultive messages varies; some of the violence expressed seems dangerous and gratuitous. In other choreography, the conscious and blatant juxtaposition of assault and vulnerability has pushed the limits and potential social influences of dance as an art form. The duets "Ties That Bind Parts I and II" by Johanna Boyce deftly mix aggression and tenderness while exploring a reconsideration of gender and sex roles. Each of these duets explores relationships between women; the first is based on two sisters and the second on two lovers. Boyce invites us to reconsider the gamut of female images as well as to accept how they operate in our own lives.

Nonmythic visions of both harmony and discord are also being applied to questions of sexuality. In Pat Graney's piece "Faith," her Seattle-based company of women worked collaboratively to evoke images of female beauty, strength, sensuality, and reverence. Amy Pivar's 1991 "NOT A CONFESSION (A True Story)" is a strident and compelling response to rape and abuse. Other sixth generation choreographers apply their work in various body therapies to redefinitions of the dancing female. Barbara Mahler in a 1992 solo entitled "In My Dreams" explored societal notions of the 'perfect woman.' Using good and bad witch archetypes, Mahler confronted our culture's fear regarding women who are 'out of control.'[19]

Victoria Marks uses group process in developing her dances, which intermix physical fearlessness and group empathy. Offering positive images of individual women and of interdependent communities as in "A Last Place" and "Acts of Omission," she layers disparate images of combat and comfort, isolation and community, harmony and discord.

Towards the Seventh Generation

Technology has had a strong impact on the work of the sixth generation but will continue even more strongly to influence the next. Computer animation programs, sound equipment, theatrical lighting, video and film expand possibilities for choreographic creation. Up to the present, video has produced the most marked results in creation and performance. Increasingly, choreographers use video technology to blur and cross borders between disciplines. Yvonne Rainer's and Twyla Tharp's early experiments with film and video explored how concerns related to structure in dance and film/ video might intersect. Other choreographers have focused on ways that film/video technology can support new conceptions of female archetypes. During the late 1980s Minneapolis-based choreographer Wendy Morris collaborated with videographer James Byrne on a videodance cycle in which an ancestress figure's relationship to earth, air, fire, and water were realized using the video medium.

Even choreographers for whom video is not an integral part of the creative process are making images of women which are altered by technology. A variety of computer graphic animation programs now exist which enable choreographers to create movement sequences and play them back, watching small figures 'dance' on the monitor's screen. Emerging virtual reality and holographic technology have the potential to extend these graphic simulations into interactive performance environments. Our actual physical selves can dance with others whose gender can be constructed by us and which we can vary from one 'performance' to another. How do these systems challenge our conceptions of dancing women? What opportunities do they provide for re-presentation? What influence will differences in cultural perspective and experiences have on the ways women use these systems? We are just beginning to discover a host of artistic, intellectual, emotional and visceral questions which result for those whose choreography

---

[19] Postperformance discussion, Swarthmore College, October 28, 1992.

employs these technologies as well as for performers and audiences who interact with them. Each collaboration provides us with new opportunities for creating, seeing and understanding images of women in dance.[20]

Conclusion

As the twentieth century opened, Isadora Duncan's hope for the scope of female choreographic vision was ambitious. Now, in the last decade of the century, the work of six generations shows that her hope was not misplaced. Female choreographers continue to break new ground, influenced by and reacting to their historic mentors but producing their own individual harmonious and discordant figures. The dances of female choreographers are affected by their mentoring relationships, the society in which they live and the choices they make regarding the content of and venue for their dances. Increasingly, issues of race, gender, age, and class inform the choices choreographers make. While nonmythic images of women will continue to dominate in the immediate future, we may see a reemergence of the mythic. New images of mythic women will be strongly influenced by cultural perspectives, social and political concerns, feminist theory and technology. The generational model presented in this essay suggests one way to continue to analyze female roles even as we expand our choreographic "tools" and become increasingly aware of the need to create inclusive communities of artists and audiences.

Bibliography

Books
Adair, Christy. *Women and Dance: Sylphs and Sirens*. N.Y: N.Y.U. Press, 1992.
Banes, Sally. *Terpsichore in Sneakers: Post-Modern Dance*. Boston: Houghton Mifflin, 1990.
Campbell, Joseph with Moyers, Bill. *The Power of Myth*. N.Y: Bantam Doubleday Dell Publishing Group, Inc., 1988.
Duncan, Isadora. *The Art of the Dance*. N.Y: Theatre Arts Books, 1969 (original copyright 1928 Helen Hackett, Inc.).
Estes, Clarissa Pinkola. *Women Who Run with the Wolves: Myths and Stories of the Wild Woman Archetype*. N.Y: Ballantine Books, 1992.

---

[20] Since 1987 the author has been using the computer animation system Lifeforms (developed under the direction of Professor Thomas Calvert at Simon Fraser University in British Columbia) as an aid to choreography and to the teaching of undergraduate courses in dance composition.

Hanna, Judith Lynne. *Dance, Sex, and Gender: Signs of Identity, Dominance, Defiance, and Desire*. Chicago: Univ. of Chicago Press, 1988.

Jowitt, Deborah. *Time and the Dancing Image*. N.Y: Wm. Morrow and Co., 1988.

Siegel, Marcia B. *Shapes of Change: Images of American Dance*. N.Y: Discus Books/Avon Books, 1979.

Siegel, Marcia. *The Tail of the Dragon: New Dance 1976–1982*. Durham and London: Duke University Press, 1991.

Articles and Reviews

Barnes, Clive."Woman's Role in Dance," *New York Times*. March 6, 1977.

Burt, Ramsay and Briginshaw, Valerie. "Turtle Dreams (Cabaret)," *New Dance*, No. 39, New Year, 1987.

Daly, Ann. "Interview with Senta Driver," *Women and Performance*, Volume 3, No. 2, #6, 1987/88.

Dunning, Jennifer. "Trisha Brown Offers Quiet Contradictions," *New York Times*, March 18, 1991.

Goldberg, Marianne. "Transformative Aspects of Meredith Monk's "Education of the Girlchild," *Women and Performance*, Volume 1 #1, 1983.

Greskovic, Robert. "Armitagean Physics, or the Shoes of the Ballerina," *Ballet Review*, 13: 2, Summer, 1985.

Kendall, Elizabeth. "Women Choreographers: A Twentieth Century Phenomenon," *On the Next Wave*, Volume 1 #4, November, 1983.

Lerner, Raissa. "Movement Metamorphosis: Victoria Marks Performance Company," *N.Y.C. Metro*, November, 1988.

Luger, Eleanor Rachel, and Laine, Barry. "When Choreography Becomes Female (Part 2): A Talk with Anna Halprin," *Christopher St.*, December, 1978.

Morris, Kelly and Leslie. "An Interview with Anna Sokolow," *The Drama Review*, No. 45.

SEXUAL POLITICS
Roger Copeland

Recent feminist scholarship tends to proceed on the assumption that history is really his story — an account of the past written by and about men. And accordingly, feminist scholars and art historians have set out during the past two decades to chronicle the achievements of women artists whose work has been systematically overlooked or undervalued. But in one art form at least, contemporary dance of the modern and post-modern persuasion, there is little need for this sort of consciousness-raising or revisionist history. In these two varieties of twentieth-century dance, women have been not only prominent, but dominant. The other major arts trace their lineage back to founding fathers. And by major arts, I mean of course, ballet as well. There, certain key exceptions like Nijinska notwithstanding, the most celebrated choreographers have been, and for the most part continue to be, men.

But in early modern and post-modern dance, the central figures are founding mothers: Isadora Duncan, Loie Fuller, Ruth St. Denis, Doris Humphrey, Martha Graham; and among the post-modern generation, Yvonne Rainer, Trisha Brown, Lucinda Childs, Twyla Tharp, and Laura Dean. There are of course, a good many exceptions to this rule — men such as Ted Shawn, Charles Weidman, Jose Limon, Paul Taylor, Merce Cunningham; as well as male post-modernists such as Steve Paxton, Kenneth King, and David Gordon — but they are, as I hope to show, the sort of exceptions that prove the rule. And the unanswered, indeed rarely asked question is why? Why are modern and post-modern dance the only major art forms in which the creators, the consolidators, the second and third generation innovators have almost all been women?

Of course, this may not be cause for unalloyed celebration. One can view this particular glass as being either half-empty or half-full. On the one hand, only a misogynist or a Philistine could fail to express gratitude for the dances of Martha Graham or Twyla Tharp; but at the same time, it's necessary to ask whether or not the success rate of women in modern and post-modern dance isn't analogous to that of black males in basketball. Are we, in other words, talking about the sort of marginalized, vocational ghetto to which women and black men have been consigned and then allowed to succeed, either because white males aren't attracted to the profession in the first place or because they feel that others are better equipped, anatomically or temperamentally, for the work? The fact that it's difficult to name a major male choreographer who isn't also homosexual suggests that the art of dance has been, and to a large extent still is, shunned by heterosexual males who regard it as a womanly activity.

But at least anatomically, it makes little or no sense to claim that dance itself is a feminine rather than a masculine pursuit. Again, it's like claiming that blacks have a natural aptitude for basketball; as if dedication, discipline, and grueling, repetitive rigors of practice had little or nothing to do with the accomplishments of a Dr. J. (basketball player Julius Erving) or Kareem Abdul-Jabbar. And, as already mentioned, in the world of ballet we encounter an almost exclusively male pantheon: Noverre, Petipa, Fokine, and more recently, Balanchine, Ashton, Tudor and Robbins (gay men for the most part, but certainly not women). It's also worth noting that two of those prominent exceptions cited a moment ago, Cunningham and Taylor, have, in effect, "reballeticized" modern dance. So even if their contributions have been, technically speaking, in modern dance, they've had the effect of nudging that once earth-bound form increasingly in the aerial direction of ballet, the traditional realm of male choreographers.

In the early 1980's, two revivals, fortuitously juxtaposed, set me to thinking about the relationship between modern dance, post-modern dance and sexual politics. In April of 1982, the Pennsylvania Ballet performed a program of dances at the Brooklyn Academy of Music choreographed entirely by women. Among them were several reconstructions of Isadora Duncan solos performed by Annabelle Gamson. Later that same month at St. Mark's Church, a number of early post-modern dances from the mid-sixties, including Yvonne Rainer's highly influential *Trio A*, were restaged in conjunction with Bennington College's Judson Project.

Here was a golden opportunity to compare and contrast the principles that animated the pioneers of both modern and postmodern dance and to compare as well the vastly varying conceptions of sexual politics that prevailed at the time these forms were founded. At first glance, the work of Duncan and Rainer would seem to have little, if anything, in common. As danced by Annabelle Gamson in her revival of *The Blue Danube*, Duncan's movement sings the song of the body electric; it luxuriates in its own physicality and basks in the gaze of an adoring public. Rainer's movement in *Trio A*, by contrast, is considerably less voluptuous. Some would call it puritanical. Certainly it is cold, uninflected, almost "unperformed," as if the performer is merely marking it rather than executing the dance full out. In contrast to Duncan, who races on several occasions toward the audience in an open-armed embrace, Rainer "averts" her gaze and remains coolly oblivious to those watching.

But despite such stark contrasts, these two dances share something essential: Not only were both choreographed by women; more significantly, both dances reflect the prevailing feminist ideologies of their respective eras. And feminist concerns may well be the missing piece of the jigsaw puzzle, the key to the question: Why have women choreographers been central to modern and post-modern dance, but not ballet?

Let's begin with Duncan: In an age still dominated by the dictates of Puritanism, Duncan dared to dance uncorseted. Dressed in a loose-fitting, free-flowing tunic, she rebelled not only against the corset per se, but also against everything it symbolized: the constraints — both physical and psychological — imposed upon women by Victorian culture. Rainer on the other hand, is the product of a very different moment in time, ironically, one inspired in large part by the example of Duncan and others like her, but which she rejects rather than embodies: I refer of course to the so-called "sexual revolution" of the 1960's and '70's.

Unlike the feminists of Duncan's generation who longed for sexual freedom and who viewed puritanical repression as an obstacle to the emancipation of women, many radical feminists of the '60's and '70's eyed the sexual revolution with considerable suspicion, fearful that it hadn't really liberated women, but had simply made them more "available." According to this argument, the Victorian obligation to be passive had merely been replaced by the contemporary obligation to be sexually alluring. Many feminists began to practice what Midge Decter calls "the new chastity."[1] They began to dress "down" rather than up; they became suspicious and resentful of what's come to be known as "the male gaze." They railed against the so-called "objectification" of women, the reduction of woman to the status of object, sexual or otherwise. In 1965, Yvonne Rainer published a statement which has since been elevated to the status of manifesto. And it reads in part: "NO to spectacle, no to virtuosity, no to transformations and magic and make believe...no to seduction of spectator by the wiles of the performer..."[2] These words were intended as an aesthetic — not a political — statement. But Yvonne Rainer's insistence upon saying "no" to so many of the voyeuristic and erotic pleasures that dance has traditionally offered

---

[1] Decter, M. *The New Chastity and Other Arguments Against Women's Liberation.* N.Y.: Coward, McCann and Geoghegan, 1977.

[2] Rainer, Y. *Work: 1961–73.* Halifax: Press of the Nova Scotia College of Art and Design, 1974, p. 51.

begins to assume feminist implications when viewed against this ideological backdrop. Still, Rainer's feminism is implicit.

Needless to say, not every pioneer of modern and post-modern dance waved a feminist banner as openly as Isadora Duncan, who once declared that her art was "symbolic of the freedom of woman and her emancipation from the hidebound conventions that are the warp and woof of New England Puritanism."[3] In the work of choreographers such as Doris Humphrey and Martha Graham, the issue of women's rights is often subsumed into a concern with women's rites. Neither *Primitive Mysteries* nor *The Shakers* is about matriarchal societies as such, but both depict women functioning independently of men and fully capable of entering into a state of ritual-induced ecstasy.

The early years of modern and post-modern dance were contemporaneous with two great waves of feminist thought. Thus it's entirely possible that one of the principal reasons modern and post-modern dance were pioneered by women is that they are probably the only major art forms prior to the 1970's to derive so much of their energy, their inspiration, indeed their imagery, from the feminist movement. To these choreographic pioneers, a new way of moving helped set the stage for a new mode of being. Early modern dance is first and foremost a repudiation of late nineteenth century ballet. And it is essential to recognize that this repudiation is boldly feminist in character. Even the most cursory glance at the voluminous writings of Isadora Duncan reveals how closely the topics of women's emancipation and dress reform were related to her virulent criticisms of ballet. Like the dreaded corset, ballet transformed and deformed a young woman's body: "Have you seen the little girls who are studying ballet today?" she asks in an essay called "What Dancing Should Be"…"Their tender little bodies already are being forced into tight bodices and baby corsets, while their natural graceful movements are being tormented into unnatural straight kicking of the legs, toe walking, and all sorts of awkward contortions which are directly contrary to what a child's natural movement would be if developed in the line of reason and beauty."[4]

As attested to by such passages scattered abundantly throughout her writings, Duncan's objections to ballet were not exclusively or even primarily aesthetic in nature. They were essentially moral and political. In her well-known essay "The Dance of the Future," she reproaches the balletomane

---

[3] Isadora Duncan quoted by Joseph H. Mazo, *Prime Movers*. Princeton: Princeton Book Co., 1977, p. 58.

[4] Duncan, Isadora. *The Art of the Dance*. N.Y.: Theatre Arts Books, 1928, p. 73.

in the following way: "To those who still enjoy (balletic) movements for historical or choreographic or whatever the reasons, to those I answer: They see no further than the skirts and tricots. But look under the skirts, under the tricots are dancing deformed muscles. Look still further, underneath the muscles are de-formed bones. A deformed skeleton is dancing before you. This deformation through incorrect dress and incorrect movement is the result of the training necessary to the ballet. The ballet condemns itself by enforcing the deformation of the beautiful woman's body! No historical, no choreographic reasons can prevail against that!"[5]

Duncan's broadside against ballet may strike us as wildly exaggerated, but there can be no denying the basic truth of her comments about the unhealthy nature of fashionable Victorian dress. Turn of the century dress codes mandated that women wear tightly laced whalebone corsets, a minimum of six full petticoats, and long trailing skirts that gathered vast quantities of debris as they swept along the unsanitary streets. In her book *Where She Danced*, Elizabeth Kendall cites a late nineteenth century grammar school where most of the little girls were corseted and none could raise their arms above their heads. In addition to restricting the flow of air through the lungs, corsets placed excessive pressure on the area of the solar plexus, contributing in all likelihood to the frequent pelvic disorders experienced by Victorian women. It's probably no coincidence, suggests Kendall, that the portion of the body most directly affected by the corset became the focal point of Duncan's new aesthetic. In her autobiography, Duncan refers to the solar plexus as "the central spring of all movement, the crater of motor power, the unity from which all diversions of movement are born..."[6] Significantly, Duncan once suggested that her real contribution to the future of civilization was to have helped free women from the tyranny of the corset. And the quality that pervades Duncan's exuberant dances like *The Blue Danube* suggests the exhilaration of a woman recently released from bondage.

Of course, Duncan was offended by ballet not only because she thought of it as corseted movement, but also because it projected what she believed to be a socially pernicious image of women. The popular stereotype of the ballerina — woman as virginal, disembodied, sylphide, an image that dominated ballet from the heyday of Taglioni to that of Pavlova, corresponded closely to the Victorian ideal of womanhood: Woman as a

---

[5] Ibid., p. 56.

[6] Duncan, Isadora. *My Life*. N.Y.: Garden City Publishing Co., 1927, p. 67.

frail, sexually passive creature apt to suffer from the "vapours" and likely to faint at the slightest provocation.

In place of delicate, chaste women who die of unrequited love or romantic betrayal (*Giselle*), or lie waiting to be awakened from their passive slumbers by a handsome prince (*Sleeping Beauty*), or mechanical toys who, unlike Ibsen's Nora, remain confined within their doll's house (*Coppelia*) — in place of these charming but ineffectual heroines, Duncan and the early moderns created images of strong, self-reliant women, a tradition that would culminate in the powerful, mythic heroines danced by Martha Graham. As Arlene Croce has observed, "No Graham heroine dies unillumined. The difference between her and the fated heroines of 19th Century ballet, a Giselle or an Odette — is that the Graham heroine possesses herself the key to her mystery. She does not entrust it to the hero. She herself must unlock the inner door."[7]

In 1902, Isadora Duncan predicted that the dancer of the future "will dance not in the form of nymph, nor fairy, nor coquette, but in the form of woman in her greatest and purest expression."[8] One of the most radical and decisive differences between nineteenth century ballet and early modern dance is so obvious that its far-reaching implications are easily overlooked. The early moderns, almost all of whom began their choreographic careers by creating solos for themselves, were using their own unballetic bodies rather than someone else's body as the raw material of their art. It's significant that, at least in conversation, we continue to refer to artists such as Martha Graham or Mary Wigman as modern *dancers*, not modern dance *choreographers*. This habit of speech has the effect of emphasizing how often these choreographers tended to perform in their own dances. They didn't stand apart from the choreography and view it as external to themselves. In nineteenth century ballet by contrast, the choreographer, almost invariably a man, imposed abstract patterns on the bodies of others, usually women. There is, after all, no male equivalent for the corps de ballet; and the choreographer who manipulates that corps stands apart from his creation.

This distinction between the male ballet choreographer who visually surveys his work from a distance and the female modern dance choreographer who rarely stands outside of her own work provides a striking parallel to the recent writings of those feminist theoreticians who equate analytical detachment with the prerogatives of patriarchy. These writers also assume

---

[7] Croce, Arlene. *Afterimages*. N.Y.: Alfred A. Knopf, 1977, p. 53.

[8] Duncan, Isadora. *The Art of the Dance*, pp. 62–63.

that a deep, abiding connection exists between patriarchal culture and a tendency to "privilege" the visual over the tactile.

The French feminist Luce Irigaray writes that "Investment in the look is not privileged in women as in men. More than the other senses, the eye objectifies and masters. It sets at a distance, maintains that distance. In our culture, the predominance of the look over smell, taste, touch, and hearing has brought about an impoverishment of bodily relations. The moment the look dominates, the body loses its materiality."[9] This latter notion seems particularly relevant to romantic ballet, where the sylphide is woman de-materialized, existing quite literally and exclusively as a sight, an apparition. Our relationship to her is purely "specular." As James learns so painfully in *La Sylphide*, she is unattainable, she resists all tactile contact.

By contrast, modern dance placed a much higher premium on kinetic empathy than on visual experience per se. Many modern dance choreographers proceeded on the assumption that the visual orientation of ballet, rooted in the principle of en dehors and proscenium framing, precluded the sort of tactile response they wanted dancegoers to experience. Tactility was thought to reduce the physical and psychological distance that the proscenium arch creates, thereby establishing a closer bond, or at least the sensation of such, between performer and perceiver. This belief — that the visual and the tactile are at odds with one another — was conveniently summed up in the 1960's by Marshall McLuhan in books like *The Gutenberg Galaxy*. A typical passage reads as follows: "Touch is not so much a separate sense as the very interplay of the senses. That is why it recedes in significance as the visual faculty is given separate and abstract intensity."[10] In *Love's Body*, McLuhan's close friend Normon O. Brown rhapsodically restates this argument in explicitly theatrical terms: "The garden (of Eden) is polymorphism of the senses, polymorphous perversity, active interplay; and the opposite of polymorphous perversity is the *abstraction of the visual*, obtained by putting to sleep the rest of the life of the body... like spectators in the traditional theatre."[11]

And Brown, one of the chief intellectual gurus of the 1960's, is advocating a return to ritual, which is presumably more participatory and tactile than the theater. One can easily imagine the early modern dance choreographers nodding in agreement as they sing the praises of tactile or

---

[9] Irigaray, L., quoted by Craig Owens, "Feminists and Post-modernism," in H. Foster, *Postmodern Culture*. London: Pluto Press, 1985, p. 70.

[10] McLuhan, M. *The Gutenberg Galaxy*. N.Y.: New American Library. 1962, p. 83.

[11] Brown, N. O. *Love's Body*. N.Y.: Vintage Books. 1966, p. 121.

kinesthetic experience in opposition to the purely visual impact of ballet. The English word theater is usually said to derive from the Greek "theatron" which means literally "seeing place," an architectural space that makes specific provisions for spectators, those who sit apart from the action. Everything performed in a theater is thus expressly designed to be seen. And that's why ballet is often referred to as the most theatrical of all Western dance forms. Balletic turnout promotes the goal of visibility, opening the body up so that it becomes theatrically "legible" when framed by a proscenium arch.

Balletic partnering was thought to carry this logic of legibility a step further. As the vogue for pointe work and ethereal characterizations began to dominate nineteenth century ballet, male dancers were demoted to the status of hydraulic lifts for the lighter-than-air ballerinas. The male dancer's function was thereby to display the female, to put this fully turned-out woman on display. This leads to a provocative question: Had the male dancer actually been demoted — which is what the textbooks tell us? Or did sexual politics dictate that the woman be displayed and that the man do the displaying? Was the male dancer, in other words, quite literally, a stand-in for the choreographer? In any event, there's no denying that the very image of the ballet dancer became invariably associated with femininity. But the choreographers remained, just as invariably, men. And unlike the early pioneers of modern dance, these male choreographers tended not to perform in their own works.

This state of affairs and its attendant implications are succinctly summed up in George Balanchine's notorious proclamation that "The ballet is a purely female thing; it is a woman, a garden of beautiful flowers, and the man is the gardener."[12] Underlying this statement is the time-honored tendency to associate women with the natural world and men with the forces of civilization and cultural advancement i.e., woman as flower; man as gardener, the one who tends, tames, and transforms nature. The best known formulation of this classic dichotomy is probably D. H. Lawrence's argument that women grow "down-wards like a root, towards the center and darkness and origin" whereas men grow "upwards like the stalk towards discovery and light and utterance."[13]

Nineteenth century ballet can thus be seen as a metaphor for the process in which nature, as incarnated in women, is transformed by the male choreographer into a culturally acceptable artifact. And classically, the

---

[12] Balanchine, G. *By George*. N.Y.: San Marco Press, 1984, p. 16.

[13] Lawrence, D. H., quoted by Kate Millet in *Sexual Politics*. N.Y.: Avon Books. 1969, p. 239.

Western visual arts have tended to connect women and the natural world. In both painting and photography, the female nude is usually situated in a natural setting. By contrast, male nudes are rarely depicted in a state of nature. This may or may not imply, as many feminist critics have argued, that patriarchal culture feels deeply threatened by the natural world and thereby develops a corresponding need to dominate it. But there's no denying the well-established convention that associates femininity with the forces of nature.

These attitudes toward nature permeate nineteenth century ballet. Significantly, in her off-stage life, even the most chaste ballerina often became the chased society prostitute of the demi-monde. The wealthy playboys who frequented the Parisian Jockey Club regarded the ballerinas at the Opera as their private concubines. And as the historian G. Rattray Taylor has argued, prostitutes were to the nineteenth century as witches were to the Middle Ages, a constant reminder of what women are really like in their natural state, outside the protective, domesticating bonds of matrimony.[14]

Nineteenth century ballet also illustrates the way in which male choreographers reconciled the art of dance with then prevailing Western attitudes toward the body in general. In the tradition extending from Plato to Freud, art is conceived as a mode of sublimation, an alchemical conversion of lower or bodily energy into a higher, mental or spiritual state. To create a work of art is to transcend the lowliness of the body. The poet Stephen Spender once argued that "Poetry is a spiritual activity that makes one forget for the time being that one has a body."[15] This notion of course, is also fully consistent with Christianity's conception of the body as a source of worldly sin from which the soul must be freed if it hopes to achieve transcendence. Hence the odd paradox that dance, the only art form whose primary raw material is the live human body, began to idealize the image of the disembodied woman. It's also no coincidence that for Freud, the healthy Victorian woman was thought to be sexually passive, essentially divested of body.

The movement that begins with Duncan culminates in those works by Martha Graham that re-examine and repudiate her own puritanical upbringing. The starkly dressed "Ancestress" in *Letter to the World* and the fiery revivalist in *Appalachian Spring* are two of Graham's darker incarnations of Puritanism. Significantly, these dances from the early 1940s that explore

---

[14] Taylor, G. Rattray *Sex in History*. N.Y.: The Vanguard Press. 1970, p. 219.

[15] Spender, Stephen, quoted by N. O. Brown in *Life Against Death*. Middletown: Wesleyan University Press. 1959, p. 157.

the crippling effects of Puritanism were followed by a number of unabashedly "pagan" works in which Graham portrayed a whole pantheon of Greek mythological heroines (Medea in *Cave of the Heart*, Jocasta in *Night Journey*, the title roles in *Clytemnestra* and *Phaedra*).

And in each instance, Graham reworked the classical myth so as to bring the female protagonist front and center (in *Night Journey* for example, the story of Oedipus becomes, for all practical purposes, the story of Jocasta). Graham's most impressive reversal of sex roles occurs in her reworking of Theseus and the Minotaur. Here it is a woman protagonist who does battle with the "Creature of Fear," and the fears that she successfully confronts and conquers are those of every woman who has been raised to doubt her own capabilities.

But puritanism per se is no longer at the root of these fears. Indeed, the immense popularity that Graham has enjoyed over the past quarter century testifies to a profound change in our sexual mores. Clearly, the rebellion against puritanical repression is no longer a revolutionary idea for most Americans. Puritanism is simply incompatible with the needs of a consumer economy that relies on sexually arousing images to promote habits of conspicuous consumption. And the new wave of feminist thinking that arose in the 1960s and '70s viewed this sort of sexual liberation as a mixed blessing, if not an out and out curse. In this new age of the pill and promiscuity, it was feared that women were no longer free not to be sexual. Certainly, the so-called 'dance boom' of the 1960s was very much a part of this sexual revolution. And post-modern dance can be viewed as a reaction against the facile equating of dance and sex that was so central to this so-called boom. Yvonne Rainer, in fact, once declared her "rage at the impoverishment of ideas, narcissism, and disguised sexual exhibitionism of most dancing."[16] Thus it seems reasonable to suggest that the austere, cerebral, anti-voluptuous quality of the early post-modern dances created by women such as Yvonne Rainer, Trisha Brown, and Lucinda Childs reflects these feminist concerns, if only indirectly.

For many women, theatrical dancing of any sort became suspect for dance has often been regarded as an art of pure physical presence in which women are reduced to, and equated with, their bodies. Unlike the actress, the dancer, traditionally at least, doesn't speak; and speech is the one faculty that most clearly distinguishes her from the rest of nature. To some, it seemed entirely plausible that women had been permitted to dominate modern dance because it inadvertently perpetuated yet another set of destructive sex-role stereotypes. Gabriele D'Annunzio for example is reported to have

---

[16] Rainer, Y. *Work*. p. 71.

declared to Isadora Duncan, "You are part of the trees, the sky, you are the dominating goddess of Nature." And Duncan, in a letter to Gordon Craig, declared that Isadora means "daughter of Isis," the Egyptian goddess of fertility.

By contrast, the women who pioneered post-modern dance were eager to demonstrate that they possessed minds as well as bodies. The original title of Yvonne Rainer's *Trio A* was *The Mind Is a Muscle, Part I*. This explains in part the prominence of spoken language in much post-modern dance, the fascination with abstract thought, the impersonal, objective, mathematically generated floor patterns often based on the geometric purity of the grid, and the new conception of dance as a mode of problem-solving. Trisha Brown has said that what attracted her to the elaborate mathematical formulas and diagrams that helped generate the choreography for many of her early pieces was the desire to demonstrate that women choreographers need not proceed intuitively or instinctively, constructing their dances from movement that comes naturally to the body. Rosalind Krauss, describing the sort of grid structures that often underlie the visual art of Sol LeWitt and others, notes that they illustrate "what art looks like when it turns its back on nature."[17] Lucinda Childs's collaborative work, *Dance*, with film projections on scrim by Sol LeWitt and modular music by Philip Glass was perhaps the quintessential example of choreographic gridlock.

Post-modern dances often treat choreography as an exercise in problem-solving. One of the central problems addressed by the women who pioneered post-modern dance was how to exhibit the body in public without becoming an exhibitionist. Rainer's provisional solution is evident in her solo version of *Trio A*. She "averts" her gaze and refuses to directly acknowledge the presence of the audience. Rather than saying "yes" to forbidden fruit in the manner of Isadora Duncan or Joyce's Molly Bloom, Rainer says "no" to familiar pleasures. To quote again from the best known of her mini-manifestos: "no to seduction of spectator by the wiles of the performer... no to moving or being moved."[18]

Of course, this fear of seduction is part and parcel of a more pervasive modernist desire to guarantee the spectator's perceptual freedom, to prevent the spectator from being manipulated by the artwork in a Pavlovian fashion. Malraux once spoke of the "lucid horror of seduction"; and Baudelaire, in his classic essay on dandyism, wrote that "The distinguishing characteristic of the dandy's beauty consists above all in an

---

[17] Krauss, R. *The Optical Unconscious*. Cambridge: The M.I.T. Press. 1993, p. 192.

[18] Rainer, Y. *Work*. p. 51.

air of coldness which comes from an unshakable determination not to be moved."[19] But Rainer's "no to moving or being moved" testifies to more than the persistence of dandyism.

Moreover, her use of the word "seduction" takes on a whole new set of meanings when considered in the light of sexual politics. In fact, much of Rainer's later work plays on the various connotations of the term "seduction" in life as well as in art. Put another way, the theatrical relationship between performer and audience is analogized to the social relationship between men and women. For example, in the slide-projected text for Rainer's *This is the Story of a Woman Who*, we are told that "social interactions seem to be mostly about seduction." At another point in the same piece, a projected title reads, "His very gaze seems to transform her into a performer."[20]

In dance the cinematic notion of the male gaze is less relevant and less useful to the theoretician than a more generalized consideration of the gaze itself, whether male or female, whether heterosexual or homosexual in orientation. We've already seen some of the ways in which dance scholarship can draw upon the recent work of those psychoanalytic feminists who focus on the relative virtues of a visual as opposed to a tactile orientation in the world; the gaze vs. the touch, in other words. The writings of feminists such as Jane Gallop and Luce Irigaray can be very helpful when it comes to illuminating the differences between the detached, visual bias of nineteenth century ballet and the early modern dancer's emphasis on tactility and kinesthetic experience.

But major problems arise the moment one attempts to apply such concepts to a post-modern choreographer like Rainer. Irigaray argued that "the eye… sets at a distance and maintains that distance." But Rainer herself relies heavily on the sort of Brechtian "alienation effects" that might be said to set (the spectacle) at a distance and maintain that distance. And Rainer is concerned that the spectator will be seduced by the wiles of the performer, not that the performers will fall victim to a predatory gaze.

Of course, feminists have argued that Rainer's distancing devices are themselves part of the problem, an unwitting act of complicity with deep patriarchal biases. Listen to the feminist writer Lucy Lippard discussing Rainer's work in the mid '70's: "for over a decade now an imposed — perhaps masculine — detachment masquerading as 'modernism' has insidiously denigrated feeling."[21]

---

[19] Baudelaire, C. *The Painter of Modern Life*, trans. Jonathan Mayne. London: Phaidon, 1965, p. 29.

[20] Rainer, Y. *Work*. p. 252.

[21] Lippard, L. *From the Center: Feminist Essays on Women's Art*. N.Y.: Dutton. 1976, p. 278.

Here we encounter, if only indirectly, one of the central conflicts in recent sexual/political theory: the debate over the correct attitude feminists should take toward traditional conceptions of gender difference, e.g., the belief that women are fundamentally instinctive rather than reflective, closer to and more open about their emotional life than men, innately drawn to tactile involvement rather than visual, analytical detachment, and always determined to render their experience holistically rather than to dissect it into fragments.

Should feminists set out to demonstrate that these presumably natural differences are nothing but patriarchal prejudices? Or should they turn the inherited hierarchy on its head, celebrating the very characteristics that patriarchy has traditionally denigrated, instinctual modes of knowing, intimacy, fullness of feeling, oneness with nature, etc. Irigaray, in her *Speculum de l'Autre Femme* contrasts the values of the maternal womb with the patriarchal logos and comes down firmly on the side of the former.

In a 1975 interview with Rainer, Lucy Lippard tries, rather desperately, to convince the choreographer that fragmentation takes on a different character in her work than it does in the work of male artists, that "there is a special kind of fragmentation that often surfaces in women's work... that quality of pulling together a lot of things... while still maintaining continuity." In other words, it really aspires toward organic unity. But Rainer is adamant: "It's the opposite of the gestalt," she replies, "Disjunction."[22]

That response tells us a lot about Rainer, and what it tells us applies as well to Childs, Brown and the other analytically inclined post-modernist choreographers. They reclaim rather than reject traditional male privileges. They don't celebrate the natural, the maternal, or the holistic. They strive to create movement objectively, not by tapping some internal, let alone maternal, instinct. In the so-called "vacuum cleaner sequence" in Rainer's *Inner Appearances* the slide-projected text read "Why do women value their insights more than their work, she thinks. Now she is laughing inwardly at her cliché — the old intuition bit."[23] Here we encounter yet another major difference between their work and that of the women who pioneered modern dance.

They repudiate the subjective inwardness of traditional modern dance. Graham, by contrast, spoke of "making visible the interior landscape" and Doris Humphrey described modern dance as "moving from the inside out." But inwardness is another of those qualities that have traditionally been

---

[22] Rainer in Lippard, p. 276.

[23] Rainer, Y. *Work*. p. 252.

attributed to women by the male psychoanalytic establishment. Psychologists such as Erik Erikson in his famous essay "Womanhood and the Inner Space" argue that women are naturally more inward than men and are therefore less likely to feel at home in the outside world, the world outside the home. Compare Graham's and Humphrey's emphasis on the authenticity of inner experience with Rainer's declaration that "...action or what one does, is more interesting and important than the exhibition of character and attitude, and that action can best be focused on through the submerging of the personality; so ideally, one is not even oneself, one is a neutral doer."[24]

This conception of the performer as a neutral doer is of course essential to those movement tasks that made up so much of the vocabulary of post-modern dance during the Judson era. And these tasks were rarely, if ever, gender-specific. In fact, Rainer insists (in the same interview with Lippard) that "At the time, I was interested in a certain kind of sexually undifferentiated athleticism, in using the body as an object, just in terms of its weight and mass, which was a reason why no sexual differentiation was made."[25] And by creating situations in which women lifted men as frequently as men lifted women, Rainer challenged one of the sacred tenets of choreographic partnering, and demonstrated that, at least in the realm of dance, anatomy is not necessarily destiny. Rainer refers to this sexually undifferentiated choreography as "movement-as-task — or movement as object." But her objectification of the body, her frequent blurring of the distinction between dancer's body and inanimate art object, is of course very different from the sort of reductive sexual display that feminists have in mind when they lament the objectification of women.

Of course, these days, one finds very few choreographers working in the idiom that Rainer called "movement-as task." Pina Bausch, who has become the major influence on emerging Western choreographers in the '80's, retains some vestiges of task-oriented movement in her work, but in the final analysis, she owes less to Rainer than to the psychological dance dramas of Tudor or the anguished, expressive, gut-wrenching movement vocabulary of Wigman.

No, the austerity and impersonality one associates with Rainer's manifestos have become increasingly rare in the dance world. And in order to understand what has happened to this ideological severity, we need only consider the evolution of Twyla Tharp, another woman who began her choreographic career in the 1960s as a stark, austere minimalist. Tharp now

---

[24] Rainer, Y. *Work.* p. 65.

[25] Rainer in Lippard, p. 276.

describes those severe early works as having been "resentful of physicality." Looking back rather bemusedly on that coldly puritanical period of her career, she refers to her (then) all-woman company as "a bunch of zealous broads doing God's work." Tharp, of course, would soon lead the way back toward a sensuous and virtuosic physicality which would also include a new dispensation toward the unabashedly "unnatural" ballet vocabulary as well; and many of the early post-modernists have since followed her lead. Once they had proved that dance could be unmistakably brainy, that it could affirm the conceptual at the expense, if necessary, of the sensual, it then became morally and ideologically acceptable to reassert technical virtuosity. *The Fugue* is the last of those severe dances that Tharp still performs today, and it's certainly less austere than, say, *Tank Dive*. But in order to get some sense how things have changed, one need only compare its hard-edged aggressiveness to the loose-limbed, luxuriant lushness of *Eight Jelly Rolls* or *Sue's Leg*.

And yet Tharp's, or for that matter, Trisha Brown's, recent evolution does maintain one essential link with the earlier work: the absence of that taut, muscular stretch that Rainer once described as "a more than human look of physical extension, which is familiar as the dancer's muscular set."[26] The sense of continuous flow and of relaxed transitions in Tharp's recent work or in Trisha Brown's *Watermotor*, *Opal Loop*, or *Son of Gone Fishin'* scrupulously avoids those frozen moments of exhibitionistic display that had always dismayed Yvonne Rainer. One of Tharp's great achievements was in figuring out how to make the relaxed, unstretched body look theatrically legible in a large auditorium. Of course, I'm not suggesting that feminism alone can explain or account for an innovation of this magnitude.

Obviously, none of the choreography I've been discussing can, or should, be reduced purely and simply to its feminist dimensions. The aesthetic and political path that leads from Duncan to Rainer to Tharp is long, circuitous, and complicated. Feminism is one of many influences exerted on, and reflected in these works. But the fact remains that modern and post-modern dance are probably the only art forms in which various stages of feminist thinking are literally em-*bodied*.

An earlier version of this material was published in *Dance Theatre Journal*, Vol. 8 No. 3, Autumn, 1990.

---

[26] Rainer, Y. *Work*. p. 65.

Bibliography

Balanchine, George. *By George*. N.Y.: San Marco Press, 1984.

Baudelaire, C. *The Painter of Modern Life*. Trans. Jonathan Mayne. London: Phaidon, 1965.

Brown, Norman O. *Life Against Death*. Middletown: Wesleyan University Press, 1959. *Love's Body*. N.Y.: Vintage Books, 1966.

Croce, Arlene. *Afterimages*. N.Y.: Alfred A. Knopf, 1977.

Decter, M. *The New Chastity and Other Arguments Against Women's Liberation*. N.Y.: Coward, McCann and Geoghegan, 1977.

Duncan, Isadora. *The Art of the Dance*. N.Y.: Theatre Arts Books, 1928. *My Life*. N.Y.: Garden City Publishing Co., 1927.

Foster, H. *Postmodern Culture*. London: Pluto Press, 1985.

Krauss, R. *The Optical Unconscious*. Cambridge: The M.I.T. Press, 1993.

Lippard, Lucy. *From the Center: Feminist Essays on Women's Art*. N.Y.: Dutton, 1976.

Mazo, Joseph. *Prime Movers*. Princeton: Princeton Book Co., 1977.

McLuhan, Marshall. *The Gutenberg Galaxy*. N.Y.: New American Library, 1962.

Millet, K. *Sexual Politics*. N.Y.: Avon Books, 1969.

Rainer, Yvonne. *Work: 1961–73*. Halifax: Press of the Nova Scotia College of Art and Design, 1974.

Taylor, G. Rattray. *Sex in History*. N.Y.: Vanguard Press, 1970.

FEMINIST THEORY AND CONTEMPORARY DANCE
Ann Cooper Albright

"The dancer of the future will be one whose body and soul have grown so harmoniously together that the language of that soul will have become the movement of the body... She will realize the mission of women's body and the holiness of all its parts... From all parts of her body shall shine radiant intelligence, bringing to the world the message of the thoughts and aspirations of thousands of women. She shall dance the freedom of woman."[1]

Isadora Duncan's visionary language has inspired generations of feminist-minded modern dancers. As one of the most famous written evocations of the new woman cum dancer, Duncan's essay on the "Dancer of the Future" conjures up an image of a strong, full-bodied, and uncorseted woman leaping barefoot across an open field. The dancing amazon that she envisions here is a product not only of Duncan's own vibrant imagination, personal audacity, and sheer willfulness, but also of the growing feminist consciousness in America at the turn of the century.[2]

The evangelism with which Duncan and early modern dancers raged against the physical deformation of the body and false representation of the spirit of woman in classical ballet is legendary. "The dancer [of the future] will not belong to a nation but to all humanity. She will dance not in the form of nymph, nor fairy, nor coquette, but in the form of woman in her greatest and purest expression."[3] This idealization of the natural underlying

---

[1] From "The Dancer of the Future" by Isadora Duncan, reprinted in *Dance as a Theatre Art*. Cohen, Selma Jeanne, ed. Princeton: Dance Horizons Books, 1992 (2nd edition) p. 129.

[2] For useful overviews of turn of the century feminist beginning see: Cott, Nancy F. *The Grounding of Modern Feminism*. New Haven: Yale University Press, 1987, and Cott, Nancy and Pleck, Nancy, eds., *A Heritage of Her Own*. New York: Simon and Schuster, 1979.

[3] Duncan, "The Dancer of the Future." In this essay, as in others, Duncan gets caught up in a binary logic that pits "the most moral, healthful, and beautiful in art," that is the "free and natural" movements of the human body, against the spiritual vapidness of ballet technique which, "vainly striving against the natural laws of gravitation or the natural will of the individual, and working in discord in its form and movement with the form and movement of nature, produces a sterile movement which gives no birth to future movements."

early modern dance has left a strong imprint on the development of dance training in America, which is only now beginning to be questioned. It is classic, of course, that these women who were so quick to identify and resist the ideology of ballet failed to recognize that they were also creating an essentialized ideology of the female body as inherently "natural and beautiful." Nonetheless, this conviction about the moral as well as physical benefits of dance gave the early modern dancers such as Isadora Duncan the spiritual fortitude with which to rebel against Victorian social codes concerning the appropriate behavior for middle-class women. Although in retrospect Duncan's rhetoric may seems extravagant to the modern ear, her utopian vision of a "dancer of the future," as well as the mythology surrounding her own life and dance career, has given modern dance a very special legacy — a sense that it is possible for women in dance to craft their own movement styles (and, in some sense, their own identities) in order to create a more positive and powerful vision of "woman."[4]

While much contemporary dance still holds the feminist goals of early modern dance close to heart, "woman" is no longer an unproblematic term, either in the culture at large or in the dance field. This historical shift in modern dance from universal images of "woman" to more specific, indeed, often autobiographical, situations inhabited by women reflects a parallel shift in the development of feminist thought in American culture. Twenty-five years ago, feminist scholarship was mostly devoted to the enormous task of recovering previously unacknowledged contributions by women in the fields of history, literature, and the arts.[5] At the same time, feminist political activity was primarily focused on issues of sexism and gender inequality. This included fighting a two-pronged battle to both open up greater career opportunities for women, as well as to encourage more respect for the traditional female roles of mother, caretaker, teacher, and the like. Rejecting the innumerable ways in which "woman" had been defined as "other" to men throughout Western history, many feminists of that generation were concerned with creating or reclaiming positive role models

---

[4] For more background reading on the connections between early women's movements and the beginnings of modern dance see Kendall, Elizabeth. *Where She Danced*. Berkeley: University of California Press, 1979, and Jowitt, Deborah. *Time and the Dancing Image*. New York: William Morrow and Company, 1988.

[5] Some of these seminal works in the study of literature include: Gilbert S. and Gubar S.'s *The Madwoman in the Attic*. New Haven: Yale University Press, 1979; Jacobus, Mary, *Reading Woman*. New York: Columbia University Press, 1986; ed. Miller, Nancy. *The Poetics of Gender*. New York: Columbia University Press, 1986; and Showalter, Elaine, ed., *The New Feminist Criticism*. New York: Pantheon Books, 1985.

of women. They were interested in exploring the poetics of "woman" on her own terms.[6]

It is the purpose of this essay to document certain parallels between critical issues in current feminist thought and contemporary dance. My point is not to argue a one-to-one correspondence, or a cause and effect relationship between feminist theory and contemporary dance. Nor am I suggesting that the women choreographers whose work I discuss in these pages are consciously making "feminist" dances. Rather, I am interested in exploring the interrelatedness between these two different forms of cultural discourse. Because they are both concerned at some point with articulating the relationship between physical bodies and social meaning, I believe that contemporary dance and feminist theory can be mutually informative. Specifically, feminist theory, because it asks how culture constructs bodies, can give us critical perspectives on dance, and likewise, contemporary dance, because it works in a continual process of (re)training and (re)articulating those bodies, can push feminist theory towards a more satisfying articulation of the complex relationship between individual experience and cultural representation.[7]

In the following analyses of works by contemporary choreographers, I attempt to articulate the implications of these dances in terms of certain cogent discussions in feminist theory. While I am interested in how dancing bodies at once reflect and create social meaning, I am also aware that dance is not simply another visual phenomenon. Its meanings are often encoded in the kinesthetic dynamics of the movement as well the visual images represented by that movement. Although it is grounded in live human bodies (whose gender, race, and ability immediately convey certain cultural messages about beauty, fitness, grace, etc.), dance carries the contributing possibility of being both very abstract and very literal. Some movements will give an audience only vague physical sensations, while other movement gestures have unmistakable meaning. Thus, dance can at once represent

---

[6] For more on female poetics see Marks and de Courtivron (eds.) *New French Feminisms*. New York: Schocken Books, 1981, and Cixous, Hélène and Clement, Catherine. *The Newly Born Woman*. Minneapolis: University of Minnesota Press, 1986.

[7] There is a growing body of work based on the intersection of feminist thought and dance theory. See for instance: Adair, Christy. *Women and Dance*. New York: New York University Press, 1992; Cooper Albright, Ann. "Mining the Dancefield: Feminist Theory and Contemporary Dance" in *Contact Quarterly* 15: 2 (Spring/Summer 1990); "The Body as Discourse" issue of *Women and Performance* (#6); Daly, Ann. "The Balanchine Woman: Of Humming Birds and Channel Swimmers" in *Drama Review* 31: 1 (Spring 1987); and Manning, Susan. *Ecstasy and the Demon: Feminism and Nationalism in the Dances of Mary Wigman*. Berkeley: University of California Press, 1993.

images that cite known cultural icons, as well as present physical states whose meanings are not so much visual as they are kinesthetic. Shifting consciously through these different modes of representation, contemporary dance can engage with and problematize feminist issues concerning gender and the body in ways that speak to the complexities of our time.

Performed individually or as part of a larger solo work entitled "Food for Thought," "Chicken Soup" (1982) presents Blondell Cummings as a woman whose life revolves around the community and loneliness of the household kitchen. The first image is the back of a woman dressed in a long white skirt and white shirt, swaying from side to side with her shopping bag in hand, just as if she were walking down a country lane on her way to market. This image dissolves into another picture of a woman seated primly on the edge of a chair. Then a nostalgic, wistful melody plays, and her face and hands become animated with a variety of gossipy — "Oh, you don't mean it!" — expressions. During this silent, cheerful chatter, Cummings begins to rock in a movement so old-fashioned and yet so hypnotically soothing that it is hard to imagine that she will ever stop. As Cummings banters away with herself, a woman's voice reminisces in a calm, thoughtful manner. Phrases such as "the kitchen was the same" melt into the tableau of the woman rocking in the chair. The constant repetition of rocking makes me seem somehow irrelevant.

Soon, however, the pleasant conversation turns to one of grief and pain and Cummings's body encompasses the change with full central contractions. The quick, flickering hand gestures which traced years and years of passing out cards at a bridge table and cups of tea get caught for a moment in a posture of pain or anger and then release back into the repetitious flow of rocking and talking. Joining the music on the soundtrack, a woman's voice haltingly describes afternoons spent around the kitchen table talking of "childhood friends, operations, abortion, death, and money." Cummings's character is selectively responsive to these words, periodically breaking into a stop-action series of emotional gestures which mime the spoken words and which have become a trademark of her work. "Chicken Soup" continues. Stepping away from the picture gallery of women which she animates in the rocking chair, Cummings sinks to the floor and picks up a scrub brush. Her body bobs with the rhythm of her work and the action of the bristles across the floor creates a swish-swish accompaniment. The audience sees her in profile, her body stretching and contracting with the strong, even strokes of her arms. The broad sweeps of her movement are more important than the task of cleaning the floor. Although the image could be one of contracted menial labor, there is a caring, authoritative quality in Cummings's motion that suggests that this work is immensely satisfying.

The direct, spare physicality and its affirmation of life in work diffuses when Cummings trades her brush for a long black scarf. As a nostalgic hummed melody floats into the scene, Cummings swirls the scarf in the air and crosses the stage with joyous, exalted skips and leaps. This moment of whirling happiness fades into a sad sweep of the scarf as Cummings walks to the back of the stage and waves "good-bye." Loss and mourning crush the previous gaiety. Her heavy, tired body is dwarfed by a huge shadow of herself projected on the background. The figure, welled by grief, looms behind Cummings. Then, the emotional tides change once again as a chicken soup recipe is recited and Cummings picks up a cast-iron frying pan with all the assurance and sassiness of a woman who could cook in her sleep. Like a simmering soup, there is a constant rhythm and bubble in her body. Chopping, mixing and frying actions are literally embodied by full motions that spread through her body and down into the feet as well. With cooking coursing through her body, Cummings comments on the images she has made by a series of wonderfully comic facial expressions. Innuendo wafts, like the imagined aroma of her cooking, in and around this figure and when the recipe directs her to "simmer until tender," Cummings ironically, and with a knowing smile directed to the audience, shimmies her hips.

When Cummings introduced "Chicken Soup" during an informal lecture-demonstration at Franklin and Marshall College in the fall of 1987, she spoke of her interest in food and how she could guess someone's characteristics just by looking in their refrigerator. Cummings described "Chicken Soup" as a solo about women — many different women — who use food to nourish and connect to other people. That nurturing quality is also reflected by the generosity with which Cummings moves, her ability to embrace so many different gestural styles with her own body. Her intention was to make a dance that spanned a variety of cultures — Jewish, African-American, Italian — and that desire is reflected in her choice of texts, which include pieces by Grace Paley as well as a recipe from *The Settlement Cookbook*.

Originally choreographed in the early eighties, "Chicken Soup" mirrored a feminist emphasis at that time in creating an inclusive portrait of what all women, regardless of their race, sexuality, and social position, share. Interestingly enough, however, "Chicken Soup" is generally referred to as, in the words of one critic, "a fond memory of black rural life."[8] This essentializing of Cummings's character in terms of race points to one of the most difficult issues facing contemporary theory today. Despite her intentions, Cummings is defined by racist culture as a "black" woman. Cummings does

---

[8] Goldner, Nancy. "Electric Cooking," *Saturday Review*. May/June, 1983.

not have the privilege of covering over the fact of her race the way white choreographers are often able to do. At this historical moment, one of the only ways she can refuse the labeling of racial difference is to problematize that identity category.

In fact, when Cummings presented the work on television in the "Alive from Off Center" program during the summer of 1988, the cover of the *New York Times* "Television" section announced her work as a vision of "traditional roles of black women in America."[9] A curiously intrusive interference by the television producer had Cummings performing the dance in a generic Formica kitchen, wearing a housedress and a flowered apron. The effect, especially to someone who had seen the solo in a theater space, with no set and white costuming, is quite bizarre. The tacky television realism stages a very narrow definition of "traditional roles of black women in America," removing the wonderful ambivalence of Cummings's earlier version of this dance. Unlike the stage portrayal of this solo where it is more ambivalent just exactly whose memories she is dancing, the television production reduces this woman to a generic two-dimensional figure who is trapped in the specific context of her own spic'n, span kitchen.

The critical reception of "Chicken Soup" foregrounds the myriad ways in which artists' attempts to create positive images of women are easily re-interpreted in terms of the dominant visions of "woman." As a result of this mainstream appropriation, many feminists have begun to recognize the need to become aware of (and thus take more responsibility for) the ways in which those images are represented and communicated. History has shown us that any image of women, no matter how inspired or original, is subject to prevailing cultural stereotypes of "woman." Isadora Duncan may well have intended to create a dancer of the future who was neither a coquette nor a fairy, but her ability to do that depended not only on her choreographic invention, but also on her ability to change how dance (and, by extension, the dancer) was viewed within Western culture. Although it is not my interest to reflect on the ultimate success of her project in this essay, it is clear that Duncan's use of classical music, her referencing of classical Greek culture, and her insistence on calling dance an Art (and herself an Artist), were strategies employed to redirect the way in which her audiences watched her dance.[10] This conscious realization that the aesthetic frame and social context

---

[9] *New York Times*. August 7, 1988.

[10] For a fuller discussion of these issues in terms of Duncan's American reception see Daly, Ann. "Dance History and Feminist Theory: Reconsidering Isadora Duncan and the Male Gaze" in Senelick, Laurence, ed., *Gender in Performance*. Hanover: University of New England Press, 1992.

is as important to the meaning of the work as is the image portrayed is, to my mind, one of the most significant contributions of feminist theory. Indeed, it is precisely by exploring how the very act of presenting one's gendered body in performance always already constructs certain cultural meanings, as well as by tracing the ways in which women repeatedly become essentialized as "woman" in these representations, that feminist thinking has profoundly affected contemporary dance.

In her 1992 solo "Desirée,"[11] Donna Uchizono's body takes on a frail, rag-doll quality, especially in the moments in her dancing when her head is flopping from side to side and her arms are held stiffly out in front of her. But there are other moments, as when her whole body is lashing out at some unknown force, when the intensity and clarity of her rapid-fire movement creates its own sense of purpose. The juxtaposition of these moments of claiming control over her body versus being controlled by some outside force creates the dramatic tension in this dance.

The piece begins as Uchizono, dressed in black, drops a huge bunch of red flowers over her head all the while facing away from the audience. The spotlight fades and she retreats upstage to begin a journey toward the flowers. This time she is facing the audience, her arms bent and fists clenched in furious movements that are alternately self-directed, as when she hits her torso, and directed outward, as when she randomly punches the space around her. As she approaches the pile of strewn flowers, her feet break out in a stamping pattern, crushing and scattering the flowers around her. The deluge of pain and passion is over for the time being and she is still, listening for a while before she nosedives into the flowers and back into the fury of her earlier dancing. Later, in one of the most beautiful moments of the dance, she takes off her top to reveal a long stemmed red rose running up her spine. The stark contrast of her black pants, white back and red rose creates a powerful image of strength and vulnerability. She turns to touch it and ends up spinning faster and faster, like a cat trying to catch its own tail. Uchizono finally grabs the flower and holds it in front of her, allowing it to lead her dizzily stumbling back and forth across the stage as if it were a divining rod.

It is not clear to me exactly what the flowers mean to Uchizono, but I find them to be a potent metaphor for a certain feminine beauty and physicality that Uchizono seems to be struggling with. The image of the rose on her back reminds me of a story by Maxine Hong Kingston called "White

---

[11] I first saw this solo in New York City during the fall of 1992. It was performed at Marymount Manhattan Theater on Sept. 11, 1992, and again at Movement Research at the Judson Church on Nov. 30, 1992.

Tigers" in which the heroine's back is carved with the names of her family. Applied painfully and indelibly on her skin, these names give her the strength to go forth into the world, but they also insist on her eventual re-incorporation into a patriarchal structure that confines her physical and spiritual identity. Similarly in "Desirée," the flowers evoke a history which provides both the visual space and narrative impulse for Uchizono's dancing, but also implies an image of "woman" which she is unwilling to completely accept.

In the past ten years, the whole conceptualization of "woman" as a universal category of gender oppression has been repeatedly challenged by working class feminists, women of color, and lesbian activists. These women have brought a new way of theorizing about the interconnectedness of cultural representations of race, gender, class, and sexuality into what had been an almost exclusively white academic discourse which was narrowly focused on gender issues. This recent wave of feminist thought and political practice has contributed to exciting new trends in cultural criticism, among which is an ongoing investigation into the ways cultural, biological, and personal experiences construct women's sense of who we are. Theoretical writings by Teresa de Lauretis, Iris Young, Judith Butler, Susan Bordo, Cynthia Novack, and others have sought to articulate how social roles both literally and symbolically construct bodies and how physical bodies, in turn, serve to reinforce those social identities.[12] I find this work particularly relevant to women (whose bodies have been historically overdetermined) and dancers (whose identities are often inextricably linked to their bodies).

While the power of Cummings's solo dancing in "Chicken Soup" comes from her incredible ability to incorporate so many different women's facial expressions, gestures, and movements into one dancing body, the intensity in Uchizono's dancing comes from the figurative fragmentation of that body. Whereas Cummings uses her full weight and embraces the space with her dancing, Uchizono holds onto her own weight, nervously shifting directions and slicing the space around her with quick movements of her arms and legs. The feeling I get from watching these dances is that "Chicken Soup" tries to encompass all identities, while "Desirée" battles with the essence of her gendered identity. As I have already noted, "Chicken Soup" reflects

---

[12] See, for instance: Bordo, Susan. "Reading the Slender Body" in Jacobus M., Fox Keller E., Shuttleworth S., eds. *Body/Politics*. New York: Routledge, Chapman and Hall, 1990; Butler, Judith. *Gender Trouble*. New York: Routledge, 1990; de Lauretis, Teresa. *Technologies of Gender*. Bloomington: Indiana University Press, 1987; Novack, Cynthia. *Sharing the Dance: Contact Improvisation and American Culture*. Madison: University of Wisconsin Press, 1990; and Young, Iris. *Throwing like a Girl and Other Essays in Feminist Philosophy and Social Theory*. Bloomington: Indiana University Press, 1990.

a desire to create an image of "woman" who represents a cross-section of women. Unfortunately, that multitude gets read only in terms of Cummings's most obvious identity marker. These ethnic differences become diluted in the reception of her solo as a portrayal of "rural black women." In contrast, Uchizono's body, rejects the category of "woman" (although not the category of ethnicity) as symbolized by the rose taped onto her back. But once she refuses that particular frame of identity, she seems to be in an existential freefall.

At the risk of oversimplifying a complex discussion, I would like to draw a parallel between the two dances I have been discussing and a key debate in feminist theory — that of essentialism vs. constructivism. In her exploration of the issues surrounding this debate, Diana Fuss writes: "For the essentialist, the body occupies a pure, pre-social, pre-discursive space. The body is "real," accessible, and transparent; it is always there and directly interpretable through the sense. For the constructionist, the body is never simply there, rather it is composed of a network of effects continually subject to socio-political determination. The body is "always already" culturally mapped; it never exists in a pure or uncoded state."[13]

Although her movement is a tapestry of multiple characters, Cummings's dancing in "Chicken Soup" never really questions the representation of her experience. "Chicken Soup" is immensely satisfying to watch because her portrayal of a community of women is so believable, so believably "there," as Fuss would say. Uchizono's movement style, by contrast, always foregrounds her process of resistance to an image which no longer makes sense to her. The total effect of the dance can be quite disturbing (even while some of the images are breathtakingly beautiful), because there is no resolution at the end, only a prolonged searching.

I am referring to the essentialist-constructivist debate in feminist thought here not so much to polarize these two dances (as Fuss is quick to point out, there is quite a bit of essentializing in the constructivists' positions and vice versa), but to point out how different dances work to either naturalize a performer's physical identity or to make that identity somehow odd. Given the ways in which women historically have been inscribed in dance as naturally graceful, or feminine, or beautiful, I find the current interest in foregrounding the ways in which identity is constructed in dance quite intriguing. Ultimately, I believe that these investigations will begin to tell us more about the nature of dance as a form of cultural representation, enriching the field of dance theory considerably.

---

[13] Fuss, Diana. *Essentially Speaking: Feminism, Nature, and Difference.* New York: Routledge Press, 1989, p. 6.

Blondell Cummings is a woman, a choreographer, and an African-American, but her solo dances can frame those identities very differently. In the following analysis of "Blues II," a solo which Cummings choreographed six years after "Chicken Soup," I would like to trace how Cummings moves from an essentialized portrait of "everywoman" to a complex representation of the intersecting identity categories of race, class, and gender.

"Blues II" is the final solo in "Basic Strategies V," a dance which explores how people grapple with the intersecting social webs of work, money and power. In what she terms her process of "collage," Cummings layers texts by the Caribbean writer Jamaica Kincaid and music by the composer Michael Riesman with her own choreography to create a series of connections between individual identity and communal legacies. A remarkable text by Kincaid focuses the dancing in the first section. The flowing, abstract movements of the group's dancing are juxtaposed with a story which braids the history of an indigenous people with that of a colonial Anglican cathedral. Smooth and liquid, the taped narrator's voice loops back on itself repeatedly: "My history before it was interrupted does not include cathedrals. What my history before it was interrupted includes is no longer absolutely clear to me. The cathedral is now a part of me. The cathedral is now mine."

During a brief interlude, another text by Kincaid begins to describe with encyclopedic detail the habitat, production and reproduction of the silkworm. Read like an article from *National Geographic*, the information seems tame enough, at first. As the interlude finishes and Cummings's solo begins, however, the context changes and this scientific discourse transforms into a series of metacomments on the politics of colonial enterprise, cheap third world labor and the production of Western luxuries.

At the beginning of her solo, the lights come on very slowly to reveal a statuesque Cummings, wearing a shimmering black evening gown and cape. Slowly raising and lowering a champagne bottle and fluted glass, she turns in a curiously disembodied and vague manner, as if she were a revolving decoration in the middle of the ballroom floor. Her impassive face and glittering dress are reflected in the large mirrors which fan out to either side of her. Functioning as a kind of "Huis Clos," these mirrors confine her movements, meeting each change of direction with multiple reflections of her own body. Sometimes Cummings moves with proud, grandiose strides, covering the space with a confident territoriality. Other times she seems frantic and possessed, pacing the floor in this prison of mirrors where she can neither confront nor escape the reflections of the woman she wants — was — intended to become.

In the midst of a luxurious, waltzy section where she is swirling around the stage, Cummings abruptly drops to her knees and, drawing her skirt over her face, begs for money. The split-second transformation of her body from ease to despair reminds the viewer of the fragility of that seductive, glamorous world. While the early fracture is quickly smoothed over by the romantic music and Cummings's lyrical dancing, this crack in the illusion widens as photographic slides are projected on a screen above her head. Alternating images of third world famine refugees with Western signs of wealth and power depicted in Ralph Lauren-like advertisements, these slides throw Cummings's whole intention into question. Is she trying to insert herself into these white, patriarchal images? Or is this whole scenario a conscious attempt to point out the problems inherent in such assimilation?

Cummings's solo forces the audience not only to confront the issues at stake in being a black woman in a white man's world, but also to see the difficulty with representing that experience. No one image, sentence, or gesture can describe an identity that must always shift between cultural icons. With each movement, Cummings introduces an image of herself which is simultaneously vanishing and reappearing in another direction. Her physical presence — the constant turning and turning again — compounds the vertigo of watching both a live body and its multiple refractions. Confronted by their own inability to follow just one image, the audience must shift their attention to the spaces between the mirrors — the space of her dancing. Because the impact of her performance is located in neither her "real" physical body nor its surreal reflections, but rather in the transient movement between these poles of representation, Cummings can fashion a self which insistently exceeds the visible. Turning, and turning again, she is always in the process of re-creating herself, at once suggesting and refusing the boundaries of her own identity.

For me, Cummings's performance in "Blues II" represents a critical moment in both recent feminist theory and in contemporary dance. Historically separate from the portrayals of Duncan's universal dancer of the future, and ideologically distanced even from the communal portrait of women in "Chicken Soup," "Blues II" defies any easy identity labels and constructs instead a self-conscious referencing of those labels which refuses the traditional separation of self and other, nature and culture, black and white, rich and poor, individual and social. The gowned woman in this dance is at once connected to and disconnected from the many narratives suggested by the visual images and Kincaid's texts. Because her body is a figurative screen for the contradictory meanings of these visual images and the powers who control their representation, it is impossible for her to find a stable identity or a comfortable way of moving. The mirrors amplify her spatial (and psychological) disorientation, reflecting and fragmenting the visual definition of her self. Even when she rejects the "lie" of the dress, even when she takes off the costume of "high" culture, there is no reassuringly "natural" self underneath it all. The dance ends without closure, continuing its ambivalence about how to represent the conflicting identities contained in this body.

What, then, are we left with? Does deconstructing universal, communal, or essentialized representations of "woman" always leave us with only fragmented or contradictory images? What are we to do with these pieces of identity that no longer fit neatly together? Although these questions are prompted by watching "Blues II," they echo similar uncertainties in contemporary feminist thought. As we have seen, the relationship between women's bodies and their sense of identity has become increasingly problematized over the last ten years. If in the course of a rigorous questioning of the cultural constructions of "woman," for instance, we lose the category of women altogether, then how can we form any kind of political coalition focused on the rights of women?

One response to this dilemma is to recognize that while gender may be a social construction, it is nonetheless experienced as a real factor in one's everyday life. In her essay on what she terms "the identity crisis in feminist theory," Linda Alcoff frames the issue in terms of historical practice: "Gender is not a point to start from in the sense of being a given thing but is, instead, a posit or construct, formalizable in a nonarbitrary way through a matrix of habits, practices, and discourses. Further, it is an interpretation of our history within a particular discursive constellation, a history in which we are both subjects of and subjected to social construction."[14] What I want to emphasize here is the dialectic process which she points to in her last sentence, the notion that "we are both subjects of and subjected to" cultural constructions of identity.

Turning back to dance, we see that contemporary dance not only reflects culture, but it can create it as well. Although women dancers' bodies have been historically overdetermined by prevailing social assumptions about just what kinds of bodies constitute a dancer's body (dictating the color, the size, the gender, the weight, etc.), it is important to realize that dancers can consciously take responsibility for reshaping the modes in

---

[14] Alcoff, Linda. "Cultural Feminism versus Post-Structuralism: The Identity Crisis in Feminist Theory," in Minnich, O'Barr, and Rosenfeld, eds. *Reconstructing the Academy: Women's Education and Women's Studies*. Chicago: University of Chicago Press, 1988.

which that body is represented. Once we see through modern dance's rhetoric of the "natural body" (and I believe that feminist thought has helped dance scholars to do this), we realize that all dance is a technology of the body, a way of physical training that results in certain kinds of social meanings. But it is also a form of representing that physicality. It is the slippage between these two modes of cultural meaning — between what the body is (short, tall, fat, thin, female, male) and what the body is doing (pirouetting, rolling on the floor, standing still, spitting) — that makes much contemporary dance extraordinarily rich to think about. "Blues II," for instance, does not seek to replace the stereotypes of black, woman, rich, poor, etc., that it deconstructs with new visions of those identities, but it does offer in their stead a physical reality of being there that, although kinesthetically unsettling, is not unaffective. Cummings's dancing presence is powerful and palpable even in the midst of its own instability. It is the kinesthetic reality of that movement that speaks to the audience and affirms her subjectivity in spite of her refusal to name it.

Because it is an ongoing discourse of live bodies that can work constructively in the space between set positions and because it can foreground the extraordinary pleasure of moving from one place to another, contemporary dance offers us several ways to rethink the metaphysical conundrum of identity issues in current feminist thought. By articulating how that body moves, as well as what it signals when it moves, dance can help feminist theory understand the dialogue between the physical and social constructions of "woman." Dance can literally and figuratively destabliize the representation of gender without losing the material specificity of the body. While the various contemporary dances analyzed in this essay do not necessarily give us a clear vision of the "new woman" as early modern dance sought to, they do help us ask critical questions about the relationship between physical bodies and cultural identities. Indeed, these works create physical images and kinesthetic experiences which consciously resist oppressive cultural ideologies of the female body, thereby suggesting new possibilities of moving and being in the world.

Bibliography

Adair, Christy. *Women and Dance*. N.Y.: N.Y.U. Press, 1992.

Butler, Judith. *Gender Trouble*. N.Y.: Routledge, 1990.

Cixous, Hélène and Clement, Catherine. *The Newly Born Woman*. Minneapolis: University of Minnesota Press, 1986.

Cohen, Selma Jeanne, ed. *Dance as a Theatre Art*. Princeton: Dance Horizons Books, 1992 (2nd. ed.)

Cott, Nancy F. *The Grounding of Modern Feminism*. New Haven: Yale Univ. Press, 1987.

Cott, Nancy F. and Pleck, Nancy eds. *A Heritage of Their Own*. N.Y.: Simon and Schuster, 1979.

Fuss, Diana. *Essentially Speaking: Feminism, Nature and Difference*. N.Y.: Routledge, 1989.

Gilbert S. and Gubar S. *The Madwoman in the Attic*. New Haven: Yale Univ. Press, 1979.

Jacobus M., Fox Keller E., Shuttleworth S. *Body/Politics*. N.Y.: Routledge, Chapman and Hall, 1990.

Jacobus, Mary. *Reading Woman*. N.Y.: Columbia Univ. Press, 1986.

Jowitt, Deborah. *Time and the Dancing Image*. N.Y.: William Morrow Co., 1988.

Kendall, Elizabeth. *Where She Danced*. Berkeley: Univ. of California Press, 1979.

de Lauretis, Teresa. *Technologies of Gender*. Bloomington: Indiana University Press, 1987.

Manning, Susan. *Ecstasy and the Demon: Feminism and Nationalism in the Dances of Mary Wigman*. Berkeley: Univ. of California Press, 1993.

Marks and de Courtivron, eds. *New French Feminisms*. N.Y.: Schocken Books, 1981.

Miller, Nancy, ed. *The Poetics of Gender*. N.Y.: Columbia Univ. Press, 1986.

Minnich E., O'Barr J. and Rosenfeld R., eds. *Reconstructing the Academy: Women's Education and Women's Studies*. Chicago: Univ. of Chicago Press, 1988.

Novack, Cynthia. *Sharing the Dance: Contact Improvisation and American Culture*. Madison: Univ. of Wisconsin Press, 1990.

Showalter, Elaine, ed. *The New Feminist Criticism*. N.Y.: Pantheon Books, 1985.

Young, Iris. *Throwing like a Girl and Other Essays in Feminist Philosophy and Social Theory*. Bloomington: Indiana Univ. Press, 1990.

Plate 1 Dorothie Littlefield in *Barn Dance*, 1938. Photographer – Maurice Seymour. Photo courtesy of Ann Barzel.

Plate 2 Catherine Littlefield, August 1938. Photographer – Maurice Seymour. Photo courtesy of Ann Barzel.

Plate 3 The Littlefield Ballet in *Viennese Waltz*, 1938. Photo courtesy of Ann Barzel.

Plate 4 The Littlefield Ballet in *Café Society*, 1938. Photographer – Maurice Seymour. Photo courtesy of Ann Barzel.

Plate 5 The Littlefield Ballet in *Ladies' Better Dresses*, 1938. Photographer – Maurice Seymour. Photo courtesy of Ann Barzel.

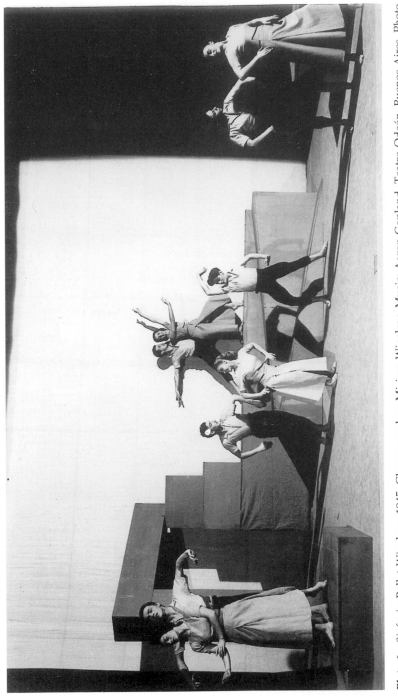

Plate 6 *Sinfonia*, Ballet Winslow, 1945. Choreographer: Miriam Winslow. Music: Aaron Copland. Teatro Odeón, Buenos Aires. Photo courtesy of Renate Schottelius with thanks to Stephanie Reinhart.

Plate 7 *Little Women* (*Las 4 Hermanas*), 1944. Choreographer – Miriam Winslow. Dancers: Renate Schottelius, Margot Guerrero, Elide Locardi, Cecilia Ingenieros. Photo courtesy of Renate Schottelius with thanks to Stephanie Reinhart.

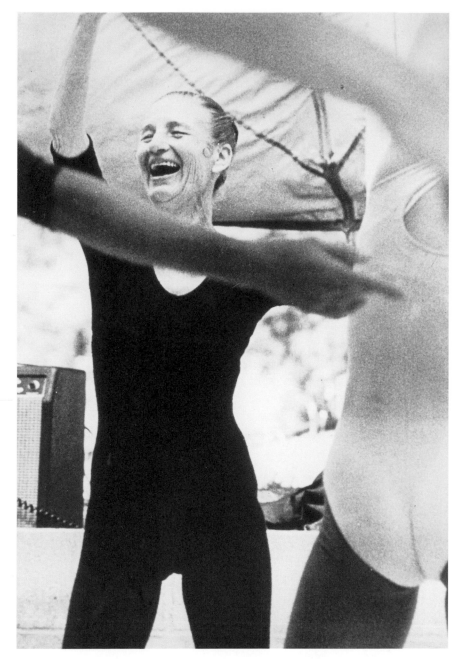

Plate 8 Bella Lewitzky in rehearsal, c. 1965. Photo Courtesy of Bella Lewitzky Dance Company.

Plate 9 Willie "Span" Joseph and Edith "Baby" Edwards as the team "Spic and Span." Photo courtesy of Edith "Baby" Edwards.

Plate 10 Edwina "Salt" Evelyn and Jewel "Pepper" Welch. Photo courtesy of Edwina "Salt" Evelyn.

Plate 11 Louise Madison. Photo courtesy of Ludie Jones.

Plate 12 Mildred "Candi" Thorpe. Photo courtesy of Jewel Welch.

164

Plate 13 Ludie Jones. Photo courtesy of Ludie Jones.

Plate 14   Merian Soto. Photographer – Beatriz Schiller.

Plate 15 Blondell Cummings. Photographer – Beatriz Schiller.

Plate 16 Billie Kirpich on "Exercise with Billie." Photo courtesy of the Dade County Division of Elderly Services/TV Channel 17, Miami, Florida.

Plate 17 Brenda Way, Artistic Director, in rehearsal. Photo courtesy of ODC/San Francisco.

Plate 18 Sally Hess in *Subway Music*. Photographer – Beatriz Schiller.

Plate 19 Kariamu Welsh Asante and Dancers. Photograph by Patented Photos, Philadelphia, Pa. Photo courtesy of Patented Photos/Pat Armenia and Ed Seiz.

Plate 20 Jawole Willa Jo Zollar in her *Bitter Tongue*. Photographer – Cylla Von Tiedeman. Photo courtesy of Urban Bush Women.

Plate 21 Eva Enciñas. Photo courtesy of Ninotchka Bennahum.

Plate 22   Ananya Chatterjea. Photographer – James P. Murphy.

Plate 23   Yunyu Wang performing the *Long Sleeve Dance*. Photo courtesy of Yunyu Wang.

Plate 24 Sharon E. Friedler and Susan B. Glazer, co-editors and peer mentors. Photographer – Beatriz Schiller.

BOOK II

THE PHYSICAL BODY
THEORY AND PRACTICE
AND USING THE
KNOWLEDGE

PART V

DANCERS TALK ABOUT THE PHYSICAL BODY, THEORY AND PRACTICE AND USING THE KNOWLEDGE
Sharon E. Friedler and Susan B. Glazer

The most important creators in dance are those who make us see things differently; their works advance history. Moving into the twentieth century, Bronislava Nijinska made us see how women could use the pointe shoe as an instrument of aggression. Isadora Duncan made us see the single, unfettered female body in a new technique; Martha Graham made us see movement built on women and charged with their sexual energy; Katherine Dunham introduced us to the power of African-based vocabularies and diverse images of African American female performers. Twyla Tharp made us see speed; Laura Dean made us see duration and tolerate it in a different way; Senta Driver made us see dancers bigger than they used to be. The work of these women and others demonstrates that there are many approaches to the female body and that they can change.

In a broad theoretical context the 'body' can be defined and read via physical, theoretical/practical and cultural constructs. The conception of these constructs varies from one culture, context and time period to another. In the most literal sense, body issues are those that have to do with the actual physical functioning of the body as well as with perceptions of the dancing body. Traditionally, such factors as height, weight, sex, relative proportion of various body parts, flexibility, agility, age and stamina have all been areas to which fixed boundaries have been applied. In the figurative sense, discourse about the 'body' extends beyond the physical. In Book I numerous women describe how mentoring relationships figure heavily in their lives in dance. In Book II, women consider the ways that their physical body, their theory and practice and cultural identification have helped shape their careers.

The Physical Body

Weight

The current ideal female dancer in many Eastern and Western theatrical dance styles is thin, delicate and vulnerable looking. She has long legs and arms, a compact torso, and small breasts. This image, most pronounced in classical ballet, is supported by training regimens which value mastery of a codified movement vocabulary, highly specific muscular development, extreme joint flexibility and stamina, all of which must be mastered within severe weight limitations. The rigors of this kind of training lead to a preoccupation with weight that can become obsessive in terms of how women view or distort their personal images.

George Balanchine was renowned for his preference for the very thin ballerina, whom he considered ideal for communicating his technique and performing his steps. This predilection was apparent both in his professional aesthetic judgment and in his personal relations. In dancing schools and companies throughout the United States, the Balanchine ballerina became the physical ideal. If this ideal is taken to excess, especially among adolescent girls, physical problems may occur. Nevertheless, being thin and fit is the aesthetic norm for most Western concert dance.

Toni Bentley, author of *Winter Season*, was a member of the New York City Ballet who worked with Balanchine for many years and considers the physical rigors she endured enormously worthwhile: "People say dancers are always in pain. Well, I picture my life in my head and there was a lot of pain, but I'm glad I had it. It's part of who I am. People who have been through a lot of pain in their lives are the people who are also able to experience the most joy. The idea of saving dancers from their pain is patronizing. Dancers don't need saving by company directors, nor by feminists, nor anybody. They choose their lives. If they don't like it they can get out of it, they can write nasty books about it. They don't need saving by people who can't even get in a toe shoe. If dancers want to starve themselves, they do. They are all mature individuals. To treat them like they're put upon, that they are not intelligent, that they are under Balanchine's thumb, is really irritating. Everyone should be so lucky."[1]

To have a slender and taut body instrument, to be in tune, is an ideal not only for classical ballet, but for most Western concert dance. Witness the female dancers in the companies of Merce Cunningham, Martha Graham, Paul Taylor, Alvin Ailey, Hubbard Street, Dayton Contemporary, Trisha Brown, Garth Fagan, Bella Lewitzky and numerous others. Early modern dance portrayed strong, grounded women, not overly thin by today's standards. Pearl Primus created an image of physical strength and power in her moving portrayal *The Negro Speaks of Rivers*. Martha Graham's early company of women used weight to accentuate the pull of gravity. Her dances *Primitive Mysteries* and *Heretic* reveal the potential for physical and emotional

---

[1] Personal interview, September, 1992.

power in a female community. In response to their choreographic imperatives, Wigman, Graham, Humphrey, Dunham, Primus, and Holm developed techniques that required women to convey physical, spiritual and moral strength. Bonnie Bird, one of the dancers in Graham's first company, remembered the physical power required to execute the 'new' floorwork invented by Graham and often performed outdoors on hard stages or surfaces. A 1938 film from her personal library shows Bird performing the Graham technique outdoors on a makeshift concrete stage, and vividly demonstrates the physical toughness required at that time.

At first, modern dancers devoted themselves to mastering a single technique, but beginning in the '60's, dancers trained in a variety of techniques, resulting in a body that was stronger, leaner, increasingly thinner, more flexible and turned out. With the advent of post-modern dance in the early '80's, muscularly defined female bodies reappeared. The pragmatic task a dancer set for herself in performance included how she could physically accomplish rigorous feats. This focus on physical stamina broadened the definition of the acceptable and beautiful dancing female body.

Senta Driver is the female choreographer whose work established a standard during the 1970's and '80's that valued strength in women. "I like to see flesh. I hire people who have discernible flesh. That's not fat, but I'm attracted to mass. I find it just as exciting to watch any dancer press the pubic bone forward regardless of what's on top of it. I have taught women and small men to do feats of strength that they thought they couldn't do. We never have the big one lifting the small one. We challenge the assumption by varying that convention."[2]

Jawole Willa Jo Zollar, the director of the African American female company Urban Bush Women, deliberately selects women capable of projecting physical and emotional strength. "I like to see women feel good about their bodies. Women who have large breasts or big hips or thick thighs should feel that they can use those parts of themselves in dance. African dance uses the expressiveness in the hips as a core part of its work. Awareness of the movement of women's breasts and hips is also an integral part of our work."[3]

Choreographer Molissa Fenley has developed both solo and group works which require women to have considerable upper body strength and overall physical stamina. In order to physically meet her own choreographic needs she incorporates weight lifting into her daily 'class.' "I've used Nautilus

---

[2] Personal interview, February, 1989.

[3] Personal interview, December, 1991 and January, 1992.

weights for years. ...I was interested in having the upper body be very different ...to define the contours of the sculpted body rather than have the normal ethereal body which seems to be in vogue for so much dance. ...If you want to be able to make an hour-long piece where you stay on stage the whole time and do a lot of activity, then you have to be in shape aerobically."[4]

Pregnancy

Pregnant women in a number of non-Western cultures in which dance is part of community life participate and play an active role in community performance. In Western theatrical dancing, however, the proscenium stage separates the performer from the community. On this stage, the historical norm for a woman has been an adolescent girl's shape. Therefore, the pregnant woman must disguise her swollen body, lest she not conform to the physical standard of the concert dancer.

For Toni Bentley, pregnancy and a ballet career are incompatible: "Having children and coming back physically in ballet doesn't work. It diverts your energy. Some people want to put more into dancing and they give up kids. Most people can have a child, but there is only one Suzanne Farrell."[5] This concern, however, is not supported universally either by ballerinas or their audience. Despite apprehension that Natalia Makarova would lose her performing brilliance after having a baby, audiences were delighted to see her return to stage as strong as ever.

To return physically is one of several challenges in a dancer's decision to have a child. American Ballet Theatre ballerinas Christine Dunham, Lucette Katerndahl and Cheryl Yeager, after having babies, feel they are fully capable of performing roles they danced in the past, but do not receive the parts. Christine Dunham laments: "I don't get the roles I had before. I used to dance the Swan Queen in *Swan Lake*, and I did *Symphonie Concertante* and *Etudes*. I feel I could dance these roles again, but I have not been cast in them." Gary Dunning, executive director of American Ballet Theatre, noting that the dancers' contracts have no provisions for maternity leave, claims that pregnancy leaves of absence have nothing to do with casting. "Ebb and flow is normal for dancers. They have busy seasons and they don't have busy seasons." Cheryl Yeager, while disappointed with her current

---

[4] Kreemer, Connie. *Further Steps: Fifteen Choreographers of Modern Dance*. New York: Harper and Row Publishers, 1987, p. 216.

[5] Op. cit., Bentley interview, September, 1992.

performance schedule, has a new set of priorities: "I look at people who are consumed with ballet, who say, 'I have to do this role' and I know that there are other things in life: I get to go home at night to Noah."[6]

When post-modern choreographer Twyla Tharp first began making dances in the 1960's she was known for her unorthodox choreographic structures and performance practices which challenged prevailing ideas about dance and dancers. But about her pregnancy, she exhibited ambivalence. While the advent of motherhood led her to explore new sources as a choreographer, her changing body caused her great anxiety as a dancer. At first, she panicked.

"Up until now I had been able to call upon my body as I wished... working more slowly daily, I decided to compensate by working longer.... I documented what I could do with my new sense of weight, ways of moving that I had known nothing about before... I continued to dance as hard as possible in order to guarantee the success of our Oberlin engagement. I refused to let my body take its natural course, tapering off into a peaceful and quiet late term."[7] Tharp attempted to deny the effects of her pregnancy and to continue to work as she had previously.

In contrast, New York-based post-modern choreographer Roz Newman recognized the powerful change and reacted accordingly, accepting the physical reality and using it to discover a new way of training and of enhancing her creative impulses. The first dance she choreographed after the delivery of her child dealt with the archetypal woman. She described it as a private journey intimately connected with her being a woman. It differed from her previous work; it was heavier, simpler and more minimal. After pregnancy, she discovered a new way of working: "Because of the baby, it's harder to get free time, so I get right down to work when I am free. I took a class with Joan Skinner and got interested in release work and Laban/Bartinieff. My movement became very free as a result. It doesn't feel as if I can use my old methods or structures. My vocabulary is different."[8]

In other cultures pregnancy is accepted as a normal aspect of a woman's life and recognized as an important contribution to the balance of society. Women in many Middle Eastern countries practice bellydancing in preparation for childbirth in order to strengthen their abdominal muscles and build the stamina necessary for giving birth. This dancing, which

---

[6] Lawson, Carol. "And Baby Makes Pas de Trois." New York *Times*. June 3, 1994. pp. C 1 and C 10.

[7] Tharp, Twyla. *Push Comes to Shove*. New York: Bantam Books, 1992. p. 140–142.

[8] Personal interview, March, 1989.

originated in pre-Biblical times, was performed by men and women as a part of religious rites honoring motherhood. In certain parts of the contemporary Arab world, the dance is still performed during labor and birth. During labor women of the tribe dance around the bedside in order to motivate and inspire the pregnant woman to imitate the movements of the dance with her stomach and pelvic muscles, thus facilitating delivery and reducing pain.

The Maoris of New Zealand and the Hawaiians also have dances which use the pelvic and abdominal muscles. The 'ohelo,' a form of hula dance, is done in the reclining childbirth position. The original purpose of these various belly dances has significantly altered throughout the ages and, to the dismay of purists, by the evolution their original intent has been eroded.[9]

Age

If pregnancy in Western theatrical dance is an anomaly, so too are women performers over the age of forty. The principal roles for women in the traditional ballet repertoire reinforce images of female beauty and youth. Older women are often cast as witches or evil crones in ballet. Some styles have somewhat extended the acceptable age and role range for both female and male performers; nevertheless, the norm remains the youthful image. Only recently have there been examples of older women who actually look mature taking over the stage in dynamic performance.

At age fifty-six Alice Tierstein won critical acclaim for her role as the mother in Stephan Koplowitz's *Thicker Than Water*. Valda Setterfield, a thirty-year veteran of American modern dance, recently expanded her stage career with a glamorous portrayal of Marcel Duchamp in *The Mysteries* and *What's so Funny?* Trisha Brown in her early sixties remains an energetic force on stage. The subtlety that enhances her performance in her recent *For M.G.: The Movie* and *Foray Forêt* is due to her maturity. Brown's new solo, *If you could see me*, prompted critic Anne Tobias to observe that Brown "seems to have no other point than to keep on moving and in so doing she shows the way in which a dancing body can be ageless."[10]

Annabelle Gamson, born in 1928, is renowned for her sensitive performance of Isadora Duncan's dances, particularly those Duncan made later in her life such as *Marche Slave* and *The Mother Etudes* which proclaim

---

[9] Varga-Dinicu, Carolina (Morocco), "The Dance of Birth." *Medical Dimensions*, V. 3, # 9, October, 1974.

[10] Tobias, Anne. "The Clock Is Ticking." *Dance View*. V. II, # 4, Summer 1994, p. 70.

the power of the mature woman. Gamson is a third generation Duncan dancer. She studied Duncan dance as a child and, after a diverse twenty-five-year career in musical theatre and modern concert dance, resolved in her forties to learn the Duncan repertoire. "The way I dance now is not how I started. ...I think I dance more beautifully now. ...There's a certain pleasure in having works you've done for a long time. ...I may not be dancing as athletically as I used to, but that may not matter. It's inappropriate at my age to pretzel myself. If I put my leg over my ear, what would that prove?"[11]

At what point does chronological age become an issue for women in Western concert dance forms? Beth Davis, Washington, D.C.-based choreographer, faced this question when she was relatively young. "When I turned thirty, I quit dancing. Now I'm thirty-six and dancing again. It is the choreographer's, the critic's, and the community's responsibility to value older dancers so that they will continue to contribute."[12]

When do emotional maturity and technical competence converge? Members of many major companies are in their thirties; this seems to be a common time for the nuances of technique and performance presence to coalesce. One usually associates classical ballet with young ballerinas and certainly youth is an asset. Yet the highlight performer of the fiftieth year celebration of American Ballet Theatre Gala was Alicia Alonso, who performed the "Black Swan" pas de deux at age seventy, and on pointe! Margot Fonteyn in the second half of her long career showed just how a mature dancer's less tangible attributes of phrasing, musicality, presence and experience can make a youthful technical performance almost look limited. Virginia Johnson is an original member of the Dance Theatre of Harlem and has been with the company for more than twenty-five years. Her rendition of *Creole Giselle* is the result of her years of experience. She knows her body so thoroughly that she can use exactly the right amount of energy for each movement, wasting not a breath. Like other older dancers she understands the depth of each gesture so fully that meaning is absolutely clear and precise. Transcending the limitations of the aging body, these dancers deepen our viewing of the dance by revealing the spirituality of the mature woman.

Older people can bring an understanding and depth of feeling due to their life experiences which are valuable both in performance and in teaching dance to others. Kaye Bardsley, President of the Isadora Duncan International

---

[11] Laine, Barry. *Ballet News*, p. 22.

[12] American Dance Guild Conference panel, June, 1989.

Institute, worked with Maria Theresa Duncan and has devoted her later years to preserving the Duncan repertoire. Bardsley reconstructed *Lamentosa* with a group of young students. "It was 1978 and we were in the middle of restaging the piece. I had come from the hospital; my husband had just died. The young dancer on whom I was setting the piece was absent; I took the part. I could not talk to them, but the dancers needed the rehearsal and I felt I had to work with them. They gathered around me. Tears streamed down my face but we danced. After that they felt very connected to the experience and it was very easy to teach them this movement."[13]

Julia Lopez, now in her late fifties and performing regularly, maintains that age is irrelevant in flamenco. "Basically, if you are a good performer you can be seventy or older. If you go to Spain you will see the lead woman either dancing or clapping and supporting the others, enthusiastically shouting 'Olé!' and other words traditional to flamenco. She is a lady, overweight, perhaps in her fifties, sixties, or seventies. What is important is how well she interprets the music, how she gets the idea across, how she projects. If she is sensuous, that is great, but we make a big point of never being vulgar."[14]

Liz Lerman and her company, Dancers of the Third Age, embrace the reality of the aging performer and use it to create a positive and dynamic image of older people. Lerman believes that everyone can dance, that dance is a birthright to be performed within the range of each person's movement ability. One of her dancers, seventy-four-year-old Bea Wattenberg, notes: "When we go into a school, one of the young dancers usually leads the show. The first question the children are asked is, 'Do you see anything unusual about this group of dancers?' Invariably they say, 'Yeah, they're old!' You can see the stereotypical image they have of older people; they find it hard to believe we're going to dance for them. By the time the hour is over we've changed their image of older people."[15] Liz Lerman's choreography explodes the stereotypical vision of who should dance, and what a dancer should look like. It deals a blow to the myth that older people can't dance.

THEORY AND PRACTICE

Spiritual expression motivates most creation. In dance, that expression is manifested physically. Female choreographers in acknowledging the unity

---

[13] American Dance Guild Conference panel, June, 1989.

[14] Ibid.

[15] Ibid.

of the spiritual and the physical probe the role of their own sensuality and sexuality in their work. The body/mind/spirit connection is relevant to contemporary dance teaching as well as creation. Students of dance study Alexander Technique, Bonnie Bainbridge Cohen's Body Mind Centering, Contact Improvisation, Feldenkreis, Joan Skinner's Release Technique and yoga in an effort to grasp this connection. Women are in the forefront of the theoretical development and training in these relational approaches to dance.

Spirituality

"I have learned to acknowledge in the creative process the sense of outer, inner, and secret journey that I have learned from the Buddhist heritage. I present an outer journey and acknowledge that there will be an inner journey, and that the inner journey will have an emotional content. The secret journey is not something that can always have a language."[16] This is the philosophy of Barbara Dilley, who toured internationally with the Merce Cunningham Dance Company and designed the Movement Studies Program at the Naropa Institute, a center for holistic movement studies.

Cleo Parker Robinson who, for more than thirty years has been the artistic director of her own company located in Denver, hopes that the artist can help to unite and mend the fissures in our society: "What is most important is to understand the artist's role in the twentieth century. With extraordinary division between culture, gender, generation, religion and race, we are living through the most challenging time because of these polarities. The artist is a healer who understands the holistic need of the individual. Unless we are united in mind, body and spirit, there will be an imbalance with each other and nature itself."[17]

Sexuality and Sensuality

Concepts of female sexuality and sensuality have changed in the course of time. Hawaiian hula dances exalt female sexual power. Katherine Dunham's *Shango* forges a link between female sensuality and magic. In the dancing during Shaker religious services or in the staid and formal court dances of the European Renaissance, female sensuality is largely ignored or subverted.

---

[16] Butler, Diane. "Exchange/Interchange: Interviews with Lisa Kraus and Barbara Dilley." *Movement Research Performance Journal.* # 8, Spring/Summer, 1994. p. 7.

[17] Parker Robinson, Cleo. "Art 21." *International Association of Blacks in Dance.* V. 7, # 1, p. 5.

The contradiction inherent in many traditional passive/aggressive roles for ballerinas is most evident in the nineteenth century romantic ballet *Swan Lake*, in which Odette the good swan and Odile the bad swan are danced by the same woman.

In some dances, sensuality moves from a subtle to a central position, becoming a deliberate exploration of the erotic. The word erotic derives from the Greek eros, the personification of love in both spiritual and physical aspects. Confusion abounds in Western culture about the erotic as a source of power and information. In dance, public attitudes have resulted in viewers conflating female eroticism solely with the physical body. During the twentieth century female choreographers have been increasingly fascinated by the erotic. In Ruth St. Denis' 1906 solo *Radha*, she portrayed the lover of the Hindu god Krishna. Later, Bronislava Nijinska created an entire society of erotically powerful women in *Les Biches*. (1924) Currently, many choreographers are rethinking the use and context of eroticism.

"I have to physically enjoy what I do," points out Puerto Rican choreographer Merian Soto. Her duet for a male and female in *Broken Hearts* was called 'steamy' by one negative critic while another found that she had successfully depicted the actions of love-making in dance. Soto said, "This piece is all about the pelvis. When we were making the piece, I would get turned on."[18] French Canadian choreographer Marie Chouinard takes the use of her own actual physical pleasure in performance to a disarming conclusion. In *Marie Chien Noir* she masturbates on stage.

Not all contemporary choreographers treat women as self-actualized, strong and in control of their sexuality. In fact, in some works woman continue to be portrayed as victims. Myriam Herve-Gil, French choreographer and artistic director of what began as an all-female group of three dancers, first collided with American feminist sensitivities in her 1991 dance, *Jeux*. She was aghast when, contrary to the French audience reaction of laughter on seeing her increasingly swollen and bruised body, Americans found her piece very disturbing and not at all funny. "I thought my piece was a failure when it was performed here," she lamented. "I was trying to show, in a French way, the difficulties of a typical male-female relationship."[19]

The German choreographer Pina Bausch presents images of female and male victimization in her work: men brutalize women while women humiliate men. Bausch combines techniques, stereotypical gestures and repetition to achieve narrative collages which strip away the veneer of polite

---

[18] Personal interview, January, 1992.

[19] Personal interview, July, 1992.

behavior and reveal the ambiguity and violence which reside just below the surface. In the 1976 *Don't Be Afraid*, a male seducer softly says "Look at me... don't be afraid" before throwing a woman down and raping her. Again, in the piece entitled *1980*, a female performer repeats five times the story of the abuse she experienced as a child. She explains how she would cry out when left alone in the dark and that her caretaker would "turn on the light... and she would hit me, she would hit me, she would hit me." The grotesqueness and the reiteration of violence grows as Bausch's work develops. When asked about this Bausch replied, "We must look again and again... maybe the saddest things about our obessions is that they look so cheerful."[20] The violence in her work raises questions about the relationship between art and morality.

Intimacy

Physical and emotional intimacy in relationships between dancers is inevitable, unavoidable, desirable, and can serve as a positive source of energy and creativity. Intimacy cannot be separated from sensuality and sexuality. The act of creating a dance requires vulnerability, mutual investment, and trust on the part of dancers and choreographers. This trust extends to physical reality. Can a dancer run any faster? Is a choreographer willing to suggest and a dancer willing to attempt a movement that is perhaps impossible? Will a group of people be there to catch one another? After spending the many hours in close physical proximity which dance-making requires, it is natural and inevitable for both platonic and sexually intimate relationships to develop.

Platonic Intimacy Martha Graham + Amanda Warren

Although married, ~~Ruth St. Denis and Ted Shawn~~, the acknowledged mother and father of American modern dance, were in actuality a platonic pair. Despite their lack of sexual intimacy off stage, on stage they presented the illusion of sexual intimacy. Denishawn founded a school, choreographed together, established a company, and toured internationally to great acclaim.

Presenting a similar paradoxical on-stage image of a heterosexual couple, Doris Humphrey and Charles Weidman worked together platonically for many years. Paralleling their mentors, they also founded a school, choreographed, established a company, and toured. Professionally

---

[20] Birringer, Johannes. "Bausch, Pina: Dancing Across Borders." *The Drama Review*. V. 30, # 2, 1986, pp. 85–97.

Humphrey and Weidman were linked as a couple despite Humphrey's marriage to another and Weidman's affairs with numerous male partners. The technique they developed is still taught as the Humphrey-Weidman technique.

Fred Astaire and Ginger Rogers embodied a romance which was visualized through supremely sophisticated couple-dancing in Hollywood films of the 1930's and '40's. Like Humphrey-Weidman and St. Denis and Shawn, they too projected an image of romantic and sexual intimacy to an adoring public. Yet fan magazines and gossip columnists continually wrote about Fred and Ginger feuding. In fact, their partnership was preserved partly because they kept their personal lives separate. At that time, Astaire was married to his first wife Phyllis and Rogers was married to tennis-playboy Lew Ayres. During the course of Astaire's career, he continued illusory romantic partnerships with twenty-one different female dancers, including Joan Crawford, Rita Hayworth, Audrey Hepburn, Leslie Caron and Cyd Charisse.

Platonic intimate relationships usually rest on a foundation of mutual liking, respect, and attraction. Judith Jamison goes further to suggest that platonic collaborations can be so powerful as to mirror a marriage. "Working with Alvin (Ailey) was terribly personal. It was like a marriage. You don't want anybody stepping into the studio while the intangible creative force is going on. Alvin choreographed *Cry* in only eight days, an hour and a half a day. In those days, after a six-week tour, we would go into the studio, close the door and bang it out quickly. No time for verbalizing. He did the movement; I repeated it in my way and it was done: an equal exchange between two 'married' people."[21]

Sexual Intimacy

A couple married in law as well as spirit, Eiko and Koma, have been presenting duet work for over fifteen years. Born in Tokyo, they met there as college students, began their study of dance in Japan, traveled to Germany in 1972 to study with Manja Chiemel, a former student of Mary Wigman's, continued their study in Amsterdam with Lucas Hoving and moved to New York in 1976, which remains their home. Discussing the patience and time necessary for their continued growth in both personal and professional arenas, Eiko said: "We collaborate by talking through — and we spend much time just talking about choreographing. And that process reassures us that we're talking about the same thing. We share the basic issue. And then,

---

[21] American Dance Guild Conference, keynote speech, June, 1989.

movement-wise, I usually make my movement, and Koma usually makes his movement, and we look at one another, and then we give suggestions. Now, what Koma suggests to me — I may not like it, but after fifteen years of work together, I don't argue. ...It's about how Koma and I agree that this is a very important issue. ...I'm not really talking about 'my art' or 'my expression'; we're talking about a common ground or common concerns."[22]

If the images that Eiko and Koma create as a result of their intimate personal relationship allow us to contemplate the slow unfolding of universal commonalities between men and women, the work of Bob Fosse and Gwen Verdon registers the immediacy of the differences between the sexes. Fosse and Verdon, a renowned Broadway dancing couple, shared a commitment to hard-hitting precision and exacting movement. This was the foundation of their dances. This excerpt written by a dancer/actress who worked with them throughout their careers demonstrates the unity of their intention. "Fosse and Verdon were so much on the same wavelength that they were always talking in shorthand to each other. Fosse would say, 'I don't know about this step. What if we ...' and Verdon would answer, 'That's a good idea, but do you think ...' and Fosse would say, 'Sure, if everyone will just...' and Verdon would interject, 'You don't have to worry about that. I'll be sure to ...' and Fosse would answer, 'I know you will."[23]

Even though Fosse was credited as the choreographer and Verdon as the dancer, each acknowledged the influence of the other on the creation of the "Fosse look." Their first show together was *Damn Yankees*, which opened on May 5, 1955. They were married during the road show of *Redhead*, in which Verdon played the leading role. Verdon was assisting him in a reconstruction of one of their most successful collaborations, *Sweet Charity*, when Fosse died of a heart attack in 1987. Critics and performers readily agree that no one has ever performed Fosse's choreography as well as Verdon. Fosse's movement vocabulary was a breathtaking and complex combination of sensual and technically virtuosic steps from a wide variety of dance styles that required a strong and accomplished acting technique, the very abilities that defined Verdon's art.

Whereas much of the world operates from a model in which heterosexuality is the norm, dance relationships reveal other realities. Homosexual and heterosexual intimacy are present as themes in choreography. Since the 1970's gay male dance artists have regularly proclaimed their sexual preference and have used it thematically. However,

---

[22] Windham, Leslie, "A Conversation with Eiko and Koma." *Ballet Review*. Summer, 1988, p. 51.

[23] Beddow, Margery, "Bob Fosse, Part Three: Redhead." *Dance Magazine*. November, 1992, p. 71.

because of the historical lack of recognition of female sexual couples, contemporary lesbian dancers and choreographers do not have many models to call upon. Few choreographers acknowledge their lesbianism or its relevance to their creative work.

Choreographer Amy Pivar and her partner/artistic colleague Freda Rosen are an exception. They are forthright in noting the significance of their sexuality and personal intimacy. Amy: "We began collaborating in 1990. Freda and I have a very intimate and close relationship and wanted to do something creative with it." Freda: "We work together to build a multicultural community that is humanistic, pro-woman, and pro-gay."[24]

Seattle-based choreographer Pat Graney states: "I know major choreographers who are gay and hide it; I don't. I don't care what people think about my identity as a lesbian, yet I'm not responsible for representing lesbians as a group or as a cultural entity. I don't feel that everything I do has to be politically correct lesbian stuff either. If I want to go fuck some guy on stage, I will. I'm not going to lie and say I'm married with two children, but I object to everything I make being identified as specifically representative of lesbians. When are we going to move on from making sexual identity a political statement? My audience is not totally lesbian — my work is for people, it represents being human; it doesn't have to exclude anyone."[25]

USING THE KNOWLEDGE

Ideas about women are embedded in cultural traditions. Culture influences the ways in which women use that knowledge in their art. Since the elements of choreography — time, space, and energy — are culturally informed, dances which portray women in a particular way in one culture may not be perceived that way in another. Dance provides an opportunity for a cross-cultural exchange which allows individual artists to share their attitudes.

More and more, cultures merge and occasionally collide. One can belong to a tradition and work to move that tradition forward. Or one can come from one tradition, adopt another, and advance the new tradition. However, borrowing movement vocabularies from other cultures is always accomplished through one's own cultural filter. Political aspects of appropriation raise these questions: What dilutes a traditional dance and what energizes it? How can individual women speak in a new voice using a traditional movement language? What does it mean when women trained in traditional movement vocabularies combine that knowledge with vocabularies and techniques of various new dance forms?

---

[24] Personal interview, January, 1993.

[25] Personal interview, January, 1992.

"Going back to older cultures does ground you. It anchors you regarding what things you might portray or communicate and what images you choose. But it is interesting to ask and acknowledge how much friction you will make when you are rubbing up against rituals and traditions," says dance writer C. S'thembile West.[26]

Contemporary choreographer Blondell Cummings's work reflects an awareness of the realities of tradition. Her choreography combines political and social beliefs with intensely personal feelings which she connects to her cultural heritage as an African American. "My first piece was based on my own menstrual cycle. One of the things I found fascinating about this was that it crossed all cultures and all people could relate to it. This was the beginning of a whole series of pieces I made to attempt to cross cultures. This has always been my intention... I believe that you are an accumulation of your experiences."[27]

Sandra Burton, working in Massachusetts, is trying to find a marriage between the aesthetic considerations of African dance and American modern dance. "Neither form alone expresses what I'm after, but mixed they do. Also, because of my years spent with Chuck Davis' African American Dance Ensemble, singing and storytelling are very much a part of my tradition. Watching the newsreels from China and Tiananmen Square in 1989, I kept thinking about how the events in China related to a piece I had made. I'm interested in dance and theater as a living document of what happens to people and how the performing arts can document something about our existence, our struggle as human beings."[28]

Taiwanese choreographer Yunyu Wang defines her professional voice through her cultural identity: "What makes me special as a choreographer, a performer and a teacher are my deep roots as a Chinese person. I'm not just talking about my training in dance and other art forms. I'm talking about my heritage. I carry it on; sometimes it's heavy, too heavy. It's five thousand years old. I try to use that heritage wisely. To me, Oriental work is very beautiful. Beyond the beauty I want to show what happens now in my nation. Only one time in two thousand years has there been peace in my country. I hope to be able to see that again one day. I want to show the struggles of the people. It's the philosophy of Tai Chi; the balance I seek shows the beauty and the struggle."[29]

Wang Mei, a member of the recently established Guangdong Modern Dance Company in Canton, China, made use of choreographic techniques

---

[26] American Dance Guild Conference panel, June, 1989.

[27] Ibid.

[28] Ibid.

[29] Ibid.

common in Western modern dance to critique current social and political practices regarding women in China. "Performed in silence, a woman writhed claustrophobically on a steeply inclined slab of bright white wood which may have represented a bed or an operating table. Had the title been less evocative... one might have interpreted this dance as a 'purely' formal exploration of the body-in-confinement. But given the title and the intensity with which the work was performed, something of a more inward, personal, and deeply troubling nature appeared to be going on."[30] This solo, *The Long Night* (originally titled *Artificial Abortion*), is an effort to criticize China's regular use of abortion as a form of birth control.

Evelyn Velez Aguayo, a Puerto Rican choreographer who works in New York, Puerto Rico, and Arizona, uses text and dance to explore the impact of cross-cultural realities. Aguayo has created an autobiographical solo, *Evelina Ampelina*, in which she focuses on "the unacknowledged conflicts created by my status and identity and memories as a Puerto Rican and a Spanish speaker living in the U.S." She says the solo, which she has continued to develop since 1988, "raises conflicts around issues of family, dance, and buttocks, all in some way seen through the lens of language. Dance for me is the holistic experience that synthesizes my split concerns: the butt, body reflections, ancestry, history, learning experience, movement, body, and language."[31]

Approaching the twenty-first century, a woman in dance presents a very different profile from her predecessor. Throughout this century but especially within the past ten years, choreographers, performers, teachers and writers have been reconsidering the images they create, the ways they show the body, the ways they incorporate dance into their daily lives, the intimate nature of their professional relationships and the manner in which cross-cultural exchange helps refocus their work.

Progress has been made in addressing the physical and psychological problems of adolescent female dancers, specifically in terms of health issues and eating disorders. Audiences have a greater appreciation and tolerance of the presence of diverse female bodies on stage — women can be larger, taller or shorter than they once were permitted to be and can dance longer. The contributions of older dancers merit respect for the wisdom of their physical performance and their creative perspective. These changes are the result of

---

[30] Copeland, Roger, "The Bull in the China Shop." *Contact Quarterly*. Summer/Fall, 1992, pp. 26–27.

[31] Aguayo, Evelyn Velez, "Evelina Ampelina." *Movement Research Performance Journal*. # 9, Fall and Winter, 1994–95, p. 9.

the work of several generations of female dance theorists and educators who developed new ways of training the body that take the emotional, spiritual and psychological needs of dancers into consideration.

In the same way that women are more forthright about their bodies, so do they represent themselves psychologically and spiritually in more honest terms. Choreographers and performers acknowledge their sensuality and sexuality and may reveal their intimate relationships without fear of reprisal. Women are solo artists, traveling independently, finding fulfillment on their own. During the last twenty-five years, women dancers of color have asserted their right to determine the context in which they are seen and the criteria by which their work is evaluated. Women choreographers, performers, educators and writers share their own cultural perspectives with the knowledge that they will inform the future.

PART VI

THE PHYSICAL BODY

What makes people say, "She looks like a dancer"? The chapters in "The Physical Body" examine this question and others related to the actual physical body and the images it produces. Julie Sandler sums up various perspectives in "Standing in Awe, Sitting in Judgment" and offers positive suggestions for the teacher and student in this practical, down-to-earth article. "Dance Has Many Ages" is the result of septuagenarian dancer Billie Kirpich's interviews with older artists about their current work. The point of departure for Carolyn McConnell's chapter is the cultural gaze. "The Body Never Lies" challenges commonly held theories about the passivity of female bodies in dance and constructs an argument which affirms the female body as a source of power and pleasure.

STANDING IN AWE, SITTING IN JUDGMENT
Julie Sandler

What is a dancer? She is and is not her body. She cannot be reduced to her body, but she is not separable from it. Just as mind and body are 'not one and not two,'[1] so the dancer's body and the dance are not one and not two. If the body is the instrument on which the dance is played, then the woman who dances, being both player and played, is a mysterious whole greater than the sum of the parts.

The female dancer feels with particular keenness the contradictions felt by most women raised in Western culture: how can a woman be an active subject when so many messages have indicated that she ought to aspire, above all, to be a beautiful object? How can she enter into the dance experience when so often she has been taught that the most important part of dance is being looked at? At the core is the question of how to be at peace with the body she has when the body types conventionally defined as right for a female dancer are a narrow band on the vast human spectrum. Another band on the spectrum defined by mainstream culture as sexy for a woman is equally narrow and often at odds with the conventionally defined right body for a dancer.

Ironically, the prevailing cultural standards for the ideal female body shape are constantly changing. They have nothing to do with what makes someone a dancer. What makes someone a dancer is her daily embarking on the practice of attending ever more deeply to the flow of movement through the body. This practice demands heart, discipline, perseverance, muscular strength, stamina, focus, inner resolve, power, delicacy, responsiveness, and sheer raw nerve. I believe this has nothing to do with body type, shape, weight, features, age, race, coloring, sex, gender, or the fact of being able-bodied or disabled.

The values discussed here are entrenched in a specific Western culture and its dance world. Although things are changing, the exceptions

---

[1] Suzuki, Shunryu. *Zen Mind, Beginner's Mind*, New York: John Weatherhill, Inc. 1976, p. 25.

still sadly serve to prove the rule. This issue plays itself out differently in ballet than in modern dance, in a post-modern group and in improvisation circles. The experience of every individual is different, as nothing holds uniformly true. On the other hand, these issues affect women across every line and there are more underlying commonalities than we might at first suppose.

Body as Object

A woman's body is not so much an object as it is part of a living, breathing subject. The mystery of a dancer is the interaction between the physical and the non-physical, the inner which manifests through the outer. This means that when any one thing changes inside a dancer, there is a transforming outer radiance. This change may happen in an instant or over time, but inner being and outer moving body continuously interplay. The body-as-object view is static by comparison and does not recognize this primordial flow. There are, of course, many choreographers and dancers who have been grappling with these ideas for a long time. There are people who have actively challenged cultural stereotypes about body, beauty, gender, and the audience-performer relationship: Meredith Monk and the House (which included the three electric female performers Lani Harrison, Lee Nagrin and Blondell Cummings), Bebe Miller, Urban Bush Women, Jennifer Monson, Pooh Kaye and the Animals, Wallflower Order, the Dance Brigade, Elaine Summers, Simone Forti, Johanna Boyce, Senta Driver, Marta Renzi, and numerous contact improvisers and performance artists like Karen Nelson and K. J. Holmes.

Body Matters

How does the body matter? What creates a moment of breathless wonder in performance? Is it not the subtlety, variety, and inner depth of a person's movement that draws us? Its relatedness? The sense of presence? Can that which makes dance compelling ever be said to be one thing? A transitory juxtaposition of limbs, the aching beauty of a barely glimpsed arc through space. As dancers, it is an essence of motion we seek — an impulse which travels through the body, changing its form with the moment, rippling like water — now fluid, now seemingly frozen still, now spiraling into a vortex. The qualities required to serve as a channel for such motion — presence, attention, attunement to inner and outer rhythms, a responsive bodymind — have little to do with body type, or body-as-object.

Women's Bodies and Dance

Although images are slowly changing in some circles, a professional female dancer must still be thin. This is baseline: if the dancer isn't *thin*, she is usually dismissed out of hand. Any fine, even virtuosic dance qualities she may have aren't worth discussion because, on the level of body, she is unacceptable. One would think that fluidity, strength, quick reaction time, flexibility, improvisational intelligence — any number of more necessary qualities would come up first — but they don't. The obsession is with thinness.

Young women considering a dance career will also often be told that they are too short, or too tall — that they won't fit into a company. Proportion of torso to legs, and of breasts, hips and thighs are also very important. Rather than being a whole, a dancer seems to be a collection of parts. Although there are well-known dancers and choreographers who have succeeded in the profession despite these prohibitions, the prohibitions nonetheless continue to define the status quo. These strong dance world conventions have affected us all. Whether we were praised and glorified, mocked and snubbed, or treated indifferently on the basis of body, whether we were the cruel taunters, the taunted, or the impassive observers, all of us have been affected by the single standard of youthful, air-brushed beauty held up by mainstream Western culture. Whether we swallow that standard whole or rage against it, not a single one of us remains uninfluenced by it.

Taking a Look at Looking

Dance is a movement phenomenon. Yet most of us have been taught to consider how our bodies look as something completely split off from the sensory and kinesthetic experience that is our body. What does it say about a culture if the body is valued above all as object — for form independent of function? What does it say specifically about the female body in our culture?

Most of us were taught to objectify our bodies and to consider their beauty/ugliness, sexiness/non-sexiness according to quite rigid, media-defined values. Mainstream American culture places little value on our bodies as the medium of our spirits, or as miraculous life-sustaining organisms. It does not teach us to respect our physical processes — breathing, digestion, circulation, etc., as integral to ourselves. These functions are typically taken for granted as unimportant. This is the very antithesis of the sense of the body as whole and sacred, which is central in many other cultures. A deep, connected celebration of sensuality is also not encouraged in mainstream

American culture. The joyless sexuality touted in the media takes a young person ever farther from real bodily connection.

Our cultural obsession is merely with how the body looks. If what it can do is praised, then the doing too is quantified: how many times, how high, who beat whom, who won, how much was the bet, how much was the ticket? Ability is objectified as a status symbol. While this may be easiest to see if we apply the image to sports — tennis, gymnastics, etc. — it's true in dance too. Some self-styled critics, if they get beyond a girlie-show evaluation of the bodies of the ballet dancers on a stage, will continue only so far as to count the number of turns made in a row. The language of dance criticism bears out how the female dancer is seen. A critic will often criticize a dancer's body for being too plump or chunky or heavy even when while, oddly enough, applauding her movement! The language of the critic describes an object, a body shape, and then, secondarily, what the object can do. It is important to note that there is a new breed of dance critics who are shaping a less culture-bound language of criticism which treats dancers, and the bodies of dancers, in a new way.

Is there a right, even a necessary kind of body for a female dancer? We all know the current politically correct reply is, "Of course not!" — and we may even think we mean it. But what really goes on underneath the lip service? The idea here is not that we pretend to feel any differently that we do. The proposal, rather, is that we study what we do think and feel until we know it very clearly; that we let ourselves hear ourselves. If we allow ourselves to listen to our uncensored thoughts and feelings, there may be a rush of relief. After all, it takes energy and tension to deny, to rationalize, to explain, to fabricate — to make it all Okay. At the same time, going inside ourselves honestly and ruthlessly is no easy or appealing process. We won't like everything we see.

Teachers and Students

In more than twenty years of teaching, I have watched either the expressions of doubt, fear, despair and self-disgust or alternatively, of contempt and self-righteous smugness in supposed bodily superiority move across the faces of my female students when the issue of the dancer's body arose, or when they faced the studio mirror. The forms of being bodily wrong that students despair over are endless. They find themselves to be too short, too tall, too fat, too thin (in Near Eastern dance classes), too flat-chested, too busty, disproportionate, too big in the hips, thighs or shoulders; too short in the neck, or too long in the torso relative to the legs.

Yet, often, the students who've inspired others were those whose bodies were far from right by conventional standards. There was one young woman in a technique class many years ago with a gentle movement spirit that shone and soared. She was physically quite heavy, and I wagered to myself that for her to take the class at all had demanded a good deal of courage. The other students appreciated that they were in the presence of real grace of movement, and this young woman blossomed under the honest admiration of her peers. She was born with a rare innate grace; she simply was a dancer.

On the other hand, I have often felt powerless while teaching in the face of a fait accompli. Enjoyably watching another student warm up one day, I inquired as to whether she had ever danced before college. "Oh yes, I used to, seriously," she told me in a noncommital monotone, "but I had a teacher who told me I was too short to be a dancer, so I stopped. I'm just taking this class for fun." I sat there struggling with how to comment in the face of her impassivity and all that I sensed it was covering, and of my own rage at the careless bulldozer of that early unknown teacher.

What can a teacher do for her female students? What ought she not do? She can respond seriously to every student who is devoting herself seriously to dancing. While being very realistic and pragmatic in discussing the life of a professional dancer or choreographer, she can let the decision about continuing to dance be the student's own. She can try to be aware of her own body prejudices, and to learn to see a student's way of moving, not just her bodily appropriateness. She can ensure that positive reinforcement in her class is given on the basis of movement, not body type. She can send her students away from the mirror for a while. Let them learn to work at dance improvisation and technique by attending to proprioceptive sensations. When they come back to the mirror, they can see that its real job in the studio is for checking specifics: "Is my back arched in the way I feel it is?" "Does that leg in back of me look like I think it does — whoops — no; it doesn't! " Send them away from the mirror and back again, so they can use it to see unnecessary tension in the neck, or hands, or eyes which stops the flow of movement. The mirror has a purpose, and its purpose has nothing to do with reinforcing the obsession with body shape. She can make it clear that she does not consider the body issue a silly one.

Since the body is also a symbol, a metaphor, a physicalization of things, it is often a battlefield on which conflicts are played out. The lack of confidence, the feelings of inadequacy, the self-hate that students feel as a result of being wrong become physical tension. "I'm clumsy... I'm awkward... I can't flow" and ultimately, "I can't dance." These are self-fulfilling prophecies. To try to look lighter or sexier or in any way different than what one is, tenses and constricts the whole musculature, and then in plain truth, one does not dance well.

Sometimes, a self-destructive turn of mind becomes physical. Anorexia, bulimia, compulsive eating, wild weight swings, and ruined metabolisms are rife in the dance world. The common dance-world convention of equating thinness with discipline and the obsession with body shape and weight leads a young dancer away from physical discipline. The rigor of daily practice demands energy and the ability to concentrate. Without fueling the body, and without some measure of self-acceptance, one has neither. Perhaps the healthiest thing a teacher can give students is a framework of ways to work, to return again and again to the practice of movement, no matter what else is happening in their lives.[2]

Dancers and Power

Being a dancer is hard. The work is hard, the living conditions are hard, the competition is hard and the economics are hard; it's a life only for the hardy. A dancer with a nonstandard body simply needs to be encouraged by a teacher to feel she has a right to take her chances with the others, that's all; the right to work, against the difficult odds that are any dancer's lot, to sweat, fail, succeed, make mistakes, fall down, get up, and try again.

There is no dance, and no dancing, without power. This takes us to the heart of another paradox in the lives of many women dancers: that of using enormous power to dance the stereotypical roles in which they appear powerless. At its most physical, this contradiction manifests itself in the irony of the muscular strength, energy, sweat, stamina and guts it requires the ballerina, that icon of frailty, to appear to effortlessly float and leap around the stage for two hours. Just as often, though, there are women dancers who, while dancing, show physical power clearly — jumping, somersaulting, grunting, running up the wall — but who off the dance floor are unable to apply any of the experience of that power to their personal lives.

Why is this? Somehow it has been all right for female dancers to be sexy, but not too powerfully strong or powerfully sexual. The act of dancing, by definition, is intertwined with sexuality and sensuality in the broadest

---

[2] There is a useful consideration of both women's body types in dance and the range of movement choices for women in "Roundtable Interview: Post Modernism and Feminism in Dance" by Marianne Goldberg and Ann Cooper Albright in *Women and Performance*, Issue 6, V. 3, # 2, 1987–88, pp. 41–56.

and deepest sense of those human qualities. In mainstream American culture, however, dance has often been dissociated from sexuality; or it has been associated with an ersatz, commercial sort of sexuality which has little or nothing to do with a woman's experience of her own body, but only how it appears to others.

There is all the difference in the world between an active, initiating sexual being and a passive, sexual object; between images of woman who only give sexual pleasure and those who passionately, powerfully claim and exchange such pleasure between acceptable, kittenish sexiness and deep sensuality. Even the words have such different connotations. We can see this paradox in the history of painting as clearly as in the history of dance. In *Ways of Seeing*, using the painting "Venus, Cupid, Time and Love" by Bronzino, and going on to discuss the paradox in general, John Berger says: "This picture is made to appeal to his sexuality. It has nothing to do with her sexuality. (Here and in the European tradition generally, the convention of not painting the hair on a woman's body helps toward the same end. Hair is associated with sexual power, with passion. The woman's sexual passion needs to be minimized so that the spectator may feel that he has the monopoly of such passion.) Woman are there to feed an appetite, not to have any of their own."[3]

The body's torso is the place in which dance — and life — begin. This center holds the mysteries: the center of gravity, the "hara," the "seika tanden," the "kundalini," the lower "chakras," the uterus, the intestines, the anus and the vagina — the organs of the most primal functions of sex, reproduction, digestion and excretion. The center is where the action is. Martha Graham felt and talked about contraction in a powerful, primal way. We saw it in the Russian dancer Ulanova, preparing to fly ethereally into the wings; we see it in Pooh Kaye's Animals, springing about the stage on all fours. Yet how often has anyone heard it described by women dancers, verbally or in writing? How did Martha Graham's contraction — the 'Slap of Life' she once called it — get sanitized into a tightening of the rectus abdominus?

Every woman dancer must have felt this sense of power in the pelvis, but how often do you hear a woman dancer, her face twisted in fierce exhilaration like a bacchante's, say, "Damn! that felt great!"? There is no feeling like the feeling of a movement uncoiling from center, or coiling back into center. There's nothing like breathing deep into the abdomen, feeling it contract and release. There's nothing like a jump which explodes upward from a movement of the pelvic floor.

---

[3] Berger, John. *Ways of Seeing*. New York: Penguin, 1972. p. 55.

This pleasure, however, is usually unexpressed; more often it is a secret pleasure in Western dance. Martha Graham and Isadora Duncan talked openly about it, but neither is quite a role model for a powerful woman. As extraordinary and astounding as they were, both of them, in different ways, subscribed in their daily lives to an exaggerated kind of womanliness that left their physical power unintegrated.

This is another important role of the dance teacher: to bring young women into many experiences of the body's center, the place from which babies are born, and battle cries are uttered, the place where the loins are girded for battle, and revealed for pleasure, the place of the lioness's roar and the snake's hiss, the power behind a guttural moan, or a teeth-baring snarl. Rarely are women in our culture encouraged to revel in such extremes and, indeed, it may be that the admirable impulse to pacifism among women plays a role here. But there is infinitely more chance for peace and serenity when the human impulse of aggression is acknowledged and responsibly claimed than when it is denied and left to run amok.

Conclusion

A teacher can provide a variety of movement experiences that lets young women explore a spectrum of different ways of moving that speak to them. The student's training should include structures that allow her to experience a variety of physical and emotional states: explosive, powerful, gentle, deft, violent, angular, jerky, smooth, fiery, aggressive, water-like and responsive. There should be classes that require brute force, classes that require the least amount of tension possible, sessions that focus on a quickness that builds endurance, and forms teaching true slow motion. We want to see more and more of the rich tapestry of human movement.

It is an important act, then, to challenge and question prevailing attitudes, to stop blindly accepting the values, pigeonholes and pecking orders that divide us from one another. We have been taught that one side, one group, one idea must win. If there is only one right way to look, then there is only one right way to be, and we all lose. There is an old Zen proverb: "In the landscape of the spring, there is nothing superior, nothing inferior; the flowering branches grow naturally, some long and some short." For a dancer's unique form of dancing to flower, she must accept herself, her body and all her contradictions.

Bibliography

Berger, John. *Ways of Seeing*. London: Penguin Books, 1972.

Browne, Maya. "Dying to Be Thin." *Essence*, June, 1993.

Elliot, Diane and Wendy Morris. "Bodywork." *Utne Reader*, # 51, May/June, 1992.

Faludi, Susan. *Backlash: The Undeclared War Against American Women*. New York: Anchor/Doubleday, 1991.

Foster, Susan Leigh. *Reading Dancing*. Berkeley: University of California Press, 1986.

Gilligan, Carol. *In a Different Voice: Psychological Theory and Women's Development*. Cambridge: Harvard University Press, 1982.

Goldberg, Marianne, ed. "The Body as Discourse." *Women and Performance*. V. 3. #2, 1987–88.

Hatfield, Elaine and Sprecher, Susan. *Mirror, Mirror: The Importance of Looks in Everyday Life*. Albany: State University of New York Press, 1986.

Henley, Nancy. *Body Politics: Power, Sex and Nonverbal Communication*. Englewood Cliffs: Prentice-Hall, 1977.

Henley, Nancy and Mayo, Clara. *Gender and Nonverbal Behavior*. New York: Springer Verlag, 1981.

Lamb, Lynette, ed. "Your Body; Friend, Foe or Total Stranger?" *Utne Reader*, # 51, May/June, 1992.

Nader, Ralph and Katherine Isaacs, eds. *Being Beautiful – Deciding for Yourself: Selected Readings*. Center for the Study of Responsive Law. P.O. Box 19367. Washington, D.C., 1986.

Novack, Cynthia. *Sharing the Dance! Contact Improvisation and American Culture*. Madison: University of Wisconsin Press, 1990.

Pape, Sidsel. "Work in Process, Words in Process: Experimental Dance as Performance." *Contact Quarterly*, Summer/Fall, V. 19, # 2, 1944.

Suleiman, Susan Rubin. *The Female Body in Western Culture*. Cambridge: Harvard University Press, 1986.

Tolmach, Robin Lakoff and Scherr, Raquel. *Face Value: the Politics of Beauty*. New York: Routledge and Kegan Paul. 1984.

Ussher, Jane M. *The Psychology of the Female Body*. New York: Routledge and Kegan Paul, 1989.

Wolf, Naomi. *The Beauty Myth*. New York: Anchor/Doubleday, 1992.

Young, Iris Marion. *Throwing like a Girl and Other Essays in Feminist Philosophy and Social Theory*. Bloomington: Indiana University Press, 1990.

DANCE HAS MANY AGES
Billie Kirpich

Martha Graham was ninety-six when she undertook a fifty-five-day tour of the Far East with her troupe. At the age of sixty-five, she choreographed and performed the title role in her masterpiece, the full-length evening work *Clytemnestra*. Miss Graham was eigthty-seven at the time she made these comments during a video filming of three of her great contemporary works: "The life of a dancer is by no means simple; it's short, comparatively. I'm not an example of that. But I can see that beyond a certain time I could not do certain things. The body should be pliable to start with and it should be eager."[1]

This self-reflective remark of Martha's applies as well to a constellation of some revered female performers, who danced in their later years, choreographed some of their best works and were activists in dance-related fields. If only a few are singled out here, it is not intended to offend those wonderful artists who are unmentioned. For the joy they afforded us, they are well known to their audiences, students and colleagues.

Katherine Dunham, the toast of Europe and America, returned in the '60's from Haiti to her place of birth, East St. Louis, an economically depressed area, where she established a high-standard Academy of the Arts for underprivileged children. In her eighty-fourth year, Katherine went on a hunger strike for the cause of beleaguered Haiti. She has recently launched an environmental project to save the 35 acres of lush jungle surrounding her home in Port au Prince from ecological ruin, thus conserving an oasis of peace and abundance in that tragic country. She has given the same love for people that was the core of her scintillating theater to her projects in East St. Louis and Haiti.

Agnes de Mille, with genius, transformed the American musical theater. Her writings on dance and for television programs opened the hearts of the American public to dance in its many forms. Her talents of communiction — simple, direct and pragmatic — were a stimulus and

---

[1] Martha Graham in "An Evening of Dance and Conversation with Martha Graham," from the PBS *Dance in America* series, 1984.

inspiration to young dancers. Performer, choreographer, writer — these gifts and a fighting spirit sustained her into her eighty-eighth year.

Maria Tallchief, prima ballerina, danced well beyond her forties, as did many of her colleagues: in America, Ruth Draper, in France, Marie Jeanne; in England, Margot Fonteyn; and in the Soviet Union, Maya Plysetskaya. Maria Tallchief is still teaching and mounting works on other companies and on her students.

Doris Humphrey, pioneer of modern dance in America, in spite of a relatively short life — she died in her late fifties — left us a voluminous dance legacy. First, she constructed a theory for a new technique of dance and a keen analysis of the process of dance composition, which she shared with budding choreographers in her book *The Art of Making Dances*. Second, she created a repertoire of dance works based on the human experience that are still being performed by many companies throughout the world.

On the magical stage, I well remember being thrilled by two very different dancers in their middle fifties, each engulfing me with the dance forms of her particular heritage. Pearl Primus, who was so awesome to the people of West Africa and to us in America as the holder of the flame, the priestess of African dance, a crown she wore into her seventies. The other was Ekaterina Maximova, an exquisite young Russian ballerina who, in her later years, when she no longer was on pointe, danced an incredibly fragile and daring *Pathetique*.

Reprise: "But I can see that beyond a certain time I could no longer do certain things" — a typical Graham understatement! In performance the young body takes off, it sings, it flows, it leaps and it is radiant. In aging, some of this is gone. The legs may no longer be as supportive, the lift sinks some. As Paul Draper put it so well: "The behind is closer to the ground."[2] Endurance is lessened and strength may be weakened — but the songs, the flow, the radiance live forever. All is not lost…. The harvest of the years has brought knowledge, faith and understanding. Experience, years of experimentation and hard work are the pillars upon which the older dancer stands and from which she takes flight. Some have continued to dance into later years. Choreographers often do their finest works when older. Countless schools have been founded and directed by aging dancers who teach, inspire and produce the incredible young dancers that we see everywhere today. Other dancers have gravitated to areas of dance less technically demanding: folk dancing, movement therapies, working with seniors and staging works for such groups.

---

[2] Ibid., Draper, *Dance in America*.

"The rigors of existence and the erosion of the years moderate, but do not extinguish, the dancer in man. He is no longer given to bacchanalian abandon; he is more sober. He dances a sedate waltz or even a discreet derivative of a conga. Dance as ritual is vestigial with us."[3]

In *The Coming of Age*, Simon de Beauvoir suggests that the so-called "inescapable" factors of old age are the result of social expectation, not necessity. Because the body ages, conventional thinking has it that dancers should retire by the age of forty. But many of us don't. Dancers do not ordinarily pay attention to such commonly held advice; they are more prone to listen to the dictates of their own body and mind.

The dance and the dancer are one — they cannot be perceived separately. If circumstances dictate that the dancer must stop, it is a wrenching time in her life since for the most part there is still so much left to explore. Many dancers beyond forty, buoyed by their own determination and high spirit, still perform in their own works or works by other choreographers — witness Chita Rivera at sixty plus. It is an exhilarating thing to see them still on stage.

As may be expected, dancers face the turning point in different ways; it seemed therefore appropriate to let them tell us in their own words about dancing into the later years. Except for Hadassah and Alonso, a letter was sent to a small number of dancers asking: What are you doing in dance now? What does this mean to you? Following are their written responses.

Jean Erdman, now in her late seventies, is living in Hawaii, where she was born. Back in the '50's, at the New Dance Group in New York City, Jean, a recognized artist of whom I was in awe, was taking classes with Jean Leon Destiné and Hadassah, from whom she sought the essence of other cultures. These were sources upon which she built her enchanting works rooted in the mythology of the universe.

"I have just now completed a six-year project of videotaping my early choreography. It would not have been possible without the performances of Nancy Allison and Leslie Billingham, to whom I taught my solos of that period. This three-volume video set is entitled *Dance and Myth, The World of Jean Erdman*. I continued to perform these solos through the sixty-seventh year of my life and taught them to younger dancers while I was still able to demonstrate the movements. Now, nearly ten years later, I am contemplating a type of performance to suit my whims and capacities.

---

[3] Jose Limon, from "Encounter with the Performing Arts." A report sponsored by the New York State Education Department in cooperation with Lincoln Center for the Performing Arts, 1967, p. 48.

"It has been a most gratifying and even a fulfilling experience to discover that choreography created over fifty years ago is meaningful to the young dancers I have been teaching. The creative American Dance gives each individual the privilege of 'starting out fresh,' thus forfeiting the idea of preserving a style and choreography as is done in ballet. I did not plan to preserve my dances nor to teach dance technique in a Jean Erdman stylistic manner. When my dancers asked me to teach them my solos, I discovered that mysterious as this creative, personal and individualistic art is, when the form of the dance is identical with its content, the nonverbal essence and spirit of the choreography could be communicated to those who have been soloists in my dance theater companies."[4]

Carmen de Lavallade, West Coast dancer, was known to us in the 1950s as a leading soloist in the Lester Horton Dance Theatre. Lack of money kept the brilliantly innovative Horton company confined to the West Coast, so few of us had the good fortune to see Carmen de Lavallade in the critically acclaimed roles that were created for her — Medea, Salome, Prado de Pena. She migrated to New York at the end of the '50s, when we were at last introduced to her magnificent presence. She was recognized especially for the revival of *The Beloved*, one of Horton's best known ballets. Since that time, she has had a remarkable career in the theater as dancer, actress and choreographer. Following, in her own words, is the Carmen of today:

"I am still performing my own material, guesting with dance companies and choreographing for operas and plays. For my own work, I am now sixty-three, I have adjusted my movements to fit my needs. My body is still agile but old injuries keep me from deep knee bends and side laterals. Imagination with choreography takes care of the rest.

"I am now the director of the dance department and professor of performing arts in the College of Arts at Adelphi University and will be teaching and choreographing for young people. Although I have never been in this position before, it feels like a continuation of my career, except now I have more of a hand in guiding futures."[5]

Alicia Alonso returned to Cuba, the country of her birth, in 1959 when she was at the height of her fame in the United States. In her mid-seventies, she is still dancing today, thrilling audiences with her impeccable technique and her undiminished discipline. It is all the more breathtaking because she is blind. Nothing could speak more of the power of the authentic dancer to soar above the limits of smaller imaginations. Agnes de Mille said

---

[4] Personal correspondence, letter to the author dated January 26, 1994.

[5] Personal correspondence, letter to the author dated June 23, 1994.

of her: "Alicia is famous, not because of her blindness, but in her own right, compared to the sighted... She is a militant revolutionary and has contributed to the social history of her country. ...Finally she has built a ballet company that is a national institution and has world prestige."[6]

In September 1977 at the age of fifty-five, she returned to American Ballet Theater for an unforgettable guest peformance of *Giselle*; in 1982, at the age of sixty, she traveled to Austin, Texas in honor of Igor Youskevitch's farewell to the University of Texas where he had been head of the dance Department and where, to the joy of the audience, they performed one of their treasured duets. In 1990, at the age of sixty-nine, on an historic occasion in Madrid, Spain, Alicia danced with Rudolf Nureyev; in 1992, she appeared in Spain to perform *Carmen* in celebration of Spain's quincentennial. De Mille raised a question: "Will she be able to make the enormous gesture of yielding to history and bowing aside so that Ballet de Cuba can develop and progress? To step aside requires the creative vision of a prophet, the humility of a saint."[7]

Sophie Maslow, soloist in the Martha Graham company from the '40's on, was co-founder of the Dudley, Maslow, Bales company and the director of the Sophie Maslow Dance Company. Sophie is a recipient of many awards: Doctor of Humane Letters Honorary Degree, Skidmore College, 1984; a Resolution of Tribute to Sophie Maslow, Legislature of the State of Michigan, 1985; Testimonial of Sophie Maslow for Her Contributions to the Art of Modern Dance, Detroit City Council, 1985; Award of Artistic Achievement, American Dance Guild, 1991.

When asked what her present work in dance means to her, she replied, "Most of my life I've been dancing and choreographing because that's what I love to do and that's what I do best and that's what I shall continue to do in whatever capacity I can.[8] Sophie just now must be reaching her eightieth birthday — she performed with her own company well into her fifties.

Sophie has not received the official title of restorer of Graham's repertory but she certainly merits it. Because of her remarkable dance recall, she has been the key person in bringing to light many of the early Graham works. She is once again teaching at the Graham school and worked on the restoration of a selection from *Chronicle* (1936), one of Graham's earliest works.

---

[6] De Mille, Agnes. "Cuba's National Treasure: Viva Alicia!" *Dance Magazine*, August 1990, p. 33.

[7] Kumin, Laura. "Alonso Surfaces in Madrid." *Dance Magazine*, October, 1992, p. 22.

[8] Personal correspondence, letter to the author dated June 2, 1994.

In a period spanning fifty years, Sophie has created more than one hundred works. Her ballets are very much in demand in other companies and she criss-crosses the country to teach her dances. From early on she had a love and appreciation of folksong and music because as she says, "it comes from the people and has great beauty and feeling."[9] *Folksay* and other works are considered American classics. As a member of her company for many years, I loved these ballets and their life-sustaining qualities.

Hadassah, a performer of special eloquence, made her professional debut in 1945 and continued to perform Indian, Javanese and Balinese dance through the mid 1970s. She was born in Jerusalem and died in 1992 at the age of eighty-three in New York City. She stopped dancing only when she was almost eighty. The following information, sifted from the memoirs of her husband, Milton Epstein, her friends and the media, attests to her vigor as an older performer.

At the age of sixty-five, in 1974, she performed in a Gala Evening of Dance, directed by Walter Terry in celebration of the 100th anniversary of the 92nd Street "Y," sharing the program with Carmen de Lavallade, Allegra Kent, Sara Yarborough and Agnes de Mille's Heritage Dance Theater. In 1983, when she was seventy-four, *Arabesque*, the magazine of international dance, wrote: "Hadassah's respect for the power of the spiritual and the power of art seems to have brought her many blessings, among them a long-lived career."[10] Before her debilitating illness set in she was much in demand for her highly stylized folk dances. For example, with the Columbia University Folk Dance Group and with groups up and down the East and West Coasts, she led workshops in classical Hindu, Moroccan, Persian and East Indian folk dance.

Lorna Burdsall in her seventies is still dancing in Cuba. "After years of teaching, performing, choreographing and directing at Danza Contemporanea de Cuba and the National School of Modern Dance, I find myself still a performer, choreographer and director but this time, of my own six-member alternative dance group called 'Asisomos,' meaning 'The Way We Are.' Though we do occasionally perform in large theaters in Havana and abroad, I prefer to dance in the intimate and unique space which is my home. The prologue for this intimate venue is an exhibit of art works created by my mother from her childhood until her eighty-sixth birthday, which served to reflect the personality of an early feminist who influenced

---

[9] Ibid.

[10] *Arabesque*, Volume 9, #3, Sept.–Oct. 1983, p. 6.

me in my own creative endeavors. It means a lot to me to be able to meet people from all over the world who come to our performances. These experiences make for a wonderful dialogue and strengthen cultural ties."[11]

Ethel Winter, one of the most beloved teachers at the Juilliard School, soloist in the Martha Graham company from the '50s, now divides her time between New York City and Florida. "As of now, I enjoy teaching a part-time schedule at the Juilliard School and guest teaching here in the States and abroad. Thankfully, the limited schedule allows me to stay fresh, enthusiastic and caring for even the slowest of learners. In my early career, trying to balance teaching class, taking class, performance and family became a bit overwhelming. Teaching was more of a job. Now it is a joy.

"Young dancers today can accomplish technically extraordinary feats. I find it important and rewarding to emphasize that dancing for performance is communication and for this we must cultivate the spirit as well as the physical. It is in these areas where I feel I, as an experienced dancer, can and should contribute."[12]

As an older artist/teacher, I relate to and share the perspectives of the women speaking above. Following are excerpts from an interview on this subject with Susan Glazer at the University of the Arts in Philadelphia.

SG: What are you doing now?
BK: In 1979 I closed the door of my studio and bid goodbye to the young dancers of the Grove Dance Theater. I started and have continued to teach older people because I believe everybody should dance regardless of age. These senior adults are either mobile and come voluntarily or they are bused in under an arrangement with the Federal Older Americans Act. I approach these students no differently from my younger students. Though the work is suited to their physical and emotional abilities, the standards are kept high. Eventually, my involvement led to the development of a national television program that won a national award. So I was launched into a new career on the tail of my dancing kite.

SG: How did you feel seeing Martha Graham dance in her later years?
BK: She never thought of herself as an older person. She had something to say and, like all great artists, she was compelled to create, sometimes as many as four works a year. I would never think that Martha or Erick

---

[11] Personal correspondence, letter to the author dated February 15, 1994.

[12] Personal correspondence, letter to the author dated May 14, 1994.

(Hawkins) or Merce (Cunningham) should not be performing. For artists who have the courage to continue, that is when they do some of their best work. As for the others, they have bowed under the mantle that has been placed upon them as being older.

SG: Do you feel there is discrimination that prohibits older dancers from continuing their participation in the field?
BK: If dance in our society had a central role in the shaping of the well-being of the group as it does in other cultures, there would be no limitations concerning how much and how long older dancers could and should perform. As in Hawaii, Trinidad, Haiti, Brazil, Africa, Asia, older dancers would be respected as keepers of the tradition. If dance were not regarded merely as a product for entertainment, the perception of dance and dancers, especially those of age and experience, would be different. Dance would not be reserved for the young alone, and older dancers would be cherished for their knowledge and contribution to the total good of the nation. Dancers would be less youth-hungry and could, in an accepting society, continue to fulfill their roles as healers and teachers.[13]

---

[13] Personal interview, September, 1991.

THE BODY NEVER LIES
Carolyn McConnell

Labour is blossoming or dancing where
The body is not bruised to pleasure soul,
Nor beauty born out of its own despair,
Nor blear-eyed wisdom out of midnight oil.
O chestnut tree, great rooted blossomer,
Are you the leaf, the blossom, or the bole?
O body swayed to music, O brightening glance,
How can we know the dancer from the dance?
　　　— from "Among School Children" by W.B. Yeats (1927)

"Movement never lies." — Martha Graham

If the body never lies then either it always tells the truth or it says nothing. If it always tells the truth, then it speaks. An entity which speaks — if speaking means understanding what one utters and not simply emitting syllables of sound — must understand the negation of its utterances, and therefore is just as capable of proposing the negative as the positive — the true as the false — and understand them as such. That which speaks must be capable of lying. Therefore if the body never lies, it does not speak.

Yet Graham's statement implies that the body does speak. The statement itself and her entire career imply that it more than speaks, it makes poetry. Only subjects speak. Language, as expression of consciousness, is peculiarly human. Language differentiates us from animals because it is created/creative, is the essence of mediation as opposed to the immediacy of animality/materiality, and allows relation between humans as subjects. Yet the body is that part of us which we understand as mere materiality, it is that which links us to animals and supposedly mires us in the 'muck of bestiality.'

Graham's statement is thus profoundly paradoxical. It sounds radical, for it ties the body to the height of human achievement, high art, and morality, and in so doing subverts our cultural construction of the body as at once amoral, immoral, objectified, and bestial. At the same time, the above argument shows that the statement also presupposes the body as silent. The remark presupposes the body as some precultural, underlying primordial substance upon which we can draw for eternal truths free of culture's deception.

I want to use this deconstruction of Martha Graham's infamous statement as a jumping off point for an examination of embodiment and its effect on women, and in particular the ways that duplicity is connected with women's bodies. Body and woman are always on the same side of Western culture's dominant dualities and are the most enduring members of that list of dualities because they are associated intimately with each other, because they define each other reciprocally, and because they share many of the same constructed qualities. The problem of the body is one which all feminists must deal with in their theories, because the body is the primary locus of gender. "It is through the body, too, that women in our culture learn their own particular form of self surveillance… Through the body women collude in their own oppression."[1] Yet for these very reasons the issue of the body is so problematic that it has been dealt with in diametrically opposed ways by various of these theorists, and inadequately by most. Both feminists and philosophers of the Western canon have worked themselves into all sorts of contortions when forced to deal with the body.

However, I believe that the practice of dancing yields clues to a way past these apparently intractable dilemmas. Because in dance the body is so inextricably present that we are forced to deal with it and yet it is present as the vehicle for artistic expression, dancers cannot be dualists in the same way that academics who merely philosophize about the body can be. Philosophers get into these contortions because they can theorize about the body while forgetting this lived-in body right here with which I am typing these words.

Graham's stance is an example of one tack feminists take, that of affirming the body as a source of power untouched by culture's oppression of women. This position is attractive, for it directly attacks the very assumption by which that oppression is justified. If woman is immoral and worthless because she is associated with the body, which is immoral and worthless, then celebrating the body is subversive of that definition of woman. Women have also been denied control of their bodies and have been denied the pleasure and power of their bodies. Martha Graham strove to create an art form unlike ballet in being centered on woman as subject rather than object and in using an unabashedly sexual and strong movement vocabulary for women. No longer would dancing be a mere leg bazaar for male titillation (in the nineteenth century, the ballet was typically a place where the aristocracy went to seek its mistresses, and in the "green room" salons backstage, rich

---

[1] Wolff, Janet. *Feminine Sentences*. Berkeley: University of California Press, 1990, p. 126.

men would bargain with ballerinas' mothers over the price of their daughters). Modern dance would not necessarily even be pretty — its implicit claim was that women could be 'sublime' rather than merely beautiful — and its protagonists would be women. Graham's movement was angular, staccato, based upon the body's internal rhythms of breath, and explicitly sexual. She used Greek myths in a transformative way to create dances centered on female protagonists. For example, in *Errand into the Maze*, Graham transformed the story of Theseus and the Minotaur into a story of a woman's journey within the maze of her own psyche. Graham's work began the process of inventing an art form that would be created and controlled by women, and for women as much as for men. Graham's dance form implied that women's bodies would be reclaimed for themselves and their own pleasure.

However, affirming the body also reinforces women's traditional relegation to the bodily and fails to question the association of women with the body. Dancing may be an outlet for women's artistic and intellectual expression in a society which allows women few such outlets, but it is open to women because it is a marginalized art form and vice versa. As well, while women have been confined to the bodily, men have still determined that realm. While most dancers are women, most choreographers and directors of ballet companies are men, and even in modern dance women only control companies which are not in the big time financially. In 1984, of the seventy-five U.S. dance companies with budgets of $100,000 or more, including ballet, modern, and ethnic companies, three-quarters were run by men, and no company run by a woman or female choreographer had received any of the grants over $70,000.[2]

Women have paradoxically been relegated to and denied the body. Women typically hate and/or fear their bodies, because they view their bodies as responsible for their oppression: if a woman is raped, it is because her body was too attractive; if she is dissatisfied with sex, it is because her body does not respond the way a "real" woman's is supposed to; her body does not come up to the standard of beauty which is the only quality for which women are valued, and yet is a quality no real woman possesses as the ideal woman does. To the anorexic who uses her control over her body to replace genuine power and who looks in the mirror and sees nothing but hideous fat, the body most certainly does lie. The body is not an immutable given; women have tortured their bodies into the "proper" shape through everything from corsets, to dieting and throwing up, to rigorous ballet or

---

[2] Hanna, Judith Lynne, *Dance, Sex, and Gender*. Chicago: University of Chicago Press, 1988, p. 127.

athletic training which often has the effect of interrupting the menstrual cycle and hormonal balance (in the quest for idealized femininity, women thus make themselves like pre-adolescent boys), to foot binding to clitoridectomy. While associating the body with nature, society has attempted to transform the body into various culturally constructed ideals.

Thus the body cannot be some eternal underlying substance which can provide power for women if we just ask it. This implication of an interrogation of the body to force it to yield its secrets is highly revealing. Duplicity and mystery are paradigmatic predicates of both body and woman. Adrienne Rich argues that patriarchy is held together by women's lies, secrets, and silence, and Norine Voss writes: "Deception means survival for the powerless: to be successfully feminine means to learn concealment, deceit, the graceful falsehood."[3] Not only is woman and therefore sexuality mystified, but mystery is sexualized, which in turn sexualizes violence. By mystifying women and their bodies, patriarchy removes the possibility of consent: if she is a mystery to man, communication of consent is impossible, and further if she is a mystery even to herself, how could she herself know what she wants? At the same time, the male conqueror is celebrated for his power to reveal to woman her truth, which neatly obfuscates the humiliating reality that because man has required her to lie, he will never know if she is faking her ecstasy. Further, by mystifying women's bodies, patriarchy imbues them with danger, which makes the conquest of them that much more heroic. Writing on a decade of theories of the body, Arthur Frank said, "The... body contains truth but it is secretive, the task is to compel this truth."[4] Thus knowledge, sex, and power are interpenetrated and interdefined — by constructing women and the body as liars, patriarchy constructs knowledge =possession=sex=rape. Supposing truth is a woman, then in the interests of knowledge, we must go to her with the whip.

This logic also explains the phenomenon of anorexia. As Ellen Probyn writes, "anorexic bodies are notably duplicitous"[5]; not only must the anorexic continually say she is not hungry when she is quite literally starving, but she sees her body as having betrayed her. It is that duplicity which makes anorexia less a deviance than a taking of society's demands of

---

[3] Voss, Norine. "'Saying the Unsayable': An Introduction to Women's Autobiography," in Judith Spector, ed., *Gender Studies*. Bowling Green: Bowling Green State University Popular Press, 1986, p. 229.

[4] Quoted in Probyn, Ellen, "This Body Which Is Not One: Speaking an Embodied Self," in *Hypatia*, vol. 6 #3, Fall 1991, p. 115.

[5] Ibid., p. 113.

women to their conclusion. Lies are required of women by men and yet also serve as the only way for women to express their subjectivity in an oppressive culture; anorexics simultaneously express their power over a treacherous body with which they have been identified, and therefore transcend a culture which objectifies them; and accept and reinforce a culture which demands that women and their bodies lie for male pleasure and in which the power to attempt to mold one's body into an unattainable ideal is the only power open to women.

Milan Kundera, in *Immortality*, uses the notion of a gesture as the motif of his novel. He argues that there are fewer gestures than there are souls, and that therefore gestures come to imprison subjects within a limited meaning. We all have the experience that our bodies are somehow not expressive of who we really are inside. But what Kundera failed to understand is that experience has less to do with the limitations and determinacy of the body than with the limitation of our cultural definition of the body. Any dancer could tell Kundera the amazing fact that no two persons can do any movement exactly alike. Even the corps dancers in classical ballet, who are trained from childhood for unison, precise movement, cannot achieve perfect, machinelike unanimity. Every person's movement is as perfectly individual as his voice or thoughts. It is our culture's constructed interpretation and formation of the body's text which is oppressive, not the body itself.

Another tack some feminists have taken is to reject women's association with the body by rejecting the body itself. They recognize the way women's bodies have been used as instruments of torture, and have seen the body as the source of women's oppression. Shulamith Firestone, for example, believes that women's connection to reproduction is the source of sexism, and therefore it should be abolished, via test-tube reproduction. This of course assumes that being freed from reproduction frees one from the body. It fails to question the assumption that women are more connected to the body than men and that biology has some determinate meaning. However, to paraphrase Quine, the body underdetermines our theories. The fact that it is women who give birth to babies does not have a determinate and eternal cultural consequence. Seemingly objective facts that Firestone points to like the vulnerability of women to pregnancy and death in pregnancy before technology are not actually such. Male-controlled technology has in fact resulted in making women vulnerable in new ways, if not in making them more vulnerable, to reproductive hazards. Control of fertility and healthy pregnancy requires less technology than simply women's knowledge of their own bodies, folk knowledge of which medicine has systematically robbed women.

It is paradoxical that women are associated with the body and yet it is men who are more at home in their bodies in sexist society. This association of women with the body seems to have less to do with any objective reality than with male reaction to the spiritual power of women's bodies. The power of a woman to bring forth life out of her body is as easily seen as heavenly as bestial. Mary O'Brien, a philosopher and former midwife, argues in *The Politics of Reproduction* that women are intimately and immediately connected with their species-being, the continuity of human history, and therefore with their immortality by virtue of childbirth, a connection which is much more tenuous and mediated for men. In the same way that capitalism alienates workers from that which is most human, their labor, sexism alienates women from that which is most human, their reproductive labor, both in bearing and raising children. Human reproduction is highly distinctive from animal reproduction both in that it pushes the limit of brain size possible to come through the human birth canal and in that children are born totally helpless and underdeveloped. So why is it considered that which links us to animals more than anything else? Eating, excreting, and sleeping, all of which men do as much as women, are more obviously bestial than human reproduction. Perhaps the argument from women's connection with reproduction to her debasement should be reversed to an argument from reproduction's connection with women to its debasement. Even this female connection with reproduction is tenuous, since human reproduction is barely begun when children are born, if reproduction means producing another independent generation.

Even without accepting any essentialism about women's bodily nature, many theorists accept the inevitability of the objectification of the representations of women's bodies. Feminist filmmakers such as Laura Mulvey have shown that the 'gaze' of films is male because the frame directs the viewer to see women's bodies as sexualized objects. In attempting to disrupt the pleasure our culture constructs us to feel in seeing such images, feminist filmmakers remove beauty and pleasure from their films altogether, a stance which accepts patriarchy's claim that the oppression of women and nothing else is inevitably erotic. In *The Man Who Envied Women*, Yvonne Rainer responded to the apparent impossibility of representing a woman in film as a subject rather than an object by removing the representation of a woman's body altogether — the heroine Trisha appears only as a disembodied voice. The implicit message is that women will be objectified as long as they are embodied — hardly an encouraging message.

I am not so pessimistic. I do believe that women must and can re-possess and redefine their own bodies and the body in general. Arguing from Hegel, I believe that the body is essential to a notion of self, for without a body we would have no notion of the limits of self, no notion of not-self, and therefore no way to distinguish self from not-self. It is only through the body that we can interact with the external world and with other subjects, interaction without which consciousness cannot be, and without which we would have no way of expressing our subjectivity in the world. The body makes us acutely aware of our own lacking. It provides us with our first experience of resistance, resistance which later also comes from other people, and which is essential to consciousness. The body is ludicrous, it is humiliating, it is often inadequate, and it is also a joy. It forces us to laugh at ourselves, it provides a reality check, and it humbles us. All these aspects are necessary to self-awareness, but because they are inconvenient and constraining they have been traditionally relegated to women. Thus at the same time that we affirm the body, we must affirm men's as well as women's connection to both its humbling and exhilarating aspects.

Hegel seems to suggest that embodiment, at-homeness in the body, is further along the path of development than rejection of and division from one's body. While realization of the power of our minds and freedom from mere materiality was necessary in the course of human history, it is also necessary that we recognize that a mind is necessarily embodied, and that it is only through our bodies that we can express our freedom.

The experience of dancing has provided me with a glimpse of what Hegel might have meant by perfect self-consciousness united with perfect self-accord. To dance is at once to make the body more controllable, to make one more conscious of the workings of the body, and to make one more at home in one's body, more one with it. The greater the training of the dancer, the more she[6] can do without any mediation of thought, and yet at the same time the more she can consciously understand about the body. Dancing is art, and as such expressive of the highest yearnings of consciousness, but also sexually, physically, primally satisfying. Dancing unifies form and content, for it uses the body as its instrument, its voice, and its subject.

For all that many poststructuralists call for a re-insertion of the body into texts, they seem to forget about this body here with the eyes burning from staring at the computer screen and the back aching from hunching over the keyboard. In an article on essentialism, Vicki Kirby describes the

---

[6] I have still not solved the problem of pronouns in any categorical way. What I have come to is a flexible sensitivity to the requirements of the context — the pronoun should be honest about the gender realities of the situation. In this case, since most dancers are women, it seemed most honest to use 'she,' though I also recognize the power of using a surprising pronoun in order to disrupt the reader's assumptions.

experience of attending a conference at which a paper on Luce Irigaray's work was presented:

"In anticipation of the charge of essentialism that is commonly leveled at this particular French feminist... we were told that corporeality in Irigaray's writing was to be understood as a decidedly literary evocation... I was left wondering just what danger this exclusion had averted. What does the nomination "biological or anatomical body" refer to?... When I asked a question to this effect, it was met with a certain nervous incomprehension. Deciding, perhaps, that I must be still immersed in a precritical notion of the body, the speaker dismissed me with a revealing theatrical gesture. As if to emphasize the sheer absurdity of my question, she pinched herself and commented, 'Well, I certainly don't mean this body.'"[7]

Because she disassociated herself from her body, and viewed the body as mere recalcitrant materiality, the speaker equated assigning any importance to the body with an oppressive essentialism. But since we live in our bodies and can only assert our subjectivity via our bodies, the body is inescapable. "This abode recalls a body that demonstrates its anti-essentialism by pinching its essentialism."[8] No dancer can ignore the body, nor imagine that it is irrelevant to who one is, yet because dancers have trained their bodies to free themselves from a socialized body and increased its capacity for 'true speech' in Martha Graham's words, they cannot see the body as simply inanimate, subsistent, or essential matter. I was given an experience of the dramatic difference between the experience of dancer's bodies and the bodies of academics who merely theorize about the body when attending a class guest taught by Ann Cooper Albright. She combined a standard lecture class with several exercises, one of which was to imagine that we had pens on the tops of our heads, and to move while imagining that we were drawing in the three dimensional space around our head. This was followed by her asking us to partner each other in pulling each other around by the tops of our heads. She did this, she explained, in order to dissolve the division between writing and dancing, and to accept a kind of trust and disorientation required to be led by our heads. She was surprised to learn that none of us were nauseous or dizzy, as many of the non-dancing body theorists she has taught had complained bitterly of these symptoms after performing the exercise. It is important to note that we were all dancers, but that none of us used any technique to keep from getting dizzy — it was simply that we did not experience deviation from vertical and from physical

---

[7] Kirby, Vicki. "This Body Which Is Not One," *Hypatia*, v. 6 #3, Fall 1991, p. 10.

[8] Ibid., p. 10.

control as frightening. As colleagues of these same theorists who were made sick would be quick to point out, there is no bodily experience that is not socially constructed.

I am not so naive to think that merely dancing itself will liberate us. Ethnic and ballet dancing were invented as reflections of the culture(s) they came out of. Ballet came out of the courts of Europe, and therefore reproduces the rigid hierarchy and gender roles of that culture, as well as the romanticized infantilization of women of the nineteenth century, when ballet was popularized, codified, and entrenched. Venerability is not simply the issue — Balanchine's emphasis on bones (read anorexia) made his revolution of American ballet in many ways more oppressive than traditional ballet, and even Graham's "blood and gore" fails to move beyond the sexualization of violence. However, postmodern dance has begun to offer a glimpse of possibilities beyond gender, because it calls attention to what Ann Cooper Albright calls "the elsewhere" or "the gap" — the seams in what patriarchy attempts to present as seamless.

Postmodern dance arose largely out of the Judson Church movement of the sixties, when choreographers began to make work which was presented in informal settings — thus disrupting the hierarchical controlling of the gaze by the proscenium stage and therefore the division between performer and audience. It included movement generated by chance procedures and did not require an external narrative content but instead could simply be about the body and dancing itself. The choreographers used "pedestrian" or everyday movement, further dissolving the barrier between performer and audience, a barrier which is gendered or sexualized because it presents the performer as an object to-be-consumed by the audience as subjects. Janet Wolff writes in *Feminine Sentences*:

"Dance can only be subversive when it questions and exposes the construction of the body in culture. In doing so it necessarily draws attention to itself as dance — a version of the Brechtian device of laying bare the medium. Postmodern dance has begun to achieve this, and thus to use the body for the first time in a truly political way."[9] When Yvonne Rainer choreographed and performed *Trio A*, she denied the objectifying power of the gaze by refusing to look at the audience and by dancing without glamor, in an unprepossessing, flat style totally unlike the flash of ballet, or Broadway, or any previous Western theater dance.

The work of choreographers such as Senta Driver disproves any body essentialism by having women of all shapes and sizes lift men as well as the

---

[9] Wolff, op. cit., p. 137.

reverse. Despite a supposed natural basis of the convention that men lift women, Driver argues, and uses her work to prove, that "Lifting has everything to do with cooperation and timing, and it has very little to do with sheer strength... It's all engineering — a sensitivity to the other person's habits of timing and concentration."[10] This kind of sensitivity is precisely what patriarchy denies in men. Driver seems to be getting at a redefinition of power, one which is precisely not the patriarchal definition as the power to refuse to be sensitive to others. Instead she equates power and sensitivity.

A crucial aspect of the objectification of women is not simply that they are identified with their bodies, but that they are identified with body parts. Whereas still photos and even most film images are static, and therefore allow or even direct us to fetishize women's bodies, the simple fact that dance moves denies fetishism.[11] Even further, while much of ballet calls attention to static poses, postmodern dance rarely uses poses, never uses them unselfconsciously, and forces us to see the dancers' bodies as experiencing and moving.

Marie Chouinard's work is subversive in this way. In *Marie Chien Noir*, she thrusts her hand in a swanlike gesture deep down her own throat, forcing the audience to watch her body's reaction to this invasion — her stomach convulses — and then bringing her hand out dripping with saliva. In this piece, when she masturbates, douses her head repeatedly in and out of a bucket of water, or breathes volubly, she draws us into the inner rhythms of her body. She forces the audience to experience the dancing as experienced. Chouinard slips easily from moments of appearing the graceful balletic sylph to shocking insertions of her body's subjective experience. She both literally and metaphorically brings her body's "inner spaces out into the performance space."[12]

In "Sextet" from *Folkdances*, Ralph Lemon calls attention to the framing of his work by drawing the gaze to the wings from which dancers' limbs emerge and by leaving the stage bare for prolonged moments. In Lemon's *Phrases Almost Biblical*, a microphone is strapped to a dancer's body and we hear his labored breathing while he dances with seeming effortlessness. The packaged image is disrupted, and we are drawn into the experiencing of the effort required to present that image of effortlessness.

---

[10] Interview by Ann Daly, in *Women and Performance*, v. 3 #2 issue 6, 1987–88, p. 90.

[11] Roundtable interview by Ann Cooper Albright and Marianne Goldberg of Pooh Kaye, Wendy Perron, and Johanna Boyce, *Women and Performance*, v. 3 #2 issue 6, 1987–88, p. 45.

[12] Cooper Albright, Ann. "Mining the Dancefield." *Contact Quarterly*. Spring/Summer, 1990, p. 37.

In Lemon's work, the couplings are as likely to be two men or two women as a man and a woman, and women lift and manipulate each other. There is a moving moment in *Phrases Almost Biblical* when a very small slender woman and a tall stocky woman partner each other — it calls attention to the wide differences between women's bodies and the beauty of both. This kind of dance presents the very seams which traditional performance seeks to hide, calling attention to what Cooper Albright calls 'the gap' or 'the elsewhere.' It is precisely by finding and drawing attention to these gaps that it is possible to envision a way beyond the oppression of women. What patriarchy presents as inevitable and all-encompassing, postmodern dancing pushes us to see as arbitrary and incomplete. The works of certain postmodern choreographers are subversive in the most radical ways precisely because they draw the audience to experience as beautiful and deeply pleasurable what denies the objectification of women's bodies and bodies in general.

The truth is the whole, as Hegel said. This is why fetishism is so crucial to the construction of women as sexual objects, for it turns women from unified whole subjects into mere parts, none of which add up to form a whole person and which deny the possibility of knowing women as whole persons. To know the whole is not simply to be able to give one or many correct facts. It is not to know this or that, but how. Martha Nussbaum writes, in her commentary on love in Plato's *Symposium*:

"The lover can be said to understand the beloved when, and only when, he knows how to treat him or her: how to speak, look, and move at various times and in various circumstances; how to give pleasure and how to receive it; how to deal with the loved one's complex network of intellectual, emotional, and bodily needs. This understanding requires acquaintance and yields the ability to tell truths; but it does not seem to be reducible to either."[13]

Only an embodied consciousness, a consciousness at home in a body, can experience this kind of knowing. While patriarchal culture tells us that only in objectification can pleasure be found, postmodern dance calls upon us to realize not only that there is pleasure beyond objectification, but that it is only when we begin to re-envision persons as wholes beyond gender that we can begin to fully experience our bodily pleasure. Only when we stop making women lie to, about, and through their bodies will freedom and pleasure be fully possible.

---

[13] Nussbaum, Martha. *The Fragility of Goodness*. Cambridge: Harvard University Press. 1986, p. 191.

This essay was originally presented to the Eastern Division of the American Society for Aesthetics at a conference at the Rhode Island School of Design in March 1993.

Bibliography

Cooper Albright, Ann. "Mining the Dancefield." *Contact Quarterly*, Spring/Summer 1990.

Cooper Albright, Ann. "Writing the Moving Body: Nancy Stark Smith and the Hieroglyphs," *Frontiers*, v. 10 #3, 1989.

Diprose, Rosalyn. "In Excess: The Body and the Habit of Sexual Difference," *Hypatia*, v. 6 #3, Fall 1991.

Fancher, Gordon and Gerald Myers, eds., *Philosophical Essays on Dance*, based on a conference at the American Dance Festival. New York: Dance Horizons, 1981.

Hanna, Judith Lynne. *Dance, Sex, and Gender*. Chicago: University of Chicago Press, 1988.

Kaplan, E. Ann. "Is the Gaze Male?" in Marilyn Pearsall, ed., *Women and Values*. Belmont: Wadsworth Publishing Co., 1986.

Kirby, Vicki. "This Body Which Is Not One," *Hypatia*, v. 6 #3, Fall, 1991.

Miller, Nancy. "Rereading as a Woman: The Body in Practice," in Susan Suleiman, ed., *The Female Body in Western Culture*. Cambridge: Harvard University Press, 1986.

Voss, Norine. "'Saying the Unsayable': An Introduction to Women's Autobiography," in Judith Spector, ed., *Gender Studies*. Bowling Green: Bowling Green State University Popular Press, 1986.

Winter, Christopher. "Love and Language — Attitudes towards the Body, Sexuality and Gender — DV8 Physical Theatre," *Dance Theatre Journal*, v. 7 #2, Fall 1989.

Wittig, Monique. "The Mark of Gender," in Nancy Miller, ed., *The Poetics of Gender*. New York: Columbia University Press, 1986.

Wolff, Janet. *Feminine Sentences*. Berkeley: University of California Press, 1990.

PART VII

THEORY AND PRACTICE

Isadora Duncan started it all. In her revolt against nineteenth century norms, she advocated a change in attutudes toward the body. This section demonstrates ways in which these changes may be seen today. In the first two chapters, a sociologist and a clinical psychologist analyze theoretical and psychological issues of women's lives in dance. Susan A. Lee in "A Developmental Perspective" compares stages of life in dance and in adult developmental theory and provides a framework for understanding the chapters which follow. Marion Frank presents an informed and objective discussion of the usefulness of ballet study for nonprofessionals in "Ballet as a Way of Knowing." The following three chapters focus on the "body" in practice, i.e., the working methodology of women dancers. Brenda Way in "Governance and Vision" discusses her female-oriented organizational structure in the founding and administration of her company, Oberlin Dance Collective. Choreographer Sally Hess negotiates the vicissitudes faced by a solo artist on tour in "A Lion in the Laundromat." Wendy Perron contrasts the styles of three major female American dance critics in "Love and Power among the Critics."

WOMEN'S LIVES IN DANCE: A DEVELOPMENTAL PERSPECTIVE
Susan A. Lee

Adult development theory, while not in its infancy, is still quite young. Research has moved beyond the confines of the theory of chronological determinants of adult behavior and has begun to explore, describe, and detail the critical events that shape development, including an examination of the adult in the context of particular social systems. The point of view expressed in this essay is based on my own ethnographic study of the dance world and fifteen years of participant observation. Following qualitative research traditions, my field research on dancers' lives over these years employed life history interviews, open-ended and semi-structured interviews, and survey data. The data were subjected to content and sequential analysis and a theoretical model was constructed based on the themes and issues that emerge. Many of the interviews were recorded and transcribed for use in combination with field notes. Hundreds of hours of interview data and over two hundred survey responses have been analyzed. Sample survey questions have included references to mentors, influential figures, dreams and goals and other accepted factors found in psycho-biography and life history research. In thinking about women's lives in dance I combine adult development theory and life course issues for contemporary women contextualized in the dance world as a social system.

A study of women in professional dance reveals many of the conflicts and identity formation struggles of other professional women, but such inquiry also takes us into the realm of the special life course challenges for performing artists. This examination of the lifecourse begins by reviewing many of the developmental tasks of adulthood (Levinson 1986), noting the adaptation and coping skills that are needed in the field of dance. This thinking is grounded in a perspective that considers the physical culture of dance and the implications of the artistic conventions and training approaches historically employed in the dance world as a social system. This chapter focuses primarily on women performers in professional ballet and modern dance in the United States, in young adulthood through midlife.

What is social systems thinking in this context? The dance world, like most art worlds, is a social system. It is comprised of a series of organizations, subcultures, and institutions. The dance world is organized to accomplish a host of tasks and to facilitate a level of consistency and tradition for doing "work." This world is composed of a network of people who agree, if only by their adherence to these principles, on a set of artistic conventions and beliefs that shape process and product.

It is a professional world made up of dancers who pursue a variety of careers as well as the interconnecting groups of non-dancers (management, audiences, patrons etc.). As in all social systems there are issues of power, control, authorization and leadership for its members. Examining status within the dance world reveals a great deal about the values and beliefs that operate within this social system.

Neither the internal ordering of the dance world nor its value system for evaluation or shaping the lives of its participants was designed to be "user friendly." Complex interactions lead to a social system that presents limited options to its participants. The combination of anxiety about getting into the system (which means to some extent pleasing teachers and other boundary managers by meeting their expectations), staying in the system, earning a livelihood, or experiencing oneself as marginal within the larger society often results in fear, passivity or dependency, and lack of personal authorization to effect institutional changes. Dancers are often unaware of how they have taken these social system beliefs to be their own.

As with any system, it is possible to trace boundaries and boundary management in dance. The process for input (attempting to become a dancer), throughput (pursuing training and perhaps performing), and output (leaving the field) can be outlined for the various forms of dance. The dance world has various gatekeeping mechanisms, such as auditions, to determine who will enter and move through the system. In dance, where there is a fine line between self, identity and career, it is especially salient to examine the female dancer's life as it is influenced by social system forces.

Most writing about the dance world to date has been limited to historical treatments or descriptive narratives. Literature about women artists focuses on studies of personality, drawing mostly from examples of visual or literary artists (Gedo 1983). There is very little work that has actually focused, especially from a developmental perspective, on the lives of women in the performing arts. Supported by the emergence of the new discipline of dance science and medicine, a number of publications have addressed career transitions (Berardi 1991). With the exception of Blackmer (1989) these works fail to address the complexity of person, personality, and the growth of the self as it occurs in the dance world.

Currently women in the dance world, with the exception of a few superstars, are looking more like their peers in the mainstream cohort of working women. Social scientist Denmark states, "Women who elect to take the path of career often find themselves involved in professional education and training that consumes large amounts of time as well as energy and leaves little of these for other pursuits such as relationships, social activities, or child rearing. This is especially true for women who have selected careers that are 'front loaded,' careers that require investment of time and energy during their early stages."[1]

Assumptions that dancers made sacrifices out of dedication to their art suppressed questions about the implications for the growth and transformation of dancers. Stated even more strongly by Nancy McWilliams, "I am suggesting, then, that contemporary women are not only experiencing the kind of tensions that men have suffered for a long time; they are also handicapped by a marked lag in the culture's adaptation to them as equal partners in the workplace and they continue to have to make accommodation to their biology that men are spared. They have the worst of both worlds; the burden of limit on it and the hazards of opportunity."[2]

Influenced by the work of Levinson (1986), Sheehy (1981), Bardwick (1980), Erickson (1986), Miller (1987), and Woodman (1993), this analysis of women's lives in dance will not focus on pathology but rather attempt to present the normal peaks and valleys of the life course, illuminating the special nature of dance. The developmental agenda begins with the assumption that women should not be measured against a theoretical goal of independence and autonomy, so often cited in the developmental literature. This hierarchical perspective, assumed to be the drive toward self-actualization, was created using a male image. For women, more relevant developmental tasks are: overcoming assaults to self-esteem, becoming aware of the drive toward putting others first, and realizing that the notion of a superwoman is a myth. As more elaborate views of the feminine are chronicled in contemporary writings we are reminded of the value of interdependence and involvement in relationships as an important step in the developmental ladder (Jordan, Kaplan, Miller, Stiver, Surrey 1991).

We know very little about the psychodynamic process of why women select dance. In some cases the field is chosen by adolescents. The internalization of the occupational title and ideology ("I am a dancer and will diet and train my body accordingly"), commitment to task ("I will take technique classes faithfully"), and commitment to an organization ("I dance

---

[1] Denmark, Florence. "The Thirty Something Woman: To Career or Not to Career." *Gender Issues Across the Life Cycle*, edited by Wainrib, Barbara Rubin, New York: Springer, 1992.

[2] McWilliams, Nancy. "The Worst of Both Worlds: Dilemmas of Contemporary Young Women." Wainrib, Barbara Rubin, ed. *Gender Issues Across the Life Cycle*. New York: Springer, 1992.

with XYZ School") does little to help us assess what ego questions are being resolved or how parental wishes are being reflected.

The Twenties

Many dancers do not fully demonstrate an occupational identity until their twenties; many discover dance while in college. In the twenties, one of the first developmental tasks is taking hold of the adult world. One moves from an idealized time into adulthood. There is a significant shift from adolescent inner turmoil to a more external focus. Questions such as "What are my professional goals?" "How do I fit into the larger scheme of things?" are common.

The decade of the twenties is a more stable passage than adolescence, characterized by a tremendous number of "shoulds." Young adults, moving from still being filled with the conflict between one's own idealism and unresolved identity issues, are engaged in leaving the family of origin and establishing themselves on their own. Young adults are freer to begin making actual life course decisions, confronting both societal and familial expectations.

Another characteristic of this passage is that these decisions feel absolutely irrevocable. Every choice confronted in the twenties feels like it is part of a permanent structure, which puts tremendous psychic pressure on decision making. There is also continued tension between the wish to establish commitments, to create foundations, and to really feel rooted in one's life, and a tremendous fear of getting locked in.

In their twenties, women feel the importance of their will. They make their own choices. Given the social organization of many dance companies, there are very few opportunities for the expression of personal choice and authority. Perhaps it is this system (one which harkens back to adolescence) that encourages dancers to become preoccupied with controlling the one thing they feel they can... their bodies.

One begins to assert independence from the family of origin, tied to the continued struggles to separate physically and psychologically. Many young dancers confuse the fact that they may have been living away from home to pursue their dance training with having achieved independence, forgetting that self-sufficiency is not synonymous with psychological independence.

Maintaining a kind of psychological dependency seems to be a social-system dynamic worth noting in the dance world. In many companies, adults continue in the role of novice, earn very little money, carry limited adult responsibility, and know little about the rest of the world. This kind of dependency contributes to dancers' accepting working under such psychologically destructive factors as weight clause contracts and no life or health insurance or retirement benefits.

With the increasing trend to marry later, young women are left without the useful psychic separation that marriage often provided. The question remains, what processes will support women in this task? As I have noted in earlier writings (Lee 1989), many dance organizations create another kind of family system that allows individuals to believe that they have achieved some measure of autonomy, when in fact their adolescent dependency has merely been transferred to another kind of family. Dance companies or schools often function as surrogate families. Many learn about sexuality and body image based on feedback they have received from teachers.

Levinson (1986) suggested that having a life dream and finding a mentor to help in the refining and attainment of that dream were two of the most significant developmental tasks of early adulthood. In the dance world, day to day authority figures and mentors often take the form of master teacher/choreographers. (Recall all of the ways Balanchine or Graham have been described and remembered.) These mentors shape much more than traditional career choices. The influence of teachers, choreographers, artistic directors and even fellow performers can determine many lifestyle and body ego belief systems for the young adult. My research on health issues (Lee 1992) indicates dancers' preferences for alternative healthcare practitioners and avoidance of traditional medicine are shaped directly by influential teachers more than by family-of-origin belief systems.

Women's life dreams often have a dual focus (Roberts and Newton 1987). There is a dream that encompasses career and occupation; there is also a dream about relationships. This dual focus stays with women throughout the constant juggling of special relationships.

Some women wish to be rescued by a person who will help resolve their confusion about life choices. Many young performers believe that if they just work hard enough, or are "good" enough, or have the "right look" they will be saved from an insignificant level of professional achievement. Some have a fantasized relationship with an authority figure that helps them feel special or valued, allowing them to be protected from experiencing the loss of other significant relationships. When this mentality is not complemented by realistic assessments of opportunities for advancement, planning for the future, and honest appraisal of relationships, it can lead to very destructive consequences. In interviews, many female participants noted they were rarely under "family" pressure to get married or start a family. There seemed to be some unspoken agreement that long-term commitments were incompatible with the demands of performing, especially touring.

The Thirties

Life course transitions provide opportunities to make major changes. While not necessarily a crisis, a transition can leave the person feeling destabilized as she lets go of some aspects of the self while other aspects emerge. As a dancer begins to release the idea of her identity as a performer, she may shed the tasks and values associated with performance. She may stop attending class, withdraw from those who still identify themselves primarily as performers, change dietary habits, or lose interest in attending concerts. If the individual is especially conflicted about this transition and change in identity, she may employ a subconscious mechanism to assist or force the change. Transitions are fueled by conscious and subconscious assessments.

Especially for women, the age thirty transition is the first major phase where we see a wish to undo or resolve what happened in the twenties. Blaming occurs for bad choices and mistakes that were made in the twenties; some women ask, "My life doesn't fit anymore. How did that happen?" This causes feelings of turmoil, disruption, frustration, and anxiety. There is a new, appropriate self-centeredness. A new feeling of competence emerges from the achievements of the twenties and a wish to keep the momentum going.

There can be more disruption during the age thirty transition than in "mid-life." The identity issues for women in their thirties are more complex than a concern with the biological clock. Many women I interviewed talked about the conflict arising from having achieved professional success while not having established a stable relationship with a significant other. Nevertheless, these women find themselves having dreams and fantasies about babies. They find it disconcerting that this feeling is emerging during a time when it doesn't feel appropriate professionally or personally to act on the fantasy.

Women appear to focus on finding the missing piece of the equation: those who had careers long for relationships and those who had relationships with little professional satisfaction want to concentrate more fully on their careers. In the relationship sphere, there is the continued search for real intimacy. In the career sphere, there is fear about the future and hard work.

Many woman evade or avoid the re-evaluation of their lives during this passage, fearing that to do so would give rise to depression. For some the unexamined life is adaptive. When some women evaluate their careers, they realize women do not have access to opportunities for change. Therefore, changes in life structures can feel out of their reach.

Like many professional women trying to balance career and children during this time, dancers taking time off from the career trajectory can be considered disloyal or unmotivated. Like other working women returning to work after having a child, dancers face conflicts. Clearly the issue of child bearing is an especially complicated one in dance, where body image is central. This is not just an issue of biology. One of the concerns that is often voiced by dancers is, "If I bear children will the passion and drive that was characteristic of my before-baby choreography or performance be lost?"

There are not many opportunities for female dancers to establish an intimate relationship with a male at work. For those in the performance world, demanding schedules limit opportunities to meet men outside of dance. While some relationships, including authority relationships, within the dance world may present special conflicts, there are also many benefits including the comaraderie so often described by dancers. The experience of belonging and feeling understood by other dancers can create an important support group useful in coping with life course challenges. The dance world, especially modern dance which has a matriarchal structure, provides unique opportunities for building satisfying friendships between women that last a lifetime.

Some women working as choreographers start to be taken seriously, having hit their stride creatively. This psychological and occupational growth can sometimes be attributed to the fact that the artist has been able to successfully differentiate from the original mentor figure in whose image she might have been formed. At this point, some dancers learn that having vigorously pursued a life in dance, their development has meant moving from dependency as a novice to autonomy as an established artist.

Given the unique time pressures in dance, many performers at age thirty face a forced career transition. Dancers experience exclusion and marginalization with age. In interviews with mature artists, some expressed anxiety about how they looked or were perceived in the classroom, others lamented the limited opportunities to dance. All agreed that simply taking technique class, especially in the presence of so many younger bodies, was a poor substitute for rehearsal and performance. Many dancers pursue performing past their prime just to be on stage. Some literature discusses the need to develop backup skills but the unspoken ideal is to remain a dancer. "Too many of us retire from dancing too soon, for the wrong reasons. Having a profitable backup skill may very well come in handy if for one grim reason or another you have to quit our lovely, mad profession."[3] Those who stay in

---

[3] Nagrin, Daniel. *How to Dance Forever*. New York: Quill/William Morrow, 1988, p. 231.

performance struggle with declining opportunities due to perceptions about aging performers. They begin to mourn the loss of the idealized body. Often, approaching this transition, performers have a rash of injuries.

Nothing in the dancer's training has prepared her for this assault on her identity. Some performers will look to choreography or to establishing a company. Assuming the position of leadership implied by having a company also furthers psychological development by taking new creative risks.

Midlife

In midlife people experience death anxiety and, consequently, search for meaning in their lives. The midlife transition is a time of danger and possibility. In some individuals precipitous career changes and divorce result. Often in midlife, relationships that worked in the twenties and thirties no longer seem to fit. Midlife is also the time to begin grappling with the counter-sexual opposite, animus and anima in Jungian terms, the feminine and the masculine within us. In midlife we begin to integrate and deal with gender aspects in a new way. Women who have never been assertive or aggressive begin to discover new capacities in themselves that they find quite surprising. Some begin to let go debilitating forms of dependency and begin to move in new directions.

This is also the beginning of biological decline. Our culture doesn't embrace images of male and female aging with equal respect. During midlife women struggle once again with unresolved issues concerning the family of origin. As longevity increases, these dynamics often involve physical care for aging parents. Many dancers who have no insurance or security experience tremendous anxiety in anticipating the needs of their families.

Conclusion

Women dance artists must be able to alter their beliefs and dreams based on what they've learned at each developmental hurdle. This requires that they do more than act out or change life structures precipitously; it requires that they draw on accumulated accomplishments from earlier passages. The dance world must also change to encourage planning for the future and reconceptualize the current arbitrary and rigid boundaries between professional dance and dance in higher education.

What factors may help produce a healthier environment for lifetime involvement in dance? How do women achieve satisfaction in their lives as well as in their art? How will their professional goals be compromised by low wages that are routinely accepted as a fact of life in dance? How does a woman's need to have time to do creative work interface with her dream of career and relationship? Do women struggle in ways that men don't with traversing the life course? What kind of artistic productivity in dance is most accessible to women? How are we marginalizing women as a result of socialization? This list of issues reveals a full agenda for future research.

Psychological disruption and upheaval are normal in the life course. There are certainly many dramatic examples in the world of dance. Creativity may be one of the few areas in which we experience aging as a positive thing; it is one of the few areas in which we allow women to grow into wise old women for whom experience counts, in which it matters that you've been in the field for a long time. This essay has categorized the periods of a female dancer's life, each one filled with unique constraints but also with opportunity.

Bibliography

Bardwick, J. M., "The Seasons of a Woman's Life." McGuigan D.G., *Women's Lives: New Theory, Research and Policy.* Unpublished paper, University of Michigan Center for Continuing Education, 1980.

Berardi, Gigi. *Finding Balance: Fitness and Training for a Lifetime in Dance.* Dance Horizons, Princeton, N. J., 1991.

Blackmer, Joan Dexter. *Acrobats of the Gods: Dance and Transformation.* Inner City Books, Toronto, 1989.

Denmark, Florence. "The Thirty Something Woman: to Career or Not to Career." Wainrib, Barbara Rubin, ed., *Gender Issues Across the Life Cycle.* New York: Springer, 1992.

Erikson, E. H., Erikson, J. M. and Kivnick, H. Q. *Vital Involvement in Old Age.* New York: W. W. Norton, 1986.

Federico, Ronald, in Kamerman, Jack and Martorella, Rosanne. *Performers and Performances: The Social Organization of Artistic Work.* South Hadley, Mass.: Bergin and Garvey Pub. Inc., 1983.

Gedo, John. *Portraits of the Artist.* New York: Guilford Press, 1983.

Gordon, Suzanne. *Off Balance: The Real World of Ballet.* New York: Pantheon Books, 1983.

Jordan, J. V., Kaplan A. G., Miller, J. B., Stiver, I. P. and Surrey, J. L. *Women's Growth in Connection.* New York: Guilford Press, 1991.

Lee, S. A. "Adult Development and Female Artists: Focus on the Ballet World." *Medical Problems of Performing Artists*. March, 1989.

Lee, S. A. "Patterns of Choice, Bias and Belief: Report from a Pilot Study on Dancers and Health Care." *Medical Problems of Performing Artists*. June, 1992.

Levinson, D. J. "A Conception of Adult Development." *American Psychologist*. January, 1986, Vol. 41, No. 1.

McWilliams, Nancy. "The Worst of Both Worlds: Dilemmas of Contemporary Young Women." Wainrib, Barbara Rubin, ed., *Gender Issues Across the Life Cycle*. New York: Springer, 1992.

Miller, J. B. *Towards a New Psychology of Women*, 2nd ed. Boston: Beacon Press, 1987.

Nagrin, Daniel. *How to Dance Forever*. New York: Quill/William Morrow., 1988.

Roberts, Priscilla and Newton, P. M. "Levinsonian Studies of Women's Adult Development." *Psychology and Aging*, 1987, Vol. 2, No. 2.

Sheehy, Gail. *Pathfinders*. New York: William Morrow and Co., 1981.

Sidimus, Joysanne. *Exchanges: Life after Dance*. Toronto: Press of Terpsichore Limited, 1987.

Steinem, Gloria. *Revolution from Within*. New York: Little Brown and Company, 1992.

Woodman, Marion. *Leaving My Father's House*. Boston: Shambala, 1993.

BALLET AS A WAY OF KNOWING
Marion Rudin Frank

A metaphoric approach to dance is certainly not new. Erick Hawkins has said that "dance is a metaphor for existence."[1] Although I emphatically agree, I do not speak as a professional choreographer. My perspective comes from many years as a classical ballet student, as a musical theater dance performer, as an enthusiastic audience of all dance, as a professional psychologist and as a woman. It is my belief, now as a psychologist and once as a dancer, that ballet has much to teach us about life; for ballet training is filled with psychological metaphor.

Most of those who study ballet will never dance professionally, yet the experience is valuable in itself. Dance can be either a rewarding recreational activity or an expression of tremendous strength and physical achievement. It can be an external expression of emotions and ideas, music and movement. It can have beneficial effects on appetite, sleep patterns, and mood. Above all, it can offer a unique perspective on life and thus be emotionally therapeutic.

Dance as a therapeutic healing aid can be traced back to prehistoric times when ritual dance was used to ward off evil spirits thought to be inhabiting diseased bodies. Today, dance therapy is an important tool for the medical arts. Bodily responses to rhythmic sound not only promote healing but provide a spiritual and aesthetic insight into life. In addition, dance enhances body image, which is a fundamental aspect of all growth concepts in human development. Those who learn the control and mastery of their bodies through movement are more likely to develop minds which are more graceful and cherishing of beauty. Enhancing the capacity to dance increases the ability to live more freely and fully, builds confidence and even has implications for aging.

Wilhelm Reich had long ago theorized that defenses are rooted in the body as chronic muscular tension, and Carl Jung had proclaimed the use of art as a means by which the patient could learn to acquire psychotherapeutic

---

[1] Hawkins, Erick. *The Body Is a Clear Place and Other Statements on Dance*. Pennington: Princeton Book Co., 1992, p. 1.

distance and detachment. In the 1960's, the value of movement experiences in psychology increased in prominence. The premise that movement behavior is analogous to intrapsychic dynamics gained widespread acceptance.[2] The concept of "flow" became important, emerging at the core of such various body therapies as bioenergetics, yoga, and the Alexander Technique. Those who studied kinesthetic awareness advanced the idea that body experience provides no less than a framework for the way we structure our concepts about the world.

Psychological interest in body therapies has broadened to include such arts as tai chi and aikido, as well as other activities which utilize the body as instrument. They also have in common foundations such as discipline, technique, and stamina. They offer not only the respective skill of their art but help the student to understand that gracefulness can be learned, that stretching physical limitations encourages the general stretching and risk-taking behavior essential for psychological growth.

Although psychological attention had been paid to many types of body work, several years ago I realized that ballet had never been studied in the same manner. As a discipline which utilizes the body vigorously and focuses on the grace of movement, ballet had been, in fact, surprisingly neglected as an area of psychological exploration. My hope was that the inclusion of ballet in psychological study would confirm the assumption that people can experience life in a more fluid manner if they move more freely and flowingly. Ballet provided another method to acquire the control necessary over one's body. But it was the search for philosophical metaphors of ballet that really intrigued me.

It was in this spirit that I decided to bring my enduring love for ballet into my work as a psychologist and proposed a professional training program in 1977 entitled "Ballet as a Way of Knowing." It was developed for the eastern regional convention of the Association for Humanistic Psychology, an organization which then attracted large numbers of mental health workers in various subfields. The association prided itself on its cutting edge approach to the study of psychology.

There was some concern about the interest that such a workshop would generate, especially since I was asking mental health professionals to come dressed in leotards for ballet class. In order to overcome the anticipated resistance, I wrote the following as part of the description for inclusion on the program booklet: "You don't have to be graceful, young, a woman, or thin to participate and discover a new sense of self."

---

[2] The term intrapsychic dynamics refers to the interaction of conscious and unconscious thoughts, feelings, interaction, and the senses; or the structure of the id, ego, and superego.

The formal letter indicating acceptance of my program for the convention included a personal note from the conference coordinator: "We gave you the only room with some mirrors on the wall, although they may be frosted or marbled or something. Good luck." It was to be a challenge on many levels.

Nevertheless, it was with strong conviction that I sensed that ballet contained many of the elements that humanistic psychology sought to emphasize in its endeavor to understand and promote personal growth. My workshop would attempt to demystify the art of ballet practiced for so long by small elitist groups and encourage participation in it. It was to be primarily experiential in nature and to utilize small groups to share and process the activities. The format included a simulated beginner ballet class, followed by group discussions of implications and relevance of class procedures to training for mental health clinicians.

The workshop design was developed as follows:

1. Introduction and Brief Historical Perspective
2. Barre Work
3. Process Discussions
4. Lecturette: Ballet as Metaphor, Positive and Negative
5. Center Work
6. Small Group Discussions (Questions, Guidelines)
7. Large Group Discussion, Wrap-up, Evaluation

The response to the workshop was overwhelming, and the number of participants far exceeded expectations. Many of these respondents were therapists who, like myself, had studied ballet as children and had an intuition that their experience taught them something beyond the basics of ballet. Perhaps they, too, had a sense that ballet taught them concepts about life itself. Perhaps they, too, felt they would gain value for themselves and have more to offer the patients with whom they worked.

People of all shapes and sizes came to the workshop, dressed in whatever they remembered or imagined ballet class attire to be. Some had studied one or more of the body therapies and already understood that movement behavior affects and is affected by intrapsychic dynamics. Some had had rigorous ballet training. Others had never been in a dance class before. They all shared a desire to participate in a serious quest for ballet's analogies for psychological growth. Together we embarked on this adventure.

As participants were encouraged to attend to the responses of the body and search for metaphors; many interesting observations were made.

Stretching physical limitations of the body was related, for example, to positive psychological stretching or risk-taking behavior. Working with the mirror (unique to dance) was described as not unlike working with a therapist, toward goals of self-monitoring, acceptance of feedback, and continually confronting oneself. The posture of ballet was seen as an expression of positive feelings of calmness, strength and upliftedness, as opposed to the negative emotions of anxiety, insecurity, and depression. The ballet teaching sequence of explaining, marking, and performing was noted as being analogous to the behavioral therapy techniques of identifying the problem, modeling, and rehearsing. It was also stated that one must risk looking silly or foolish to achieve a state of grace — physically, emotionally, or spiritually.

More specific comments from workshop participants were elicited after barre work. Tendu in first position brought to mind thoughts of centering and then extending the self. Ronde de jambes triggered remarks about energy circles. Porte de bras exercises concerned one's sense of awareness of space and expanded limits. Concentrating eyes on specific points of attention during piqué turns elicited comments on the importance of a directional focus and its relationship to finding balance in life. The barre itself could be seen as the security one needs before freedom (or center work) is possible. Ballet's emphasis on intentional image began a discussion on how image profoundly affects all of one's life, including social relations, occupational success, and basic psychic functioning.

Following the ballet class experience, small groups were asked to use the following questions to guide their discussions:

1. What experiences or concepts in this workshop held special meaning for you?
2. How does the idea of discipline (control) and its relation to freedom (grace) have meaning for you?
3. How do you react to modeling as a way of learning?
4. What has been the value of planned, concentrated action in your life?
5. Do you see ballet as a viable vehicle for teaching such concepts as centering and grounding? What other concepts might you learn from its practice?

The large group discussion which followed revealed that participants were very positive about their experience of the workshop. Their comments spanned a variety of topics, and it is possible to recapture only fragments here. Participants noted how technical skill and intense control create a sense of grace and flow. Exposure to aesthetics was discussed for its importance in bringing balance and perspective in life. They also emphasized how the exercises brought out feelings which were not previously conscious. Above all, the richness of the potential for ballet work as psychological metaphor was clear, as were the implications for emotional healing.

My thinking about the potential contribution of ballet to psychological thought has continued to evolve since that workshop. Today, I believe that any discussion of ballet's metaphors should include the negative images which are also derived from the ballet experience. As a woman who brings feminist theory into the clinical practice of psychology, I cannot overlook the obvious sexist ideal of femininity in ballet that equates beauty and grace with excessive thinness. Relentless persistence of this often unnatural "ideal" body has caused many aspiring young women to engage in activities which result in eating disorders. Studies linking ballet dancers with anorexia and bulimia find that the majority of ballet dancers weigh significantly below national norms, are excessively preoccupied with food and weight, and engage in unhealthy methods of weight loss. For dancers immersed in the ballet world, these behaviors are socially and strongly reinforced.

In dance class, bodies are constantly on display. Often weight, more than talent, is the criterion for acceptability. The "sylph" look is a ballet tradition, and chances of getting into a ballet company (or fitting into the ballet "family") are dependent upon being thin, often excessively so.

These powerful pressures cause young women to develop an overconcern with normal development of breasts, thighs and buttocks and to believe that the road to success is starvation. It is not all that unusual for young ballerinas to diet to the point of losing menses or having erratic periods, compromising health, risking stress fractures and possible future osteoporosis. With an inner drive for perfection, a teenager with serious aspirations may practice up to eight hours a day, withdraw from friends and obsess about maintaining what is actually a prepubescent body shape. Those not genetically prone to slight bodies may encounter severe self-esteem issues or suffer other psychological consequences.

Moreover, ballet has mirrored the culture's ambiguity toward sexual expression and gender patterns. The ballerina is at once artist, idealization of virgin-like femininity, and sex object. Her body is the instrument of dance and thus the tool of the choreographer. Dance shares with other disciplines and career paths a gender-related prestige hierarchy. The well-recognized choreographers and managers are disproportionately male and the dancers are disproportionately female. In the studio or on the stage, male choreographers unintentionally may treat dancers like children; there is an expectation that they will be obedient and deferential. Ballet teachers still refer to female dancers as "girls" and male dancers as "boys."

Some contemporary writers believe that classical ballet has offered a legacy in which heterosexual, romantic, and chivalrous relationships validate male dominance. A recurring image is certainly the pas de deux, in which the strong male interpreted as her pedestal, dominates and supports the woman on pointe.

However, more than simply sanctioning gender-related behavior, ballet offers opportunities for fantasy. The pas de deux may be interpreted not only as man manipulating woman but as man enabling woman to have added freedom in movement, helping her to achieve her goals. Or it may be seen as a mutually interdependent image, with clear separation of duties.

Few attempts have been made to understand the impact of ballet on the adult development of female dancers. Susan A. Lee, in her exploration of the topic, concluded that the environment of the ballet world causes arrested development and supports dependency and immaturity. Normal developmental processes may be jeopardized if, for example, the mother plays an intrusive role in the career of her aspiring daughter, rendering the achievement of the tasks of separation and independence more difficult.[3]

Moreover, dancers deal with a unique peer group, one which is comprised of rivals. In spite of emerging sexuality, this group of adolescents may be striving not to mature physically, as would be age-appropriate. On the other hand, serious dancers are often forced to make decisions which are more characteristic of older midlife experiences. Before the age of thirty, dancers may feel forced to leave not only a job but a lifestyle and, even more importantly, a core identity.

In spite of potential hazards such as limited body image, old-fashioned gender roles, and out-of-step developmental tasks, dance has much to offer that is psychologically beneficial to women. It can promote the development of self-esteem, self-confidence, and a host of important understandings for managing life. Perhaps the primary lesson derived from the study of ballet and of particular value to women concerns the related themes of discipline and commitment. Adolescent women have less access to these and other important understandings, which men often gain from experiences in playing team sports. The ballet studio is an environment of courage. There is the dancer who dances despite realities of low wages, injury, or family hardship. A young woman sees that it is ultimately motivation which brings achievement and not simply potential. She also learns to strive for perfection as an individual, yet to adjust her individuality to the group.

---

[3] Lee, Susan A. "Adult Development and Female Artists: Focus on the Ballet World," *Medical Problems of Performing Artists*, Vol. 4, 1 March 1989, pp. 32–37.

Like any athlete, the ballet student must confront inevitable limitations — the stretch that is not perfectly turned out, the student in front whose kick is higher, the reality of her genetic structure. She learns that great effort enables her to achieve certain levels of technical competence, yet exceptional talent is inevitably born. Hopefully she learns to focus on her possibilities and potentials rather than on her limitations. Although the best ballet student is likely to be the one who lives and breathes ballet, a woman dedicated to it discovers what it means to find something that one loves to do. Its practice, like any worthwhile endeavor, is a matter of patience, endurance, pain and pleasure.

In my therapy work with women of various ages, the most prevalent and perhaps most profound of the themes which inevitably emerge concerns the concept of power. Lacking societal status and role models, women in our culture often struggle to take themselves seriously, to assert themselves, and to trust their own intuitive sense. Dance cultivates a way of learning and knowing which heightens this sense, as dance is centered in the body and the mind. As emotions and memories are embedded in the body, a heightened sense of body awareness may enhance access to them. In addition, it is obvious that a young woman can change quite dramatically through ballet training, that presence and grace can be learned, developed and mastered. Practiced movement brings with it a change in a sense of style, presence and confidence and an accompanying alteration in inner feeling. Ballet offers the opportunity to go beyond ego, to respect form and to reach for resources deep within in order to stir the audience outside. A woman learns that performing itself is at once an assertive act and an essential skill for life.

As mentors and role models, the influence of the ballet teacher cannot be overstated. The teacher of ballet has a tremendous opportunity to affect not only technique, but the values and lives of students. An awareness of psychological dynamics is essential to develop a teaching style which is validating and empowering to young women. As stereotyped conventions change, changes in the teaching of dance are also inevitable. Today, more flexible body ideals and fewer gender-specific steps convey a greater freedom and sense of empowerment for women, particularly in modern dance. In the future, even in ballet, more flexible teaching methods might emerge which incorporate psychological methods and concepts.

For example, small groups may be encouraged to work together before and after class, to focus on and help one another with specific steps or routines and to foster a true "esprit de corps." Or groups of three to five might be given responsibility for choreographing a piece, an experience to which too few dancers are exposed. These groups might also be encouraged to process their feelings about how they worked together and what they appreciated about the contributions from other members. Role reversal is a psycho-drama technique which may be used in dance class to better understand the essence of another's role and one's own impact in the performance. A temporary switch of dance roles might facilitate an understanding of the interdependency of those roles and clarify how differences in physical movements relate to different emotional responses. Male and female students might be encouraged to try each other's parts. This exercise also enables one to become more familiar with the masculine and feminine parts of one's own nature. (Teachers should expect to meet with some resistance when introducing non-traditional teaching methods, but their value will inevitably emerge.)

It is important that the dance teacher be aware of his/her unspoken message to students concerning diet and body image. Students will role-model a teacher who survives on diet soda and cigarettes. Attention to language is important as well. Students who are addressed as "men" and "women" rather than "boys" and "girls" will more likely act mature and assume adult responsibility. Most importantly, the teacher of dance teaches what it is to be an adult who loves dance. No matter what the subject, it is enthusiasm which determines the successful teacher. He/she must bring passion, not only to the work of dance, but also to the values of life which are inevitably imparted. A consciousness concerning ballet's metaphors is essential, for whatever can happen to the body can happen to the soul and psyche.

Ballet training may be a demanding discipline for a specified period of a woman's life, or it may be an absorbing pleasure that can last a lifetime. In an article expressing the value of dance, Armando R. Favazza, wrote, "While researchers continue their vast and complex studies of rhythms... which are intertwined with the experience of life, poets... continue their search for the perfect metaphor for life. To the latter, I would suggest that dance is as good as any."[4] As the search continues for the perfect metaphor for life, I would suggest that ballet is as good as any and that the meeting of ballet and psychology holds great promise for women.

Bibliography

Bakker, Frank. "Development of Personality in Dancers: A Longitudinal Study." *Personality and Individual Differences*, Vol. 12(7), 1991, pp. 671–681.

---

[4] Favazza, Armando R. "Ballet de Corps," *M.D., Mirror of Medicine*, October 1976, p. 180.

Barlou, Wilfred. *The Alexander Technique*. New York: Warner Books, 1973.

Brooks-Gunn, J.; Warren, Michelle P. and Hamilton, Linda H. "The Relation of Eating Problems and Amenorrhea in Ballet Dancers." *Medicine and Science in Sports and Exercise*, Vol. 19(1), February, 1987, pp. 41–44.

Favazza, Armando R. "Ballet de Corps." *M.D., Mirror of Medicine*. October, 1976, p. 180.

Frank, Marion Rudin, "Ballet as a Way of Knowing." Professional Training Program Developed for the Association of Humanistic Psychology, Eastern Regional Conference, Atlantic City, N.J., April 17, 1977.

Garfinkel, Paul. "Some Recent Observations on the Pathogenesis of Anorexia Nervosa." *Canadian Journal of Psychiatry*, Vol. 26(4), 1981, pp. 218–223.

Gargiulo, Janine; Attie, Ilanan; Brooks-Gunn, J. and Warren, Michelle. "Girls' Dating Behavior as a Function of Social Context and Maturation." *Developmental Psychology*, Vol. 23(5), 1987, pp. 730–737.

Hanna, Judith L. *Dance, Sex and Gender*. Chicago: University of Chicago Press, 1988.

Hawkins, Erick. *The Body Is a Clear Place and Other Statements on Dance*. Pennington: Princeton Book Co., 1992.

Hittleman, Richard L. *Yoga for Physical Fitness*. Englewood Cliffs: Prentice-Hall, 1964.

Kalliopuska, Mirja. "Empathy, Self-Esteem and Creativity Among Junior Ballet Dancers." *Perceptual and Motor Skills*, Vol. 69(3, Pt. 2), 1989, pp. 1227–1234.

Lancelot, Cynthia; Brooks-Gunn, Jeanne; Warren, Michelle P. and Newman, Denise L. "Comparison of DSM-III and DSM-III — R: Bulimia nervosa classifications for psychopathology and other eating behaviors." *International Journal of Eating Disorders*, Vol. 10(1), January, 1991, pp. 56–57.

Lee, Susan A. "Adult Development and Female Artists: Focus on the Ballet World." *Medical Problems of Performing Artists*, Vol. 4, 1 March, 1989, pp. 32–37.

Lowen, Alexander. *The Betrayal of the Body*. New York: Macmillan, 1967.

Lowenkopf, Eugene. "The Student Ballet Dancer and Anorexia." *Hillside Journal of Clinical Psychiatry*, Vol. 4(1), 1982, p. 53–54.

Reich, Wilhelm. *Discovery of the Orgone*. Trans. by Vincent R. Carfagno, N.Y.: Farrar, Straus & Giroux, 1973.

Vincent, L. M. *Competing with the Sylph: Dancers and the Pursuit of the Ideal Body Form*. Kansas City: Andrew and McNeil, 1979.

Walter, Sorell, ed. *The Dance Has Many Faces* (3rd ed.). Princeton: Chicago Review Press, Inc., 1992.

GOVERNANCE AND VISION
Brenda Way

Creating form is the choreographer's job and I think the organizations we make express our values as surely as our work — less poetically, less humorously perhaps but nonetheless clearly.

For me the political forces of the 1960's shaped my view of institution. Cooperative or collective on the one hand, independent feminist on the other. Limited resources did not limit imagination or ambition. We were creating alternatives. Invention and ingenuity replaced entitlement. The early collective structure of the company, Oberlin Dance Collective, which used everyone's energy and skills to make doing the work possible, gave way over time to a more conventional hierarchy but several assumptions remained: that two heads are better than one, that everyone must feel ownership, that the power of ideas rather than vested authority motivates the most effective action, that you make your own rules. The model of the extended family which the collectives of the '60's sought to establish (and which now of course has numerous corporate analogues) is still the fundamental shape of the company. Everyone has a primary function and a stake in and responsibility to the well-being of the whole.

There are basic human values that determine the structure of my organization and the style of leadership in it. They are my personal values and ones that I share with my co-director, KT Nelson, and which we look for or cultivate in everyone associated with the company from the board room to the studio: a taste for adventure and risk, initiative, a capacity for problem solving, straightforwardness, a good ear. No prima donna, business-naive nonsense here.

From the beginning in 1971, I wanted an institution that would, like an ideal family, provide the freedom for its members to grow up and change, to grow old even, that would provide opportunity, challenge and security. Somehow I see the structure as translucent. And there's a lot of passion in my notion of this ideal family. I have four children; there is nothing pallid in the word domestic.

I didn't want to tour year-round either. I don't choreograph best on the run, as the work springs from an engagement with life rather than removal from it. It was clear from the start that my nesting instinct would rule. The company would be home-based in some essential way. Indeed, all our major risks and initiatives supported this vision. We bought and built a home facility in San Francisco; we committed to paying year-round salaries rather than weekly wages for the dancers, to developing longer and more frequent home seasons instead of more elaborate productions or New York seasons. We set out to make a modern dance institution that limited touring to twelve weeks and focused on a major presence at home. The result is I can have a more mature company of dancers. They have time to become interesting artists as they can combine adulthood with their dance career. They have time to both understand and realize my movement idiom. They will follow me into the breach and they will challenge any crisis of courage I face on the way. As in the '60's, I worked for "wholeness" as a feminist goal; I pursue it now as the richest palette for artistic expression. They are not my children, they are professional artists whose abilities continue to inspire as well as serve the work. Being settled, they are free to explore.

The basic tenets are clear. The charge to the whole organization — board and staff and dancers — is how to forward this vision at any given point in time. How to hit the ground running — this is essentially an entrepreneurial undertaking and whether I see it as homesteading or the board sees it as a start-up company, it requires the same quick-footed, hard-headed, heart-felt responses. I fuel the momentum and have identified the destination, but we all forge the route. The board, staff and artists function in overlap — each with a primary charge but all attendant to the big picture. For Oberlin Dance Collective, governance and vision are one thing.

This essay was first presented for the Dance USA International Roundtable, June 1990.

A LION IN THE LAUNDROMAT
Sally Hess

Mindbody: The prologue I am writing, the words-that-come-before, is, so to speak, the spirit before the flesh. Let me enter the heart of the matter in descending paragraphs, slowly.

I would like to tell you how the one-woman, evening-length dance/story *Small Gate* was composed. I worked on it while living on the road, from 1986 to 1989, and continued to perform it on tour for the next year and a half.

The dance is divided into two sections by an intermission and a costume change. As the house lights go dark, the theater is filled with the roaring of lions. Some of the roars are throatwide into space, recorded in the African veldt. Some have a metallic ring to them; they were recorded in zoo cages. The roars spill out over each other, indicating a pride, but after fifteen seconds or so they come softer, further apart, and soon only one lion is heard. As the lights rise, the gaze focuses upstage center where I am kneeling with eyes closed, clenched fists. I follow the invisible lion's lead, and I too roar three times into space.

Now I begin to dance, then to speak and dance, early childhood memories, of where we lived:

> In my father's house were many chairs. Some for sitting, some to admire. Some gave comfort with their straightforward frumpiness.
> I learned early that chairs are friendly and supportive. Only once did I see a chair give up and crash under an inconsiderate bottom. She was deeply ashamed of having fallen apart in public and stayed hidden in the closet for weeks.
> We always assumed that it is the duty of the family to see that embattled chairs do not lose face. In return, chairs help the family maintain appearances.

And what we did:

> On rainy afternoons, on snowy afternoons, when friends came from foreign countries or on empty weekends when boredom hit the house with its screeching whines, my mother took us to the Museum of Natural History.

I was concerned with recapturing and making sense out of family configurations by "resensing," through the detail of moved words, some of the child's experiences. The segment titled Museum was suggested to me by a dream I had in South Carolina, wherein the glassed-off display case filled with wild animals blended the painted scenery into the dream-real countryside and I was able to pass freely from the diorama to the house where the museum director lived, a lovely cottage by the sea. Within the context of the dream, and upon waking, outside the dream context in writing, I explored the passage from fake to real and back again; what is trustworthy, what reasonable, what false, and of course, what is true... the child's perspective pointing up the short and oft-forgotten distance to adulthood and the fluidity of our several worlds. I remembered also with whom I lived:

> (Esther) *was our mother's helper, our dearest friend, our very own glamor-puss with a husband more handsome than Hopalong Cassidy. She wore her hair in a snood and red lipstick that always went too far in the wrong directions and stayed there.*
> *She was our beloved Esther and she would dance for us with her arms flapping and her back all round. She would sit on the edge of our beds, and tickle us beyond laughter into pure submission. In the quiet, holding the intensity of our eyes awake against our slowing bodies, she would sashay to the gray curtains that divided our room from the next, and draw them seductively across her darkening figure. Then she'd tear them open with a rebel yell and send us leaping lengthwise above our mattresses.*

And how the memories of bedtime "thorns and petals" danced me to the conclusion of the first half of *Small Gate*, along with the Prince, his Bride and a string of flung leaps to the grand waltz from *Der Rosenkavalier*.

In the first stage of development, the words seemed to appear on their own, with no definable physical locus, but almost at once I recognized the events as present sensations/feelings. In order to integrate my tales, in order to tell them properly, I had to retrieve them from the dream float and the accepted family prison frame, that is, move them below the mental system, incorporate them. While choreographing *Small Gate*, the effort was to ground the story-memories in the dancer's earth. I found that the activity of dance-making was making available a body of thought. Through it, I was enabled to offer the audience a body of history, however personal, however limited.

Sometimes, when I write, the words tumble forth without regard to meaning. What matters is number and weight of syllables, relation of vowel mass to the density and explosion of consonants. Out come words, a stream, a mob. Some shine brightly in the sentence while others shrink, but all serve the rhythm I am hearing in my head; sound precedes sense. It could be said fairly that the words hit the page dancing. Later on I ask myself in dismay, does this mean anything?

In the dance studio, but also lying in bed or standing on a subway platform, movement phrases, gestures, crowd into the mind and demand to be attended to, realized, embodied. I say, What would it look like if? What would it feel like if? And the hands or the feet indicate a fabulous twisting leap, a racing tangle of dancers or a serenity of arms. What's it about? Where does it go? And then, so what? I want both rhyme and reason, I want rhythm as well as flash. It is not a secret that mind is passion, body is craft. Sometimes. Which, when and why? The adventures intertwine as I think and write and dance.

Aged eight, I learned grammar through a technique known as "logical analysis," and it consisted, as I remember, in circling subjects with red pencil, objects in blue, green wavy underlines for relative clauses, and so on. That homework was quite fun, like coloring sense backwards into nonsense. Latin was taught the same way, to the same effect. I once eavesdropped on two teachers between classes to find out if they were speaking Latin to each other. I was convinced "one could," and that they were withholding the living language from their students as a punishment for being so unredeemably rowdy. But they were not, and Virgil, Ovid and Livy remained in their mind-coffins until I eventually dug them up into English. Performing *Small Gate*, then writing *Lion in the Laundromat*, became attempts to get low down and to come up clean, the lost language recalled through the vivifying action of a body of words dancing out the timetrip of my life.

The above thirteen paragraphs that you have just read, the introduction, are (I hope!) a fore-curtain bow to the great importance I (we) attach to the intellect's requirements of logic and coherence: no one wants to mutter about matter. And so to the next movement, into the body of the text.

Bodymind: *It's hot and I sit at my typewriter between the refrigerator and the sink. A green lamp on the table and the rotating fan on the floor, artificial wings swishing cool at my back every five seconds. Fridge busy in its deep, impersonal drone. Outside, the city cycles, cries of children and mothers at dusk, the junkies' calls take over the street and the sirens, ambulances, car alarms ring out with fear on a schedule of suffering, regulated at a rhythm beyond my ken.*

> Sometimes the world seems drenched in garbage, endlessly dirty. I travel. I move from town to town. From Charleston to New York by plane. From Paris to Brussels by train. Denver to Austin by bus.
> I dance in churches, schools, cafeterias, a modern-day troubadour. After I get off the bus and register in the motel (the Southland Inn, $12.50 a night), I have two urgent questions: where is the nearest supermarket, please? Where is the laundromat? There is no hot water in the

bathroom. There is chewing gum on the bedsheets. I travel with a spoon and a bowl. Tea and soap powder.

Today my courage leaves me, and with it, the strength to move, to roar. I feel endlessly hungry and dirty. I feel drenched in garbage. I am dragging my childhood behind me. Who will take care of me? Where is the laundromat, please? I turn towards my sister and reach for her hand. Once again, we are monkeys in our cage under the dining room table. Once more, we climb and plunge across the living room chairs, screaming high from the branches of our innocence.

As we stare at each other, we sigh, and grow older. I feel endlessly lonely and angry. I can hear the couple in the next room arguing, the truckers pulling out at 4 a.m., and the roosters, gone crazy, seem to crow all night long.

The journey I'm taking begins to repeat itself. Last year is the same as tomorrow. I'm traveling because I wanted to be a dancing troubadour, to tell my story, and maybe yours, as I lived and learned them, on the road. Instead I feel like a fake troubadour. One story equals another. Any other.

Am I a real dancer? Or is the dance fake too, and only the doubt, real?

I'm "home" now, in the NYC apartment that I've shared, occupied alone and as a couple, and sublet repeatedly for the last fifteen years. I spent the past four gone, on the road, making and presenting *Dancetales*, a series of one-woman shows. The most recent, *Small Gate*, was performed willynilly as the piece evolved, words and movement churning around each other, an attempt to dance my story while I lived it, of necessity falling behind myself, but always reaching for — hmm — a perfection of awareness, starbitten, as though I had to have been chomped on by the heavens in order to leave my safe place with no planned itinerary and no work more than a fortnight ahead.

I remember how much of this dance I wrote sitting in the laundromats of South Carolina: Shop 'n Wash. Wash 'n Wish. The Palace of Fluff 'n Fly. People who use public laundromats are poor. The clothes I pulled out of the machines were, like theirs, all-purpose raggedy. Too-thin sweatpants, shredded socks and miles of black elastic leotards. In Bishopville, a small town on the Greyhound bus route, the kids romping about while the rest of us stared bleakly at the suds 'n duds, brought me into conversation with their mothers and older sisters. "Where do you belong?" they asked. "Why are you here?" ("See! See! It's the dancing lady!"). I was, I told them, the "visiting artist" from the Arts Commission in Columbia. All week long I had been teaching, and I performed and invited the children to dance with me in the cafetorium with movement stories and some vigorous Sitting Up/Down rounds of Simon Says. Afterwards, the children asked me what it was like to be a dancer: did I mind sweating so much? How much money did I earn? "How old are you?" (giggle). One earnest group of girls took me aside after a lecture-demonstration to quiz me on why I married but had no children. Their frank curiosity touched me with its mix of concern and compassion. I haven't sought to clarify the whys of it, but have respected the sense of communion between women that arose unexpectedly among us. That was the McClellanville Public High School and I was the first dancer they'd ever seen live, off TV.

Must have been something about my size (six-foot-plus on half-toe) and the fact that actual performance presence provides a very different experience from the energyless tube. On the splintery stage in the cinderblock room filled with teenagers, I felt the intensity of their eyes so strong on me as I began to dance and to speak, increasing as I went further into the stories ("One afternoon in early summer I was walking down Broadway with my lover..."), that I changed my plan midway through the show, and instead of removing my spiked heels, large blue sweater, skirt and woolly warmups to dance in the girdle-like unitard (on a large and well-lit stage, it's called an "elegant costume"), kept on my thick and ungainly tights as a coverup. The stares were too raw for me to absorb, the one o'clock daylight too revealing as I felt the murmurs of the kids watching a real live and vitally displayed woman tippytoeing, jumping, headstanding, singing, telling of loves lost and lost again after brilliant sexy findings... I kept my clothes on. Later my sponsor and soon friend Regana, a counselor in the school, driving us back to her house, said, you were right to stay dressed, there was a lot of pressure in the room. It was, yes, a successful performance. As happened often, the questions went beyond the allotted time, and the students left the hall walking backwards. A few teachers stayed to shake my hand. After an hour and a half, I was exhausted. Proud. Energized. Deeply pleased.

Dancing my way from kindergartens to universities, I talked through the dances, danced while talking, talked without dancing and danced without talking. I told all about laundromats. One evening as I sat alone in a Coin Op Wash reading a copy of a ladies' magazine, I came across an article recounting the latest fad in teenage hazing: how you can prove your bravery. Get respect. This one is for daughters who do the family wash late at night: one girl gets into the dryer, her friends close the door and put coins in the slot, then set the temperature. They set it on low and begin moving it up as the machine turns the girl on its wheel. She's tumbled and raked by bobby pins, metal zippers, bracelets. How long can she take it? She knocks when she wants out, they open the door and grab her, laughing. The girl who stays the longest inside the burning cylinder, wins. If you can survive the scorching spin, you're in, and you know you can outlast the battering life will deal you. Your own body is the war trophy.

I watch my clothes tumbling and I feel sick and sad. I go make a long distance call to my friend Peggy in Colorado, where it's cool, mountains. I ask her if I can come dance in Colorado Springs and she says yes, you can dance here on our Thursdays at Noon program. People come to the theater with their lunches. It's free, the stage is beautiful, no lights, you dance for an hour, we'll pay you $100 and you can stay with me. Okay, I'll be there in ten days. I let the clothes dance, and go across the street to the bus station. Inquiry yields the news that a bus ticket from Charleston to the Springs costs $150. I'll have to teach several more master classes before I can get to Peggy.

I look back on the traveling and the story-writing and the figuring-out of steps in various studios — a plywood shack on the edge of a tidal marsh in the Carolina Low Country, a spacious loft fronting the Rockies — and I wonder how someone as timid as I could have undertaken such a journey. Desperation, end of a career, precipice of middle age, wasted life, last chance... Of course, being broke, too broke to pay the rent. One way of dealing with that kind of poverty is through the nomadic life. I don't think the troubadours made much money. I bet they laughed a lot.

It's getting darker outside and hotter. No rain yet.

There's a section in *Small Gate*, after intermission, which I call the Men Section. My friend Victor, who coached, poked, pleaded and pulled many of the stories out of me, said one day, "You're stuck. Why don't you write about something you already know? Why don't you write about men?" — Is this a joke? To find out, I went to the library at The New School, on Fifth Avenue and Fourteenth Street in Manhattan after rehearsal (I was in town at my friend Natalie's for a month's visit to the city with a performance of *Autobiography #72*, *Small Gate*'s predecessor). I watched men walk by, eating, smoking, arguing, being slobs and being dapper, shaven, busy, and so on. I wrote down what I saw. Then I wrote what I remembered, what I loved, missed and desired from men. Pages and pages' worth. Soon work began on the "text," with me on the road again, long distance phone calls to Victor and from, and letters filled with moans and rewrites. I didn't want anyone to see what a mess I had made of my life, yet it was here, in this rundown, the being left and left and left, no money, no men and in the end, no mystery. I discovered that I really wasn't "telling all." When I went further into personal history with encouragement to go deeper from Victor, the mystery reappeared. The spoken words began to call up their own movements. I started to block out arms and legs in space, diagonals, rolls: the breath gave texture to the words, the words found partners, a swindler hooked a piqué arabesque, a gigolo snapped into a passé and the metaphysicians in pony tails sautéed across the floor sparkling.

Then Victor came to the studio and the shaping began in earnest. Victor Byrd is an ultra-tall yogi from East Tennessee with a smile as broad as his mountain accent. Full of music, drama and street smarts, he could root out sentimentality but exploit schmaltz with the best of the farceurs. He pressed me relentlessly into focusing on process rather than outcome, to stay patiently in the moment — of writing, molding character, of performance. He required awareness and appreciation of outcome through exploration of content. It's a mighty thin plank that doesn't have two sides! He was never vague. Many rehearsals he left me in tears on the studio floor with a tape recorder and a notebook. Write more! I want it tomorrow! Choreograph! And his generous mouth would magically multiply the vowels of that Greek word and stretch it into an exotic challenge. He said to me, be real. Don't perform. Follow the rhythm of the sentence and don't break it up because of the movement. Sustaining the line brings speech into song. Let the emotion roll.

Again and again, the question of self-revelation came up, in the choreography and in the writing. How much Sally can I expose? How much do I want to look, to be seen? Why are you doing this? I suppose if there's one question I hear most in the dance world, it's that one. The answer is a sideswipe: "I'm gonna quit." There are others too, though. One, because I want to dance and I don't see any other way, any other choreographer, company, job. How large a person can pass through how small a gate? I was trying to squeeze between the bars, through the keyhole, but on bad days I just stood outside in the drizzle and waited for someone to open it for me. Why am I doing this? For the sake of the dancer. She wants to kick up her legs, leap and be still in the highlit space. Victor supplied another answer when he said bluntly, the point of this journey away from your safe (sic) New York apartment is not what is evolving in transit, not the bread and butter, and the point is not creativity. It's a Bildungsroman in the flesh, that is, *who* is emerging in transit. You are learning to pay attention.

March 21, '88, Amarillo, Texas, I wrote: "This is a journey of growing up and getting sick. The more ill I feel, the longer I will remember to look into this matter called life and death." *Small Gate* became an attempt at working towards awareness of what is, a learning to stay in touch with present action in its most vital functioning. The dance pushed me to an edge of exertion and through its elaboration and performance, I began to touch the people watching it. As in the reverse swing of the wave from shore to watermass, I was touched by them into feeling myself.

Well then, why are you doing this? I was sitting in the library of the College of Charleston, SC, blanked out after a day of rehearsal in the humid studio (did I get something done? NO!) and homesick. I like libraries. I spent the next four hours in the periodicals room, reading one issue after another of the *Village Voice*. I read six months of dance reviews, living through passionate envy to Schadenfreude to sympathetic joy as I went vicariously to concert after concert. Once I finished the *Voices*, I moved on to *Dance Magazine*. This time I ogled the photos, analyzing ankles, drinking in line and gorgeous poised/posed forms. I hadn't been to ballet class in half a year, and my cherished Maggie-tapes (from class with my teacher, Maggie Black) were beginning to distort from overuse. I thought about the people in Maggie's class and about pointe shoes, and how in some respects, ballet equals city-civilization. That's not only "Bayadère" at the Met, but "Aureole" at City Center. I felt like a country lump with my taped feet and only two costumes, a unitard and a pleated skirt. But hey, that was the premise: to dance anywhere for anyone. Boombox in my luggage, clothing for four seasons, take any space, no lights, I'm affordable, accommodating, full of words, the better to understand you, my dear! So stop comparing and enjoy the covergirls!

In the December '87 issue, there's an article by Mindy Aloff on the Bolshoi season in New York City: "In Petipa or Balanchine, concentration on technical finesse allows a dancer to show himself without a mask: to the audience if he chooses. The focus outside his own psyche is his performer's shield."[1] This bothered me and made sense. I tried to apply it to my own situation. I had left New York City in order to dance as much nonstop as body and time would permit. For that to be possible, I had to have a dance that could be seen under any conditions, a dance that I loved. I had also wanted to have a dance that allowed me to come into contact with the audience as a collection of individuals rather than as a dark mass across a great divide (apron, orchestra pit), to tear down the so-called fourth wall. I would be a troubadour, telling my stories and listening to the stories told me. People did indeed come to tell me their tales, after the show, sitting on the stage, or backstage, in coffee shops and in parking lots. Still, didn't the dance itself provide me with, if not a wall, then a mask, if not a mask, then enough energy to permit an awareness that who I was dancing, "myself" as a character, remained separate from "who I really am." One layer of self-revelation simply put me in touch with the next unrevealed levels. So in order to crumble more levels, I set myself challenges of a technical nature. Difficult balances, leaping while speaking, dancing the show in French, and most mindbending, dancing while telling the stories in both English and

---

[1] Aloff, Mindy. "Cossacks of Classicism, The Bolshoi Ballet — Metropolitan Opera House," NYC, June 30–July 18, 1987, *Dance Magazine*, December 1987, volume LXI, no. 12, p. 39.

French, switching languages from sentence to sentence. Since words phrase the movement, and the words in each language create a particular rhythm and therefore a particular style (personality) for the dancer, I felt as though mind and body were splitting apart, indeed as though the mind itself was cracking in two cultural directions like a rock under the strain of too rapid a temperature change. It was great fun for me and for the audience, francophiles and graduate students in Austin, Texas. The concert was organized by the Visiting Fellow from the University of Montpellier, my friend and translator, Jean Vache, and sponsored jointly by the French and English Literature Departments at the University, the Alliance Française and several local wine merchants.

I had been trying to strip away the performer's shield only to find that it was always moving parallel to me and therefore always beside me in my new place. But by using my resumé as a focus for the dance, while requiring also of myself that I concentrate on the form of line and verb, I made it possible, in small moments, to "show myself without a mask" as though the dancing person existed independently of the character "Me." While revealing the biographical soul, I had nonetheless maintained a measure of privacy for my psyche. The performer had used her own story as a brace, and so the private, introverted person was freed to dance. I came to understand that unmasking, on stage or off, is a process, self to other(s), self to self. At last, it involves a relinquishing of technique and biography, a level of devil-may-careness, that began with this travel.

Greyhound Bus terminal, Jacksonville, Florida, 2:30 am: arrival after several breakdowns on the highway. No air conditioning. We sit and wait for our connection to Miami. Suddenly a young man staggers in, eyeglasses askew, one lens shattered, blood streaming down his face. A woman approaches him and peers, "Can I help? What happened to you?" He turns and yells at her "What's it to you? What's it to you?" then rushes across the station and out, dripping blood onto the linoleum floor, followed by the night attendant, expressionless, mopping up the red trail in zigzag sweeps. Not a trace. Leaving not a trace.

It's okay to speak of the thinking body, and to vitalize it with the prongs of analysis, but I've wanted to activate the dancing mind, so that the sweep of grace can inform the ego's stronghold and let the phrases of motion and stillness impart rhythm to thoughts. So too, I hope for a reflective poise to flesh out physical movements when the intellect turns to shift its attention downward. I believe this is something that dancers can train to do; in fact, making dances is part of that training. Alignment, that is, active, centering awareness of relationship in the physical, helps engender a conscious inhabiting of the body/mind continuum. In my experience, it's a process that cannot be undertaken alone.

I sat in the studio for two hours, wishing I hadn't paid for three. Not an idea in my head nor a twitch from my bones. I was scrunched on my heels, tilting into an ankle stretch. All at once, the image of a roaring lion, flashing teeth and curling tongue, rushed up between the mirror and me. Inhaling fast, I dropped to my knees and answered the vision: I tensed my arms, opened my claws, stuck my tongue way down to my chin and rolled my eyes up as high as possible: aaaaaarrrrggghhhhgghh!!!! In that moment, my companion for the dance leaped towards me. I watched her approach from the mental sky, soft-padding over the blondwood floor of Douglas's loft. This lioness, the hunter who befriended me, gave me the throughline for the dance.

Now I shifted from my knees to a sideways squat on my heels with the left arm outstretched right and the right arm held overhead. Then slowly lowered the top arm, spreading fingers like sabers, to close them with the lower upreaching arm. Jaws clamping. I turned left, going into a crouch, arms on the floor, bottom up, stretching as though the shoulders would tug away from the lower back forever. Here, upside down, I remembered how I had once fishtailed myself on the tops of my feet and then flipped up straight from the head-down position. I enjoyed the topsyturvy and the quick motion from head dropped down to head-and-torso risen. I had taken my weight onto my hands and then rocked back onto the metatarsals, slight plié and then a fly up. The movement felt so good that I continued it into a sequence familiar from my 1987 long dance, *Autobiography #72*. I swooped into a fifth position relevé outside turn ending in arabesque, then let the lion play in silence. That took an hour and rehearsal was up. The next day I came back and went on, pleased to have found 45 seconds. I was delighted to be taking myself into the new dance on the toes of the old. I had become interested in leitmotif when reading Thomas Mann's *Tonio Kroger*. Mann uses certain key sentences throughout his story to offer the reader a thread with which to follow the characters as they change course. It now brought me a dancerly pleasure to repeat certain phrases not only in the body of the current dance where an onlooker could recognize the reappearances of movement material during the evening, but from one work to the next: three movement shapes were carried over from *Four Noble Attitudes* ('85) to *Autobiography #72*. *Small Gate* inherited shapes from '85 and from #72, with several new steps clustering around this old/less old group. So the dance spread out from here, following, following the lion's lead.

I'd like to prop open the fridge door and type inside it. How much exertion produces how much sweat? Weather matters.

One summer evening in New York, Margie Beals, a beautiful solo dancer, and I went out for a drink after a splendid dance concert. It happens sometimes that the choreography and the music are so blended, the dancing so full, that one can sense in one's own body for hours afterwards a lightness and an extension that grant the world buoyancy and clarity. We sat in a basement bar and talked about dancing. It's simple: Margie's passion falls into a form that is accurate to her devotion to the art: "My life is The Dance." And I? — well and etcetera: "I'm dancing my life."

Maybe I can't do this tonight in my kitchen, but I'll try, fingers zooming madly across the keyboard. Sometimes the carriage doesn't return well and oblivious to the page above me, I type eyes down, over and over the line I've just written. I'm seeing the line of kids in party dresses from Lower Lee Elementary; the angry motel clerk in Knoxville; a swollen board in Jeff's studio by the river... I'm remembering how sad and desperate I felt when I sensed myself getting further and further out of shape from the constant touring. All that stuff dancing itself out in my head while downstairs people buy bagels and yell at each other.

I'm trying to write how I danced then: awkwardly, on balance, painfully, wild-eyed, shrewd. How I made up then what I danced later, or how the movements made themselves up somewhere before "I" got involved with them, in a dream perhaps, or a forgotten meeting. Most of all, I think, I wanted to make something beautiful. A beautiful dance, a moral dance. Since beauty and morality require a climate of exchange, the solo work had to posit several of me and a severally responsive audience. We are such fragile creatures. Small Gate hoped to open us to one another before the farewell.

Despite the confusion I'm beginning to accept as the black backdrop to my clarity (isn't it the other way round, Sal?), I feel exhilarated. My task is, after all, quite simple. I need only present the various elements of the paradox, hold them fast and with trust: the dancing head tops the sitting body (which roils on inside, while the mental "activity" looks like a series of snapshots caught immobile by the typewriter), but in that instant, my shape-saving body passes riotously over her thought generator, laughing.

If I can't write my old dancing, if I lose power as the oft-told stories weigh me down and hopelessly out, still I can fashion some kind of triangle here, whose corners acutely support — sprout — solutions from the original opposites. Thinking the past onto paper jumps me above the felt here-and-now, and I triplecast myself into an eerie evolution, moving towards the apex of the three-shape, when I'm patient, of the tree-shape, dissolving into a new shape, paradox generating the next step, a glancing turn or a walk with a hand to heart. I come nose-up to a vision of Kenneth King's word/warmup: "The body," he writes, "tracks, paces, swings, pivots, gallops, darts, slashes, skewers (I think, look! He's really doing this!), scoops, scampers, vaults, jousts, rotates, balances, springs into the air." And then, "Dancing is immensity."[2]

---

[2] King, Kenneth, in Connie Kreemer, *Further Steps: Fifteen Choreographers on Modern Dance* (Harper & Row, 1987), p. 157.

I move from town to town. The lion becomes my traveling companion, and the guardian of my courage. I take strength from her instinct and her deliberate grace. Through her, I feel the world. She roars when she's trapped. She'll fight even if the battle is lost. I'm frightened now but I trust her power and her pain. I can leap beyond the stars and together, we'll roar ourselves free!

So look, here I am. I'm standing in the laundromat at 4:00 a.m. The electric light is harsh and the machines are noisy with my wet clothes.

Does the lion have a share in this kingdom?

Do you see — sometimes my lion disappears... when the hunter has missed the hunt and there's no more time left to kill...

I am sorting out loss and failure and folding them into my backpack. The bus leaves soon. I know I'm crying, for the children, for the dancer. I'm crying white tears, I'm crying sea salt, bleached tears in the laundromat, I am clean, I'm tumbling dry, white heat, red heart... I am, we are alive!

It's raining.

LOVE AND POWER AMONG THE CRITICS
Wendy Perron

In the mid seventies I was dancing, choreographing, and writing regularly for the Soho Weekly News. *I would sometimes go to a performance and sit with my friend Sally Banes, but I noticed that no other dancers and critics sat next to each other. I wondered why. It was perfectly natural for me to socialize with critics, especially since I was one (though my "beat" was performance art and not strictly dance).*

Now I understand the tension between artists and critics all too well. Having survived as a choreographer for over two decades, I'm keenly aware of the fragility of a dance career in a consumerist society. A single negative review can be financially and emotionally ruinous. Also damaging are critics who inflate their power at the expense of artists. My own personal example is the time Anna Kisselgoff, chief dance critic of the New York Times, *came to see my concert in 1991, and in her review included a definitive statement on my major strength and major weakness as a choreographer. I was astonished that she should adopt a tone of authority on my long-term career: she had not seen a concert of mine in 17 years.*

In 1991 I wrote a critique of critics in the Village Voice *in 1991 entitled "Beware the Egos of Critics."[1] I pointed out the human fallibility of critics and the destructiveness of their negligence and prejudice in the context of the marginal place dance holds in our economy. The following chapter was originally meant to be a sequel to that piece. But I eventually shifted into a more analytical mode and decided instead to examine the choices of three of our most renowned women critics.*

A big difference between critics and artists is this: critics have to show how much they know, and artists have to show how innocent they are. We look to critics for the final word on quality; we look to artists to come up with something *fresh*. As the painter Mark Rothko has said, the artist tries to see the world as if for the first time.

Critics and performers are polarized into a teacher-student relationship. Most critics assume an authoritative tone and display opinions that affect the psychical and economic lives of artists. Artists are vulnerable in the making

---

[1] *Village Voice*, April 9, 1991, p. 92.

and showing of their work. Jill Johnston said in 1981 about her position as dance critic in the '60s, "The power I wielded placed me in a diametric relation to individuals and discrete groups."[2] Although critics and artists come in all genders, I would say that the authoritative tone of the critic versus the vulnerability of the artist, and the critic's presumption of "objectivity" versus the "intuition" of the artist, echo a classic male-female opposition.

Critics have a choice, however subliminal, whether to challenge this polarization or to be governed by it. I will discuss the work of three women critics whose writing reflects their choices. They are Jill Johnston, who wrote for the *Village Voice* in the sixties and has since written several memoirs and novels; Deborah Jowitt, who has been writing for the *Village Voice* for twenty-odd years and has published several books on dance; and Anna Kisselgoff, who is the chief dance critic for the *New York Times*. Of these women, the first defied the polarity; the second attempts to heal it; and the third plays into it.

Both Johnston and Jowitt have been dancers themselves, and still felt or feel the connection to dance as they wrote or write. Johnston used this connection to bridge the gap between the performers and herself. In 1981, she wrote,

> As a critic I never adopted a removed or detached stance. I saw no reason why my role as critic should preclude activities involving those I criticized…. I was naturally attracted to the people whose work I admired, and they in turn found it amusing or useful to reciprocate my interest or initiate familiarities. I was enamored of the artists and continually found opportunities for blurring the boundaries between us.[3]

Her openness and her excitement brought her to the point of identifying with the dancers. It wasn't much of a stretch since as a dancer she had felt a little lost until the Judson explosion of the early sixties presented her with the opportunity to blow the lid off. (In fact, in an article she wrote in *Dance Observer* in 1955, she virtually predicted the Judson rebellion.[4]) The Judson project was to defy expectation, and Johnston, now no longer a dancer but a writer, joined enthusiastically in this effort. Not only in her printed column but also in her personal life, she defied expectations of herself as a writer,

---

[2] Johnston, Jill. "A Criticism of Outrage." *Judson Dance Theater: 1962–1966*, catalogue for an exhibit organized by the Bennington College Judson Project, 1981.

[3] Ibid.

[4] Banes, Sally. "Signaling Through the Flames," in *Writing Dancing in the Age of Postmodernism*, Wesleyan University Press 1994, originally printed in *New Performance*, 2/1, 1980.

a woman, and a critic. She became close with some of the dancers and organized concerts of her own; and when she spoke on public panels or went to art parties she performed outrageous acts that identified her with the free-wheeling Judson group.

Carol Gilligan, in her ground-breaking book *In a Different Voice,* holds that a woman's desire to merge is no less mature and complete than a man's desire to separate. Our culture teaches us to judge maturity by independence and "objectivity." Johnston's need to merge made "objectivity" impossible (it always is anyway) and it glorified subjectivity in a womanly way. Her style wasn't particularly respected outside the avant garde, but now we can see that she gave us some of the best critical writing on the planet. Her writing was giddy, provocative and heroic and it got a rhythm going. There's no dance criticism that's more fun to read than her anthology *Marmalade Me.* And there's no other dance criticism that captures the headiness of the moment when modern dance imploded into post-modern dance.

The peak of her storm of merging came with her review of an outdoor performance by Robert Whitman in 1966. She describes that moment: "It was written in a gushing ten minutes or so and in the eye of my second tornadic transformation of consciousness when associations were rampant and happily I was unable to distinguish myself and dreams from the dream of those events in the swamp."[5]

Her sense of merging, her confusion of identity, her living at a feverish pitch could not go on indefinitely. Shortly after writing the piece on the swamp event, her column devolved into an agitated idiosyncratic confessional in radical voice. She was later institutionalized, an experience which she later viewed as a further opening out.

If you look at the word choice in these two passages — "attracted," "enamored," "gushing" — or if you remember the wild pungency of the reviews collected in *Marmalade Me,* you can view Johnston as a woman falling in love. That she put her feverishness and impulsiveness at the center of her writing was unusual. But being in love with performers or artists is not unusual. It is clear in the writing of the legendary critic Edwin Denby, for instance, that he too was in love when he took up the pen in the service of dance. Always a gentle eros clung to his words. But Denby, being a gentleman, held his distance from the dancers and the dance world. In Johnston's case, her infatuation was more brazen and it was this energy that drove her to defy the critic-performer polarization.

---

[5] Johnston, Jill. *Marmalade Me.* New York: E. P. Dutton & Co., Inc. 1971, Preface.

In more recent statements, Johnston, even at her current distance from the downtown dance community, continues her interest in unifying critics and performers:

> *Reviewers and choreographers should be part of a mutually cooperative community, working together to help enlighten audiences, rather than the antagonists they tend to be.... Choreography itself may be in advance of other mediums, and it isn't getting the coverage it deserves. The world isn't finding out just how advanced it is.[6]*

The world isn't finding out. Johnston's idea of cooperative community is a vision for truly advancing the art of dance. Can we rise to the occasion? One of the few people who actively promote this vision is the next critic I will discuss.

Deborah Jowitt is another critic whose love for dance is palpable. But her love is a slow burning glow, capable of sustaining unconditional love. She is warm and gentle even when she scolds. Like a mother more concerned with the spiritual well-being of her children than with outward signs of success, she values how deeply we look into ourselves and measures us by our own past achievements. She is so responsive to the feelings of artists that she once used her column to publicly apologize to choreographer Marta Renzi. Three months before, she had written a mostly negative review and then, after mulling it over for the summer, wrote a self-correcting review of her own review, including six self-imposed precautions for writing criticism. After publishing this, she received responses from many quarters of the dance community. Later, she wrote, "Most of the responses mentioned my 'courage' in exposing myself. I didn't think I was being particularly courageous, although it crossed my mind that fellow critics might think me mawkish or wonder what good could come of undermining my own authority."[7]

For me, it's chilling to hear that Deborah Jowitt, whose grandeur as a critic is well known, has to consider the possibility that other critics would not approve of her exposing her own doubts. It sounds like a bunch of teachers worrying that their image of all-knowingness might get sullied by rebellious kids. Like Johnston, Jowitt is so open to identifying with the performer that sometimes a nice confusion settles in. In a review of me in 1980, she concludes by writing, "At one point I wondered if she had tears in her eyes, and discovered that I was the one who did."[8]

---

[6] "How Dance Artists & Critics Define Dance as Political." *Movement Research Performance Journal.* #3, Fall, 1991.

[7] Jowitt, Deborah. "'View and Re-View' Reviewed." *Dance Critics' Association Newsletter*, Winter 1986.

[8] Jowitt, Deborah. "How Quick Is the Eye." *Village Voice.* March 3, 1980.

One of the classic responsibilities of the critic is to situate a given artist within a hierarchy, from insignificant to great. Jowitt refuses to do this. She uses metaphors to make vivid an artist's contribution rather than rate him or her within a hierarchy. Describing Merce Cunningham's work in 1986, she wrote, "He puts movements together… and life is revealed the way a small whirlpool is created when you turn on a faucet: you couldn't have made that, yet had you not turned the faucet on, it couldn't have appeared."[9]

Not all women critics are interested in bridging the gap or healing the wounds of the conflict between critics and artists. Many accept the power that comes with the byline unquestioningly. That's fine; I'm all for women feeling powerful. But their power tends to be at the expense of artists and to play into the conventional consumerist power structure. Critics want to exercise their power by discovering talent and influencing people to buy tickets. "I talk and people listen" is the gross equivalent of this effort.

The most powerful critic at the most powerful publication reviews the most powerful companies. I don't think Anna Kisselgoff actively seeks power. She is not a mover and shaker in the dance world. Although she has championed certain choreographers, e.g., Molissa Fenley and William Forsythe, she is not an advocate in the tradition of John Martin, who, writing for the New York *Times* in the forties, introduced Martha Graham and Doris Humphrey to an uninformed public and followed their progress with loving detail. Rather she acquiesces to all expectation. She is supposed to 1) sound like an expert, 2) sound "objective," 3) plump up the most established companies and certain visiting companies, and 4) give the readers the signal of whether or not a show is worth their money. These things she does faithfully.

In accomplishing the first and second goals above, Kisselgoff relies on what Carol Gilligan calls the male mode of maturity: independence, separateness, isolation. Her writing style is detached and authoritative. She diligently provides an accurate historical context and she articulates her admiration well enough. Her reviews are balanced and she resists the lusty negativism of some of her colleagues at other publications. What is missing, though, is any sense that she is deeply affected by what she sees. She seems to me to be invulnerable to the art, invulnerable to the beauty that dance can create or reveal. She believes too completely in her hard-earned "objectivity."

The notion of objectivity in criticism has long been open to debate. No one questioned this assumption more passionately than Oscar Wilde. In his essay "The Critic As Artist" written in 1890, he celebrates the inevitable subjectivity of a critic: "It is only by intensifying his own personality that the

---

[9] Jowitt, Deborah. *Village Voice* dance review, 1987.

critic can interpret the personality and work of others, and the more strongly this personality enters into the interpretation the more real the interpretation becomes, the more satisfying, the more convincing, and the more true."[10] (He and Jill Johnston would have been great pals.) Wilde viewed the critic-artist split as an arbitrary one. He felt that the critic has some of the artist in him or her and, conversely, the artist has some of the critic in her or him: "Without the critical faculty, there is no artistic creation at all, worthy of the name.... The critical faculty invents fresh forms. The tendency of creation is to repeat itself. It is to the critical instinct that we owe each new school that springs up, each new mould that art finds ready to its hand."[11]

As I write this, the latest science news brings us the crossing over of male and female hormones: "Physicians and scientists... have begun to consider the role of so-called male hormones on the making of a female."[12] Apparently women are born with a good dose of testosterone and men with estrogen. (Carl Jung justified his concept of the anima and animus on just this sort of crossover.) One could imagine the Chinese yin-yang symbol, with each half containing a piece of its opposite. This is exactly the kind of overlap between the artist and critic of Wilde's vision. I propose a similar, but more deliberate, overlap between critics and choreographers: choreographers should write a little and critics should choreograph a little. Then perhaps dance artists could learn to apply the critical ability more assertively in their choreography, and critics could develop a greater understanding of the vast challenge of a choreographer — to create something from nothing. These new skills would foster more understanding within our community, and begin to bring about the kind of enlightened advocacy that Johnston envisioned and Jowitt embodies.

---

[10] Ellman, Richard, ed. "The Critic as Artist." *The Artist as Critic*. New York: Vintage Books, 1968.

[11] Ibid.

[12] Angier, Natalie. "Male Hormone Molds Women, Too, in Mind and Body." New York *Times*, March 5, 1994.

PART VIII

USING THE KNOWLEDGE

This section presents images of the woman dancer in particular cultures. Kariamu Welsh Asante recounts the empowering, transformative, spiritual nature of African dance in its affirmation of a woman's significance as an individual and as a member of a community in "Sensuality and Sexuality as Dual Unity in African Dance." Susan B. Glazer's "Political Issues of Jawole Willa Jo Zollar, Artist/Activist" highlights the political history and contemporary reality of an African American choreographer. Ninotchka Bennahum in "Seduction in Andalusian Flamenco" examines the exchanges of gestures and gazes in a live performance. Ananya Chatterjea calls for change in contemporary Indian dance in "How Can the Brown, Subaltern Feminist Speak?" and finally, Yunyu Wang describes Chinese traditional dance heritage as well as the current status of dance in Taiwan in "Sorceress, Imperial Concubine and Dancing Girl."

SENSUALITY AND SEXUALITY AS DUAL UNITY IN AFRICAN DANCE
Kariamu Welsh Asante

Many historians and critics have interpreted the role of women in African dance as erotic, exotic and sexually suggestive. Upon examination of selected "texts" in African societies, it is my aim to reconceptualize the role that female dancers play, both as participant and symbol. The empowering, transformative nature of African dance is spiritual and embodies a female principle. Women in African dance are expressed symbols of the natural and the supernatural and as such their bodies are instruments both rhythmically and visually as part of a holistic homily in which the female is an integrated, interrelated part of a cosmic unity.

The aesthetic and cultural illusion that women weave in African dance is artistic and functional, creating vehicles of personal and collective statements that are generational, historical and creative. This celebration of the self, the female body and all its particularisms is an affirmation of community. It is from this perspective that the female in African dance must be understood. This chapter explores images of African and African American women in dance within a womanist/Afrocentric aesthetic.

It is not an accident of history or an aesthetic anomaly that women in African dance are most often projected as bare-breasted and dancing in ecstatic frenzy. The cultural legacy that these images have spawned continues to determine and prescribe how African women are defined. The concept of the "noble savage" leads Africans and their descendants to be on the aesthetic and religious defensive. The African male still labors under the colonial cultural legacy that depicts him as hypersexual, extra physical and super strong. The African woman, being both African and female, was the source of immediate scorn and fascination from European societies that were both anti-African and sexist.

African dance provides a means through which we can examine the roles that women perform and how roles of women were misinterpreted to create an image that is antithetical and incongruous to traditional African societies. By traditional African societies (TAS), I mean pre-colonial, ancestral centered, land revered, polygamous societies which are distinguishable from one another by language, specific customs, dress and geography.

Key among the TAS is the holistic integration of functions of phenomena, social and sacred and natural and supernatural, and the attitude towards the body. Scholar Robert Farris Thompson defines the African aesthetic as "an intellectual mode of energy that is only operative when used" (Thompson, 1975). The body in TAS according to Thompson is represented by stance, position and movement. Matriarchal art, according to Heide Gottner-Abendroth, is independent of the fictional and is therefore not "art" in the patriarchal sense nor does it require special technical know-how. It is rather the ability to shape life and to change it: it is energy, life and drive towards the aestheticisation of society. It can never be divorced from complex social action because it is the center of that action (Gottner-Abendroth, 1987: 84).

If we are able to recontextualize culture, art and dance from an African-centered perspective, we are then closer to understanding the inclusive aspects of traditional African dance and the image of women in those dances. It is important, therefore, to acknowledge a broad definition of dance. Ethnologist Joanne Kealiinohomoku: "Dance is a transient mode of expression, performed in a given form and style by the human body moving in space. Dance occurs through purposely selected and controlled rhythmic movements: the resulting phenomenon is recognized as dance both by the performer and the observing members of a given group "(Kealiinohomoku, 1983: 541).

Body as Text

Sylvia Boone, an art historian, in *Radiance from the Waters* describes how young women in Mende societies have their breasts admired and even touched by both men and women. This demonstrates recognition of a woman's function as life giver, nourisher, and nurturer. In the Mende language as in most African languages, the word for beautiful is the same as the word for good. When the breasts of these young girls are admired, it is collective affirmation of the good these breasts will bring to the community. Procreation is the most significant phenomenon in TAS and because the female body is the divine vessel by which the child comes, the woman is accorded much attention and interest that focuses on her physical person.

This is not to be confused with the Western male's obsession with the breast. This preoccupation with the breasts leads to the objectification of the female body. In Western societies, function actually becomes an inconvenience. Breast feeding, while functional, is viewed as a detriment to the aesthetic beauty of the breast. So function is devalued and form is overvalued and the dichotomy is played out on the woman's body. Feminist Susan Brownmiller discusses the function of the female breast in the following passage: "Breasts are the most pronounced and variable aspect of the female anatomy, and although their function is fundamentally reproductive, to nourish the young with milk, it is their emblematic prominence and intrinsic vulnerability that makes them the chief badge of gender. Breasts command attention, yet they are pliable and soft, offering warmth and succor close to the heart. Breasts seem possessed by an independent momentum, an autonomous bob and sway that forever reminds and surprises. Breasts may be large or small, droopy or firm, excitable or impassive, and variably sensitive to hormonal change, swelling in pleasure or in discomfort or pain. Breasts are an element of human beauty." (Brownmiller, 1984: 41).

The African woman's physical beauty may be extolled in praise poetry or "oriki," but the true test of her worth lies in her ability to procreate. The female torso is often proportionally large when depicted in African sculpture. The breasts are full and the belly round, both images providing commentary on the ideal state of womanhood. As Brownmiller suggests: "An uptilted cup shape is idealized in Western art, for high round breasts are associated with youth. A strikingly different tradition, however, is evident in celebrating a figure whose breasts point downward sharply. A sharp downward thrust also typifies New Guinea and the Kwa Kluth carvings" (Brownmiller, 1984: 42). In TAS femaleness is equated with motherhood. While this equation may disturb contemporary Western women, it is still operative for contemporary African women.

The dances of Africa reflect relationships between individuals and society and between male and female. Traditional African dance is a microcosm of society reflecting a holism that unites and binds the community (Welsh Asante, 1985). Traditional dance is significant because the belief systems operative in traditional customs permit specific attitudes and cultural behaviors towards women. These attitudes manifest themselves in the examination of all phenomena, natural and supernatural.

A context for the examination of the image of women in African dance must focus on perceptions and stereotypes from within the African community and from without. Traditionally, the woman's body in Africa was neither an enemy nor sinful. The female body was an affirmation of the life force: its paramount function was child bearing. Far from being seen as separate components, aesthetics, sexual pleasure, meaning, and enhancement were equally relevant/recognized. No individual body part became a fetish or an object to be focused on. Attributes were appreciated in a mode harmonious with traditional belief systems.

How do we reconcile the image of the bare-breasted female dancing with the Western concept of civilization? How does the image of the female in African dance support the stereotype of eroticism and sexuality in the African female?

It is interesting that in the dance world many of these attitudes are continued even as various disciplines rebel and attempt to redefine themselves in attempts to take a more holistic approach toward the body. The baring of the breasts alone in African cultures cannot take full credit for confusing the Western world.

Nudity or partial nudity in Western society carries with it an attitude of eroticism, sin and primitiveness. In Western societies men are not considered nude if their chests are bare; women are. In many traditional African societies, a loin cloth can suffice for men and women as full clothing. In other societies, women wear skins or lapas and men may wear pants. In Africa, age is the factor that determines when a young girl begins to cover herself. Usually she is free to cover only her genitals until she reaches the age that she would undergo the rites of passage. The rites of passage mark the perspective from which the female is viewed at the time of transition into womanhood that is synonymous with marriage and motherhood.

In Africa the body is ontologically ordered: God, Spirit, Man, Animals and Inanimate Objects. Man is both mind and body and the traditional African celebrates his/her body as an expressed symbol of "Muntu" (humanbeingness). (Jahn, 1972). The body can be diseased, possessed, destroyed or hexed but the body as vessel is not the originator of evil, although evil or harm can enter it. No one part of the body implicitly by birth or being represents evil.

Because the breasts move when one dances and because African dance is vigorous, the movement of the breasts is pronounced. Missionaries, traders and explorers all focused on the breasts as if they were intrinsic icons. The missionaries and explorers transposed and imposed their axiological European belief systems onto the bodies of African women. This imposition led to interpretation, distortion and ultimately documentation that further cemented the image of the African women in dance as "sexual" and "exotic." Any distinction between sexuality and sensuality has to be contextualized. The correlation of African women solely with sexuality is offensive and inaccurate. By making this connection, one implies that African women are somehow more sexual than other women and that their sexuality lends to eroticism. Eroticism is not an evil in most traditional African societies and the equation of sex as erotic is only a statement of an obvious fact.

Indeed it is, as Ikot p'Bitek so poetically states in "Song of Lawino" about the African body that dances:

> *It is danced in broad daylight*
> *In the open*
> *You cannot hide anything*
> *Bad stomachs that have swollen*
> *Skin diseases on the buttocks*
> *Small breasts that have just emerged*
> *And large ones full of boiling milk,*
> *Are clearly seen in the arena*
> *Breasts that are tired*
> *And are about to fall*
> *Weak and bony chests of*
> *weaklings*
> *Strong Lion chests*
> *Large scars on the thighs*
> *Beautiful tatoos below the belly*
> *button*
> *Tattoos that have become scores*
> *on the chest*
>
> *All parts of the body*
> *Are shown in the arena*
> *Health and liveliness*
> *Are shown in the arena!*
>   *(p'Bitek, 1966: 43)*

The body as text in TAS helps to maintain the moral border of the community. It can be read as sexual but not exclusively and not obsessively so. Sexuality is accounted for and incorporated into the dances of flirtation, courtship, marriage and fertility. Male members of the Nuba Tira ethnic group are described by Nadel as dancing to attract the attention of the females. In this dance, male pride and sexual stimuli are inextricably mixed. By means of these self-praises the young men try to attract the attention of girls, who, standing in the center of the ring formed by young men, will pick out one or the other, and throw themselves against the partners they have chosen (Nadel, 1947: 248).

Judith Lynne Hanna cites a description of a sexual dance that promotes fertility. "Sandawe men and women in Tanzania dance by moonlight in the erotic 'phek'umo' rites to promote fertility." She goes on to cite Ten Raa, who describes the dance as "begun by women who go in circles. They carry their arms high in a stance which is said to represent the horns of the moon, and at the same time also the horns of game animals and cattle. The women select their partners from among the opposing row of men by dancing in front of them with suggestive motions. The selected partners then come forward and begin to dance in the same manner as the women do facing them all of the time. The women entice the men away in a southerly direction and as the dance warms up, the movements become more and more erotic, some of them turn around and gather up their gamens, to expose their buttocks to the men... (Ten Raa, 1969: 38). According to Hanna, "dancing belongs to the repertoire of resources for sex role scripting, which educates young and old alike about what it means to be a man or woman" (Hanna, 1988: 47).

The Western tendency to perceive the body as an object collides with African interpretations of both dance and gender. Feminine and masculine qualities are manifested as complementary dualities, not as opposing forces. In African societies male and female are interconnected, interrelated and interdependent. Thompson's discussion of the image of a person can be generalized for most of Africa. He states: "The image of a person... in Mali or East Africa therefore is an expression of aesthetic or spiritual principles. Such principles explain in part the mid-point mimesis which we find virtually everywhere within the African aesthetic universe" (Thompson, 1974: 43).

Thompson's concept of "mid-point mimesis" complements Richards's concept of "Dual Unity" in that they represent harmonious and humanizing functions of the society (Richards, 1989). Mid-point mimesis is defined by Thompson as "balance in the mode of representing visual reality." He defines the African aesthetic as such a mediating force. The person of moral perfection/the balanced person is the subject of African art and dance, not the representation of the individual (Thompson, 1974: 27). It follows from this that image in TAS is personal but not individualized.

Conclusion

In traditional African societies, birth, rites of passage, harvest, recreation and death are all commemorated through dance. The Western body as individual possession and therefore individual property contradicts the African concept of body as community. The "invented body" of the African woman is a body perceived by Calvinist Puritanical eyes. It is an "invented body" thrown back onto the African continent in order to have the invention perpetuated and made iconic. The "exotic" of Europe's Age of Reason is still an "exotic" today in the European American "Age of Technology." By equating primitiveness and nudity, Africa, her dances and her women, are consigned to a place called "primitive" and a time called the past.

The image of women in African dance, although rigidly divided by gender in performance, reflects a primordial belief in a cosmic order. Sexuality and sensuality are part of this order; both are acknowledged as natural phenomena. Historically, there has been a misdirected emphasis on sexuality as applied to African women in general and, in particular, to their dancing. Images taken out of context, isolated and objectified make fetishes out of male and female bodies and lead to misinterpretations of the humanistic and holistic intent of African dance.

Bibliography

Gottner-Abendroth, Heide in Ecker, Gisela, ed. *Nine Principles of Feminist Aesthetics*. Boston: Beacon Press, 1985.

Birdwhistell, Ray. *Kinesics and Context*. Philadelphia: University of Pennsylvania Press, 1970.

Boone, Sylvia. *Radiance from the Waters*. New Haven: Yale University Press, 1986.

Brownmiller, Susan. *Femininity*. New York: Ballantine Books, 1984.

Daly, Ann. "Classical Ballet: A Discourse of Difference." *Women and Performance: A Journal of Feminist Theory*, Vol. 3 No. 2, 1987.

Hanna, Judith Lynn. *Dance, Sex and Gender*. Chicago: University of Chicago Press, 1988.

Kealiinohomoku, Joanne. "An Anthropologist Looks at Ballet as a Form of Ethnic Dance." *What Is Dance?*, Copeland, Roger and Cohen, Marshall, eds. New York/Oxford: Oxford University Press, 1983.

Lacan, Jacques. "The Agency of the Letter in the Unconscious or Reason Since Freud." *Ecrits, A Selection*, translated by Alan Sheridan. New York: W. W. Norton and Company, 1977.

Nadel, S. F. *The Nuba: An Anthropological Study of the Hill Tribes in Kordofan*. London: Oxford University Press, 1947.

Sjoo, Monica and Mor, Barbara. *The Great Cosmic Mother*. San Francisco: Harper & Row, 1987.

Pasteur, Alfred and Toldson, Ivory. *Roots of Soul*. New York: Anchor Press, 1982.

Richards, Dona. *Let the Circle Be Unbroken*. New York: 1989.

Thompson, Robert Farris. *African Art in Motion*. Los Angeles: University of California Press, 1974.

Welsh Asante, Kariamu. "Commonalities in African Dance." *African Culture: Rhythms of Unity*, edited by Asante, Molefi Kete and Welsh Asante, Kariamu. Westport, Conn: Greenwood Press, 1985.

POLITICAL ISSUES OF JAWOLE WILLA JO ZOLLAR, ARTIST/ACTIVIST
Susan B. Glazer

Jawole Willa Jo Zollar is the artistic director of Urban Bush Women, an all-woman dance/theater company that presents work inspired by contemporary social, political and feminist issues, folklore and the religious and cultural traditions of the African diaspora. Ms Zollar grew up in an America that forced her to deal with victimization and oppression. She sees racism as an institutionalized aspect of society and culture that affects all African Americans. It is her mission as an artist and as an activist to overcome the destructive effects of racism, sexism and homophobia.

The impetus for Ms. Zollar's work has always been based in research and personal history. Yet, concurrent with the development of her creative work for the concert stage, her interest in exploring the creative and political aspects of popular culture has grown. She and her company have developed a model for intensive community engagements that use culture as a catalyst for social change (New Orleans, 1992; Brazil and Philadelphia, 1993; Miami, 1995). The model involves long-term residencies designed to enrich and further an empowerment process already under way in the sponsoring community. The curriculum for these community engagements is based on progressive and interactive educational lesson plans, centered around movement, music, writing, theater, media, and elements of the company's creative method of collaboration, improvisation, research and discussion. History and culture are the foundations for the development of critical analysis. The goal ultimately is to effect profound changes in individuals and in neighborhoods through the verbal and non-verbal power of dance.

SG: You were raised in Kansas City, Missouri in the 1950's. Was dance part of your upbringing?
JZ: I started dancing in a dancing school at the age of seven. My mother had been a dancer. She had stopped by the time I was born but she told me stories about her life in vaudeville and occasionally showed me movements from her shows. Dance was something that was completely around me and my sister; it was a natural part of my neighborhood. In school, I was in drill team, I ran track. Dance was a natural part of my life. As a kid, I stayed to myself and made up dances in my head. I always felt that I was guarding something more by moving.

SG: Did you perform in high school?

JZ: Oh yes, we danced in nightclubs, where we always worked with a live band. The standard for that time was that you could say, 'I want to hear this song and please play it at this tempo and I want the breaks here: eight bars before the roll' and so on. I worked with drums and drummers from the beginning. Listening to hear how the drum sounded was a very natural part of my life. My mother had also been a musician, a jazz singer, and she played the piano so we would have jam sessions at our house. We would go to the musicians local in Kansas City. I accepted this as my world and I never thought there was anything spectacular or wonderful about it.

SG: Were music and dance a natural part of your entire community?

JZ: At that time, Kansas City was segregated, so the community I grew up in was all black and the art forms within it were all black. The way that the cheerleaders did their cheers was the black style. The drill team was a different style too. There was only one white person in my high school. So in my world were church picnics, songs, dance from the African American tradition. During college Milton Myers formed a dance group called "Black Exodus" which included a gospel choir. I was part of this group of artists who reacted to the social movement of that time. Much of our work was about Black liberation.

SG: Did you have any mentors along the way?

JZ: Joseph Stevenson, who had been a student of Katherine Dunham, was my first teacher. He encouraged me to develop my own individual style that stemmed from the tap dance tradition. If you saw a step that someone else had done, you couldn't just steal that step — you had to take it and make it your own, so, whatever you started from, in terms of borrowing, the finished step couldn't look like an imitation of that person. It had to be your own thing. This concept has shaped all my thinking about what I do. Then my first modern dance teacher in college, Winifred Widener, looked at my body, which was not academically trained despite years in dancing school — my legs didn't go up high, my feet didn't point — but she saw my soul and was very encouraging to me as a choreographer. She opened my mind to the many possibilities of choreography.

SG: When did you discover your choreographic voice?

JZ: At Florida State University, I was in graduate school and was introduced to Artaud and the theater of the absurd and I realized that I wanted a theater that was not the larger-than-life Graham thing but was the simple and the familiar, that challenged you, that had an impact, but was a smaller base of movement. In one single concert, I did two pieces. One was a traditional African funga which had an all-Black cast. It was African. And I did another piece called "Crossings" which coincidentally ended up having an all-white cast. The piece was very abstract, very expressionistic and very minimal. It was about my mother's death. And people had a hard time believing that I had done both dances because they were so completely different. Some people went so far as to say, 'are you trying to say that the African Black world is happy and joyous and that the White world is depressed and dying'?

SG: Were you insulted by the racial implications?
JZ: Absolutely. I approach each work by its own grace, by its own statement; each work has its own individual style as you do as a dancer. One work may be more formal, another work may be relaxed; one may be linear, another completely nonlinear. I have never viewed this as a contradiction but that's when I understood that other people viewed it as a contradiction. Why not look at different expressions of ideas? When I moved to New York I wanted to integrate my political concerns, my choreographic concerns, my concerns about movement, my concerns with spirituality. At any given time, the expression may predominate in one form or another, but as a whole they are in unity. I think this idea comes directly from the feminist spirituality movement. The idea of not fragmenting the self in the way that many women feel, you're a housewife, you're a mother.

SG: How do your personal politics affect your choice of material?
JZ: I have been involved in radical political organizations for years. There is a didactic thinking that sometimes comes with that. I maintain the values and I am intensely interested in how we move through the complexities of life.

SG: Could you characterize a type of woman you would like to work with?
JZ: I don't ever want to put a dancer in a unitard because of the types of bodies that I work with. My work is not line focused. I prefer to look at emotional lines and their impact. I like women who are natural movers and I look for dancers to bring the power of their moves to performance. I also do not want to see a woman as a 'bitch,' a 'whore' or any other characterization where you so often have seen women unless there is a complex dynamic present. For a long time I hated ballet and I didn't want to go to ballet class because I felt philosophically opposed to every minute. Once I figured out what I was reacting to, the idea of the woman being the light little creature who could be lifted around the stage and was ethereal and helpless, I could go to ballet class all the time. I want women to feel good about their bodies.

Women who have large breasts should feel that that's okay as dancers or big hips or thick thighs. That you can use that aspect of your body because African dance uses the expressiveness within the hips as a core part of its statement.

SG: You formed your company 'Urban Bush Women' in 1984 in response to your feelings about the need to preserve your ancient roots, to explore the familiar and the distant in your culture. What is the future direction for the company?

JZ: I chose a name that would evoke an image of strong women for my all-women company who share an African heritage. I belong to several oppressed groups in this country who are programmed to be victims. I am interested in how you reclaim power. I am actually moving into education and learning in the context of the environment so that you take responsibility for how you buy into your own oppression, you take responsibility for your own liberation and that learning is centered in those ideas. The "MOVE" incident in Philadelphia (1985) brings authority into question. We ask children, "Who was right? Who was wrong?" A whole neighborhood was destroyed to evict one group of people. It was the first time in a domestic situation that we'd ever used a bomb in this country. How do you deal with people who look different from you, their values are different, they carry themselves differently, they smell different, what does that mean? This has implications on how we deal with each other. What happens if your family moves into a group where you are completely different from everyone else and they want you out? My experience with children is that they are extremely capable of handling these questions and coming to decisions and processing. I want to increase the dialogue between my work and children on their level.

Using dance for social change, as Jawole Zollar envisions her role and responsibility, has significant repercussions for the future of performance and education. The immersion into African American cultural history alongside the idea of relating personal research and community work to choreography provides an understanding of the social context in which young people live. The theoretical framework and methodologies for community work are powerful tools to begin to address some of the social problems of our time. As one of the oldest forms of expression, dance offers many possibilities as a life long process that heals, informs, transforms and delights.

SEDUCTION IN ANDALUSIAN FLAMENCO
Ninotchka Devorah Bennahum

The essence of this art is the mutual inter-penetration of races; the dual nature of Aryan and Semite; the parallel development, amazing in its precision of the musical line and that drawn by the body in response to the melody... the subtle transformation of those curves, spirals, and ellipses, those interlaced ornaments of sinuous calligrams which are the foundation of all Iberian baile... *In a foam of black-spangled tulle... the Spanish Dancer is like some heraldic serpent, undulating on its tail...*
— *André Levinson,* Theatre Arts Monthly, *Paris, 1928*[1]

Inherent in Flamenco dance is the multi-cultural mosaic of southern Spain. Nourished by five centuries of gypsy coexistence, by migrants from India, Persia, Turkey, Eastern Europe and North Africa, Flamenco dance elicits and communicates a pluralistic form of encounter on stage. A Flamenco dancer's dialogue with her singer, or *cantao*r, guitarist, or *tocaor*, as well as with her partner, group, or *cuadro*, and audience, demands the attention of those who accompany her, as well as those who observe her movements and hear her every beat. Her ruthless pounding into the floor echoes themes of love, death, poverty and persecution. Within this cultural mosaic, the female dancer speaks.

The cultural historian can trace historical and artistic visions of the woman's body in Flamenco performance. Narratives have been drawn from the visual and textual accounts of her dancing body: from the opening of the first *café cantante* in Triana in 1842, to the vaudevillian *Operisma* of the 1920s in Madrid and Barcelona, through Hollywood's exoticized Flamenco scenes in the 1930s, to Spain's own promotion of itself as a sensual land through the representation of the mysterious woman on fire to advertise its 1992 Olympics and World's Fair.

Fascinated by her ecstatic presence — her inaccessible and auspicious aura of *duende* (trance-like state) during *cantes jondos* (deep songs of unrequited love, death, pain) — writers, painters, and filmmakers have tried to capture the ephemerality of her form: her body carriage, the bird-

---

[1] Levinson, André. "The Spirit of the Spanish Dance," in *Writings from Paris in the Twenties*, eds. Acocella, Joan and Garafola, Lynn. Middletown: Wesleyan University Press, 1991.

like fluttering of hands, highly articulated fingers, wrists, elbows, and outstretched *braceo*, (arm-work) strained neck, intensely contemplative focus, and *zapateado* (machine gun-like footwork elegantly uplifted atop two-inch heels). Her costumery — *bata de cola*, (hair, earrings, shawl and fan) — form a bodily mise-en-scène, a traveling costume shop from which artists have drawn their impressions and recorded their expressions. She is shown at different periods of time, her dances rechoreographed to fit the frame. Each artist, each work of art, offers a unique history of a particular dance on a particular night performed in a *tablao*, an Andalusian pueblo or big-city theatre. Each performance becomes a reinvention of actuality, descriptions of which we trust to viewers whose thoughts, too, are informed by the personal and cultural contexts within which they live.

This will be a journey told through the iconic/symbolic imagery of Flamenco. It asks the following questions: How does the female Flamenco dancer embody shape and inhabit space as she moves across the stage? How does her body demand the attention of those who view her? How do those, carried away by the sheer ephemerality of her presence on stage, represent her? How and why are her body movements considered erotic? Does she view herself as erotic, and, if so, how does she understand her own body's movements?

Ann Daly in her article "Dance and Feminist Analysis" suggests that dance analysts are making a mistake in dubbing all spectatorship as caught within the impossible rubric of the "male gaze." In dance, the spectator has been described as the one who sees, who consumes, who possesses the image cast before him/her. This spectatorial positioning must be revised as it leaves no room for aesthetic differentiation, appreciation, or formalization of a particular dance form, performance, or performer. Dance scholars rebuild past constructions of women in performance, not within the matrixes of traditional standards of femininity in everyday life or within post-structural analyses of the female dancer. They could attack the issue of how the female dancer is seen and represented through a reconstruction of what Daly calls the "metaphorical space in which spectator and performers can share the dance together, on equal terms, rather than the one serving her/himself up for the others."[2]

Flamenco, as a non-Western form of theatre-dance, problematizes the dialectical, spectatorial relationship between performer and viewer. In a *bailaorina's* control of the rhythmic alterations of a specific movement sequence, the experience of viewing a given Flamenco performance alters

---

[2] Daly, Ann. "Dance and Feminist Analysis: A Limited Partnership." *Dance Research Journal*, Vol. 23, No. 1, 1986, p. 3.

the relationship between spectator and seen. In a performer's unexpected shifts, the audience member gets pulled deeper into the experience of the performance, as if kinesthetically experiencing her body as she moves. This physical, as well as visual, happening changes the performance boundaries, bringing the viewer into the participatory circle of performers onstage. The relationship between viewer and viewed becomes one of ritual, instead of one of linear spectatorship.

In Andalusian Flamenco performance, one hundred and eighty-pound women with long black hair, olive skin, thick legs, bulbous arms, and delicately thin, long noses dance. The intensity and ferocity with which such *gitanas flamencas* move stem from a lifetime of Flamenco fiestas and festivals dedicated at Easter time to both Jesus Christ and to symbols of the earth and the moon — in mother-goddess *deblas*, or verses. Each female performer improvises to a solo *tocaor*, or guitarist, or performs with a *cuadro* of accompanying musicians who follow her every move, respond to her every beat. On an American stage, such women would be considered heavy, perhaps ugly, and certainly not erotic. However, within the Iberian Peninsula, they are erotic and sensual.

In Andalusian fiestas, when gypsy women dance, they embody strength, fertility, beauty, passion, and love. In their acute musicality and power, *gitanas* speak for themselves and for other women in their clan. Their movements, although constant echoes of the traditional Flamenco stories, utilize tradition through rhythmic interpretation and individual performance. How well these women dance will determine how beautiful they are thought to be by relatives, friends, and by members of other gypsy clans. A woman's musicality, invention in rhythmic changes and intricacy of spatial pattern increase the audience's sense of the overwhelming beauty of her dancing. The drama becomes the mechanism through which a woman's capacity to embody beauty is judged. The heavier the woman is, the more weight she is able to press into the stage, thus appearing to shake the earth during her rapid footwork sequences, or *zapateado*. To affect the earth in Andalusian gypsy culture is to be powerful, willful, and deserving of respect: it is to be potent.

It is through the dance that gypsy Flamenco performers convey their sexuality and express their sensuality. The female body is accepted and understood as inhabiting a larger portion of the stage space than male dancers, who are generally quite thin. It is thought in gypsy communities that the larger and stronger the woman, the more forceful and convincing the performance. The *gitana bailaorina*, or gypsy dancer, assumes a role that is physical/personal, cultural/communal, and sociological throughout her life. She takes on this role in early adolescence; it continues in marriage,

through child-rearing until death. The *gitana's* status within the Andalusian
gypsy community and especially within her own clan is determined by
her physical and performing ability to meet the criteria of Flamenco dance
culture.

The *Solea* is a highly ornate, intricate and powerful solo dance lasting
anywhere from three to twenty-five minutes. Its tempo and duration are
controlled by the dancer, not by the musicians. The *tocaor's* and the *cantaor's*
roles are responsive: two or three male musicians carefully time their own
arpeggio changes and maintain a visual and rhythmic balance on stage. The
Solea's drama and power revolve around the soloist's ability to inject rhythmic
changes into the performance. The interstices of these changes of tempi
determine the way in which a female dancer chooses to interact with those
who watch her. She acknowledges the importance of tempi to those who
participate with her, yet she dances the *Solea* for no one but herself.

The *Solea* represents isolation and solitude in mournful *cantes jondos.*
Its length, repetitive rhythmic sequences, and harsh pounding of the floor
intensify the spectator's experience. At times, the dancer is seen as a rhythmic
instrument. At other moments, the *Solea* presents her as a protagonist in a
narrative, her pounding flesh, the inaccessible object of a spectator's desire.
As the performance proceeds an intimate relationship is formed between
bailaorina, cantaor — who cries out the story she dances — and accompanying
tocaor. Yet, no physical interaction exists between these men and the female
dancer; neither enters the other's stage space.

The almost complete isolation of the female dancer in *Solea* can be
attributed to the trance-like state she falls into during a *zapateado.* Such a
liminal state of being and motion is called by gypsies *duende.* As if hypnotized
by the ruthless beating of her own shoes into the stage floor, the *gitana's* total
absorption in the moment of the execution of each beat distances her from
those who watch her. Her sweat, vibrating skeletal frame, lateral shifting
from hip to hip and foot to foot, are sensual and sexual because they allow
strangers a look at an intimate performance. However, these actions are erotic
only because they are inaccessible, not because they are performed for the
benefit of anyone but the *Solea* performer. Further, the *Solea* functions as a
ritualistic dance. Those who perform and those who watch both participate
in the action on stage through clapping, snapping, and shouting and an
intimate knowledge of how the performance is supposed to proceed. It is
also the only dance in the Flamenco vocabulary in which the soloist can
break the repetition of rhythms at any time through a *llamada,* or a call to the
musicians.

The *bailaorina* can improvise steps while her musicians are forced
to comply with the rhythms she sets. Any non-compliance would disrupt the

musical flow of the performance. Such a mistake would be intolerable and unforgiven. The dancer can never be blamed by an *aficionado* or a fellow dancer for having violated the traditional form of the dance, since her improvisation, executed at unexpected and dramatic points during the performance, is integral to the dance's structure. The surge of *taconeo*, or heelwork, requires the dancer's inward intensity. Its difficulty forces a complete focus. The more intense and frenetic the movement, the deeper the trance, the longer her inattention to her audience.

The Andalusian *bailaorina* exists in a space and time outside mere spectatorship — outside the "male gaze."[3] Flamenco is politically and sexually powerful; it transcends any one performance. Flamenco presents itself as far too complex for a reductive and unimaginative reading, i.e., an objectification of the female form and male spectatorship. During *Solea*, the woman frees herself from the strictures of Spanish and gypsy culture, as well as from the stage space itself. She inhabits a universe of her own making, one we are privileged as spectators to enter, observe, and attempt to understand.

To illuminate the issues of sexuality, sensuality, and seduction in Flamenco dance, one can look at the symbiotic exchange of gestures and gazes in one particular dance filmed in Spain.[4]

De Leyenda is a ballad sung and danced by Flamenco artists. Its structure is new and it includes textual additions to Flamenco dance and music performance. *De Leyenda's* structure follows that of *Flamenco Puro* convention. The dances — *cantes chicos* and *jondos* — are framed by the songs and guitar solos. This combination of old and new makes *De Leyenda* representative of the theatricalization of Flamenco performance while preserving, for an Andalusian audience, the flavor of a Flamenco evening. Though the story is staged and does not change from performance to performance, the traditional dances which form the body of the concert create an aura of spontaneity on the part of each performer during every performance. In this way, *De Leyenda* falls in between the choreographic

---

[3] Feminists argue that for the male observer, dance becomes sexual because its primarily female performers are viewed physically. As sexual objects, they are observed through what the feminist film critic Laura Mulvey has termed "the pleasure gaze." Mulvey, Laura, ed., "Afterthoughts on 'Visual Pleasure and Narrative Cinema,'" in *Visual and Other Pleasures*, Bloomington: Indiana University Press, 1989.

[4] The author witnessed an all-female *cuadro* on the night of July 29, 1991 in the once Moorish pueblo of Alhama de Granada, a little town forty-five kilometers from Granada. The dance-drama, entitled *De Leyenda*, was performed as part of an avant-garde dance-theatre festival of gypsy creation within southern Spain at which only Andalusian-based dance and theatre companies were invited to perform. I, a young, white American woman, was the only non-Spaniard present.

strictures of *Flamenco Puro* and the modern dance-theatre. It is a complex and interesting fusion of old and new, of contemporary technique and ritualistic, gypsy dance tradition.

Directed, choreographed, and sung by Paco Moyano, *De Leyenda* presents the story of a gypsy, her daughter, her daughter's lover, and a female chorus who act as friends, onlookers, and soothsayers, predicting and commenting upon the story. The performance is both a story of the courting and deflowering of a young girl, who is then cruelly rejected by her suitor, and an affirmation of the gypsy woman as head of the home. The mother, played by a gypsy named Concha Vargas, has descended from a long line of dancers and bullfighters. Vargas's presence on stage as protagonist is powerful, both for her troupe and for the audience. Vargas is the only gypsy dancer on stage; the rest of the performers are Spaniards.

In el Patio del Carmen, an open-air theatre of a former convent, in the once Phoenician, Moorish, and now Castilian pueblo, *De Leyenda* opens with *cantaor* and *tocaor*, singing and playing. The dancers enter: Concha Vargas first, followed by four Spanish women. Concha sits at the apex of the group: two dancers sit on either side, and three more women sit at her feet. In *De Leyenda*, this *cuadro* represents a kind of ritualistic gathering of women who tell each other tales of love and loss through gesture; they are a group of women with whom even female audience members are not welcome. A good part of what is danced actually goes unseen by the audience. The dancers revel in their movements but conceal them by showing only their backs. Such concealment becomes seductive as it teases, tempts, and entertains the audience. The displaying of backs, a part of the body that one would not normally go to a performance to see, forces us to imagine what the front looks like. Such musing engages people's desires.

Strained necks, frenzied footwork, and effortless *braceo*, upwardly flying skirts and cascading shawls are sensuous feminine Flamenco symbols. The arch of the upper body creates a protrusion of the breasts and pelvis, an erotic revelation and exaggeration of these body parts. The rhythmic fierceness of the *zapateado* creates a stimulating, frenzied crescendo of music and dance.

Concha sits with outstretched legs ready to react to the crescendo of the guitar's wailing arpeggios. Her hands clap soft *palmas*, her face is flooded by a spotlight. Her all-female *cuadro* begins to dance in front of her, for her, one at a time. Concha, never looking at the audience, tilts her shoulders from side to side, up and down, echoing the 4/4 *Fandango* played by the guitarist. This is a dance André Levinson referred to as the "pantomime of love." The first singer and dancer is Mathilde Lopez, whose words echo Paco's as she performs center stage in front of Concha. Only Mathilde's back is revealed to us as she turns toward Concha to dance, while the remaining three women carry a steady, polyrhythmic meter for her to interpret with her feet and arms. As the guitar's chords rise in crescendo to the wailing of the singer, Mathilde tilts her neck backward and pelvis forward, off-axis, in an unstable extension that only Concha can see from the front. Mathilde's hips and shoulder's rock, at first slowly, while her arms continue to pierce the area above her head. As she increases her velocity and varies her footwork, her hips move faster and faster, while her upper body remains perfectly calm, although torqued.

As she continues to push her weight into the floor from her pelvis, her legs shoot from side to side, she drops her body rapidly forward and backward. Mathilde lifts up her skirt, securing it in between her thighs but the audience sees only her buttocks. Mathilde winds her skirt tightly around her body, then spins around on one leg. She jumps onto the other foot, landing on both feet only to shuffle, executing quick, soft, and small lifts of her heels as she walks, in profile, back to her place.

After all the other women have danced, Concha begins. She faces front and prepares for the spasmodic twists and spins she will execute. Although she dances for her chorus and in front of an audience, she physically acknowledges only the presence of the four women on stage. Circle after circle around the stage, arms outstretched backward as if gesturing to those left behind her, Concha's walk accelerates, her *taconeo* become harsher as she stops center stage to execute a frantic and frightening explosion of sounds that lasts ten minutes. As she dances, the audience knows that her *Solea* has begun. The merciless 4/4 beating of the floor is subsumed by a 3/4 attack that Concha alternates in cut and regular time. The sweet, soft gestures of the *Fandango* disappear and are replaced by quick circles of the arms. She dances her *Solea* as if in front of a mirror into which she peers to catch a glimpse of herself. She constantly counters rhythms given her by the guitarist. Concha dances *soledad* — her loneliness as well as her strength.

After five minutes, sweat begins to trickle down her forehead, her neck and onto the front of her costume. Her hair becomes unpinned and falls down around her shoulders, flies out to the sides when she turns her head from side to side as if in a fury of restless motion. Her skirt flies up, her *mantilla*, or shawl, moves around her body. All the while her face remains tense in concentration. Never once does Concha look at us, nor leave the trance she seems to have fallen into until she begins to slow down her footwork to a barely audible, light tapping of the floor. When she finishes, she does not bow, but walks over to her *cuadro*, acknowledges them and exits the stage.

Sitting in the Patio del Carmen on a hot, sticky night, the audience in no way understands Concha Vargas to be anything but what she reveals to us nor anything less than what she conceals. We are privileged to watch her dance but not so privileged as to create a theory of her dancing that exists outside the time and space in which she lives for these few moments.

Bibliography

Acton, Thomas. *Gitanos*. Madrid: Espasa-Calpe, 1983.

Alpers, Svetlana. *The Art of Describing*. Chicago: University of Chicago Press, 1983.

Balouch, Aziz. *Cante Jondo: Su Origen y Evolución*. Madrid: Ediciones Ensayos, 1955.

Blas Vega, Jose. *Diccionario Enciclopedico Ilustrado del Flamenco*, Parts I & II. Madrid: Cinterco, 1988.

Blondel, Eric. *Nietzsche. The Body and Culture*. Stanford: Stanford University Press, 1991.

Caballero, Angel. *Gitanos, Payos, y Flamenco, en los Origenes del Flamenco*. Madrid: Cinterco, 1988.

Castro, Americo. *The Structure of Spanish History*. Princeton: Princeton University Press, 1954.

Daly, Ann. "Dance and Feminist Analysis: A Limited Partnership," *Dance Research Journal*, vol. 23, no.1 (Spring, 1991).

Grande, Felix. *Memoria del Flamenco*. Two Volumes. Madrid: Espasa-Calpe, 1979.

Irigaray, Luce. *Le Sexe qui n'enest pas Un*. trans. Porter, Catherine. Ithaca: Cornell University Press, 1985.

Irving, Washington. *Leyendas de la Conquista de España — Cronicas Moriscos*. Granada: 1974.

Kant, Immanuel. *Observations on the Feeling of the Beautiful and the Sublime*. Berkeley: University of California Press, 1960.

Kiernander, Adrian. "The Orient, the Feminine," *Gender & Performance*. Hanover: Tufts University Press, 1992.

La Belle, Jenijoy. *Herself Beheld. The Literature of the Looking Glass*. Ithaca: Cornell University Press, 1988.

Levinson, André. "Argentina" and "The Spirit of the Spanish Dance," in *André Levinson on Dance. Writings from Paris in the Twenties*. Middletown: Wesleyan University Press, 1991.

Manuel, Peter. "Andalusian Gypsy and Class Identity in the Contemporary Flamenco Complex," *Ethnomusicology*, 33 (1989).

Molina, Ricardo. *Misterios del Arte Flamenco*. Sevilla: Editoriales Andaluzas Unidas, 1986.

Mulvey, Laura. *Visual and Other Pleasures.* Bloomington: Indiana University Press, 1989.

Nochlin, Linda. "The Imaginary Orient." *The Politics of Vision.* New York: Harper & Row, 1989.

Phelan, Peggy. "Feminist Theory, Poststructuralism and Performances," *Drama Review* (April 1989).

HOW CAN THE BROWN, FEMALE, SUBALTERN FEMINIST SPEAK?
Ananya Chatterjea

Ancient India had a rich dance heritage. The *Natyashastra*, the scripture of performance, was written between the second and the fifth centuries. Dance and dance-drama have always included a wide variety of classical, semi-classical, folk, and creative forms. From ancient times to the present, women have been the central bearers of these dance traditions, passing them from one to another.

During the continuous foreign invasions and ensuing political upheavals that shook India and culminated in the establishment of the British Raj (colonial rule) in the eighteenth century, many dance traditions and institutions disintegrated. When India regained independence in 1947 after an arduous and long-drawn struggle, the cultural revival movement was already well under way. The leaders of this movement sought to reclaim faded artistic traditions and to celebrate the ancient richness of Indian culture. The reformulation of the classical dance forms in keeping with the tenets of classical performance codified in the *Natyashastra* was part of this effort. Such revivalism was highly influenced by the writings of Anglo-European Orientalist scholars who glorified the ancient culture of Vedic India and contrasted that glory with what they saw as the current degradation of Indian culture. This celebration of cultural inheritance was linked to the search for national pride as India laboured to recover from the shame of the colonial yoke and the pain of the partition of the country. Dance, with its newly gained respectability, provided an arena where middle and upper class women could find a channel for self-expression and artistic fulfillment in post-independence India.

The ensuing years have seen a flourishing of the classical and folk dance forms, with occasional creative dance-drama projects dotting the scene. In response to different socio-cultural, political, and economic structures, the avant-garde marks its arrival not as a movement per se but in the endeavours of individuals. The work of these artists reflects regional, cultural and political differences.

The avant-garde is often marked by ambiguity: traditional forms and modes are critiqued in their contemporary incarnation. It looks beyond the neo-classical dance celebrated by "modern" or modernizing India and beyond the models of modernity created by the West. The avant-garde chooses to privilege what has been marginalized, often attends to the differentials enforced by class, caste, and gender inequities, and looks to itself to define its own aesthetics and politics.

Contemporary issues or recast and critiqued versions of traditional myths and legends are typically the subject of much avant-garde choreography. Group instead of solo forms, which were the staple of classical dance, are more popular. Traditional Indian choreography put great emphasis on time and used complex rhythms to create a rich temporal tapestry. Choreographic concerns of the avant-garde emphasize the spatiality of movement, counterpointing complex and often interrrupted spatial patterns with intricate rhythmic structures. Perhaps this shift from a focus on time to one on space is a response to contemporary conditions in which the displacement, resettlement and redistribution of land in India is paramount.

Not surprisingly, several women have been at the forefront of the emerging avant-garde. Their choreography, as is evident in the works of artists like Chandralekha, Manjusri Chaki-Sircar and Daksha Seth, often foregrounds women's issues. It seems to me that avant-garde or contemporary choreographers in Indian dance must continue to work toward reforming idiom, form, and choreographic structure. I can only speak with conviction as a middle-class, educated, Indian woman dancer and choreographer, who has grown up in the world of post-independence India.

In my work *Multitudinous Trio* the experiences of the protagonists Draupadi, Urvashi and Savitri can be expanded to resonate the lives of many women. Draupadi is the central female figure from the Hindu epic *Mahabharata* who is married to the five Pandava brothers, suffers the enemy's attempt to disrobe her in public, and vows terrible revenge for this dishonour. Urvashi is the first *apsara* (semi-divine, semi-human female), created when a sage drew her with the end of a mango leaf-stalk on his thigh. She was endowed with life by the gods because she was such a beautiful conception. Urvashi, the gorgeous dancer of the heavens, is considered to mark the pinnacle of female beauty and talent. Savitri marries Satyavan, knowing he has not long to live. She follows Yama, the god of death, when he comes to take away her husband's dead body and finally wins back her husband's life in a battle of wits with Yama.

While I had chosen to choreograph reinterpretations of the legendary figures Draupadi, Urvashi and Savitri from a contemporary feminist perspective, I had to keep myself grounded in the reality of their lived situation so as not to create a travesty of traditionally held values. Further, while I had the "epistemic privilege" of belonging to the society which formed the context for my voice and of having experienced the particular modes of oppression I was critiquing, I had to be careful to acknowledge the changed circumstances of time, place and context. Thus, while I personally may not uphold the value of *sindur* (the vermilion powder placed in the part of a woman's hair as a sign of marriage), it was imperative for me to realize its romance, richness, and prestige within the traditional value system. *Multitudinous Trio* was not aimed at arbitrarily critiquing traditional values. Taking the acceptance of these values as given, I re-present the woman's experience from my "womanist" perspective.

In India, the ability of a woman to tell a good story, through which she subtly accomplishes the moral and cultural education of her children, is highly valued. Several religious ceremonies are observed by the woman retelling the *vrat-katha*, the story related to a particular event. The *Natyashastra* upholds the importance of educating an audience about cultural and religious traditions and mythology through the *abhinaya* (expressional, particularly story-telling) aspect of performance. One of the richest sources of power for avant-garde dance in India is the narrative — not a linear, cause-and-effect narrative but one which progresses as a kind of stream of consciousness, bringing in a wealth of intimate details.

Traditionally, women have been relegated to a position where they do not or cannot assume agency for writing their own stories. I realized the importance of rewriting the patriarchial conception of my three protagonists, of allowing their embodied presence to speak. Some retelling of women's stories from a woman's point of view has happened in performance texts.[1] In recreating the mythology, I had to uncover the woman's perspective which could be described as the "un-text" — there being no documentation of any alternative ways of reading these myths. Draupadi's most wrenching question arises when her dancing body collides with the gestures of the remembered disrobing and of marital sexuality. In her horrified reaction to her own movement lies the germ of her realization that her marriages have in fact been, like the disrobing, similar to experiences of rape.

---

[1] One of the most notable instances of this is Saoli Mitra's rendition of Draupadi's story through her one-person performance, though this is not a reconfiguration of the woman's body in the mode of *l'écriture féminine*. One of the "stories" which did influence my thinking considerably was Gayatri Chakravorty Spivak's translation of Mahasweta Devi's fiction "Draupadi," which rewrites the epical story. Draupadi, in this story, is a peasant woman who is an important figure in the 1967 Naxalbari revolution of North Bengal. The Brechtian overturning happens when Mahasweta Devi's narrative questions Draupadi's "legitimized pluralization" (as a wife among husbands) by placing her protagonist first in "a comradely, activist, monogamous marriage" and then in a situation of multiple rape by her captors. Chakravorty Spivak, G., "'Draupadi' by Mahasweta Devi." *In Other Worlds*, 1987, p. 183.

A woman's consciousness of the distinctness of her body, its vulnerability and the potency of breasts, hips, and vagina served as a source for much of my movement. The body is, in the Indian context, a social construct and contains within it a realization of culture and social thought. As I move away from socially constructed, familiar dance grammar, I locate the richest source of knowledge available to me: the individual female body and its instinctive physical reactions to diverse situations.

My Urvashi, Draupadi, and Savitri rely on the intimacy of the knowledge churned from within themselves, once they have acknowledged themselves as subjects of history. This means they operate from within an acceptance of their social, cultural and political context. However, their bodies, their subjective beings and their thinking all give them information that questions the traditional structures of patriarchy. They are forced to act and open up a new powerful space for women. Thus when Urvashi, created from a male conception of the most beautiful woman, is drawn to reflect upon the nature of beauty and of its relationship to dance, she finds that her dancing body takes immense joy in distorting *bhangis* (poses) traditionally, and often from the point of view of male voyeurism, held to represent beauty. This leads Urvashi to create an alternative concept of beauty and the beautiful dance from her perspective. The particular realism of "womanist" epistemology is located in the very groundedness of the woman's mode of knowing. Knowledge comes from lived experience, with the feet planted in the ground, not from abstract ratiocination. Thus, Savitri cannot be seduced by traditional ideas of the indissoluble union of souls in marriage: she needs the practical reality of her husband's physical body. This doesn't mean that she does not recognize the grandeur of the human soul, but that her recognition has a practical dimension to it — she knows that spirituality can be experienced within the realm of human life and that it need not be set apart from physicality. In other words, she knows that *jouissance*, the essence of a woman's desire is sexual, spiritual, physical, and conceptual at the same time.

The thrust of much feminist theory regarding emotion has been to emphasize that intentional judgments as well as physiological disturbances are integral elements in emotion.[2] For Draupadi, the emotional recognition of horror at what her body's confusion has just revealed to her — the contiguity of her marriages and her disrobing — leads her to question her traditional

---

[2] As Jagger explains, these conceptions "define or identify emotions not by the quality or character of the physiological sensation that may be associated with them but rather by their intentional aspect, the associated judgment." Jagger, A. M. "Love and Knowledge: Emotion in Feminist Epistemology," in Jagger, A. and Bordo, S. (eds.)., *Gender/Body/Knowledge*, p. 149.

values and brings her to a new sphere of knowing. This knowledge which comes from emotion can also empower: Draupadi takes it upon herself to avenge her own insult.

Still, there is a difference in the "position of intimacy" that Forte (1988) calls the hallmark of Western feminist performance and the place of intimacy in the subaltern context. According to Forte, "Rather than masking the self, women's performance is born from self-revelation as a political move."[3] It is perfectly true that women performers challenge the symbolic order when they assert themselves as knowing and articulating subjects and defy the patriarchal construction of discourse. However, in the subaltern context, the female body, and particularly the performing female body, has been subject to relentless tabooing and reconstructing through the process of colonization, national cultural revivalism and the creation of a new national identity through the woman's body. In this situation, personal authorship and self-revelation do not work in the Western sense.

The position of the contemporary woman dancer in India is related to the tradition of the *devadasi*, who were banished because their sexual morals did not sit well with the new English-educated, Catholic-influenced, *bhadralok* (genteel) community of Indian intelligentsia. The *devadasi*'s body was metaphorically desiccated by this rude rejection. Laws made her lineage illegal. Meanwhile her dance was arrogated by Indian nationalists and "cleansed" in order to be representative of "high" Indian culture. Just as the *devadasis* returned to eventually claim the central place of dance within Indian religious practice, so too are contemporary choreographers revisioning and reclaiming ground in the secular performance arena.

Contemporary Indian dancers who believe in avant-garde performance and in feminism almost necessarily speak through reinterpretations of myth and mythology. Avant-garde Indian women choreographers and mythological characters they have used include Chandralekha and Sakambhari, the goddess of plants and vegetation; Manjusri Chaki-Sircar and Prakriti, the daughter of the earth; Uttara Coorlawala and Yakshi, the semi-divine nymph; Daksha Seth and Usha, the goddess of dawn; and finally my own trio, Urvashi, Draupadi, and Savitri.

In *Multitudinous Trio* I also chose to reinterpret myths so as to upset traditional conceptions. Thus, an unexpected idea is brought into the familiar story of Draupadi when her curse results from her breaking out of the protected bridal space. She becomes self-empowered and decides to take

---

[3] Forte, J. "Women's Performance Art: Feminism and Post-Modernism." *Theatre Journal*, V. 40. Number 2, p. 224.

matters into her own hand instead of relying on her husbands. The dance is stripped of all but two anthropological hand gestures (as opposed to the decorative *mudra*), the *lingam* and the *yoni*, the male and female sexual symbols. I use them to signify marriage, but also ownership and force and thereby set up tension with the traditional values associated with marriage. The lovely young bride who submits to her husband because she has been socialized to do so, in fact becomes an unwitting agent in the patriarchal structure in which she might be subjected to violence.

Clearly, I have not arrived at answers but the process of coming face to face with relentless questions remains powerful and painful. Like Draupadi, I know that new knowldge can rob one of an illusion of comfort and peace, but that once that veil is torn away, there can be no going back. At the end of this piece, Draupadi is forced to question the value of her *lajja* (literally shame, metaphorically that which prevents shame, garments). Her *lajja* symbolizes traditional associations with marriage, decency and notions of female sexuality. At the end of the dance she is left discarding the symbolic veil yet clutching it back. Draupadi's dilemma is mine and that of many Indian women in my generation: How do we strip off the skins of history?

Bibliography

Carby, H. "The Canon: Civil War and Reconstruction." *Michigan Quarterly Review*, Winter, 1989, pp. 35–43.

Chakravorty Spivak, G. "'Draupadi' by Mahasweta Devi" in *In Other Worlds*. New York: Methuen, Inc., 1987.

Code, L. "Taking Subjectivity into Account." in Alcoff, L. and Potter, E. eds. *Feminist Epistemologies*. New York: Routledge, 1993, pp. 15–48.

Diamond, E. "Brechtian Theory/Feminist Theory." *The Drama Review*, V. 32, #1, Spring, 1988, pp. 82–94.

Forte, J. "Women's Performance Art: Feminism and Post-modernism." *Theatre Journal*. V. 40, #2, May, 1988, pp. 217–235.

Fox, K. "Choreographing Differences in the Dance of Leisure." *Journal of Leisure Research*. V. 24, #4, 1992, pp. 333–47.

Hawkesworth, M. E. "Knowers, Knowing, Known." in Malson, M., O'Barr, J., Westphal-Wihl, S. and Wyer, M., eds. *Feminist theory in practice and Process*. Chicago: University of Chicago Press, 1989, pp. 327–53.

Jaggar, A. M. "Love and Knowledge: Emotion in Feminist Epistemology." in Jaggar, A. and Bordo, S., eds. *Gender/Body/Knowledge*. New Brunswick, NJ: Rutgers University Press, 1989, pp. 145–71.

Jenkins, L. W. "Locating the Language of Gender Experience." *Women and Performance*. V. 2, #1, 1984, pp. 5–20.

Karve, I. *Yuganta: The End of an Epoch*. Poona: Deshmukh Prakashan, 1969.

Kristeva, J. (1981). "Women's Time," in Warhol, R. and Herndl, D. P. eds. *Feminisms*. New Brunswick, NJ: Rutgers University Press, 1991, pp. 443–62.

Martin, C. "Feminist Analysis across Cultures." *Women & Performance*, V. 3, # 2, 1987–88, pp. 32–40.

Mulvey, L. (1975). "Visual Pleasure and Narrative Cinema," in Warhol, R. and Herndl, D. P., eds. *Feminisms*. New Brunswick, NJ: Rutgers University Press, 1991, pp. 432–42.

Narayan, U. "The Project of Feminist Epistemology: Perspectives from a Non-Western Feminist," in Jaggar, A. and Bordo, S. eds. *Gender/Body/Knowledge*. New Brunswick, NJ: Rutgers University Press, 1989, pp. 256–72.

Von Morstein, P. "A Message from Cassandra — Experience and Knowledge," in Code, L., Mullett, S. and Overall, C., eds., *Feminist Perspectives*. Toronto: University of Toronto, 1988, pp. 46–63.

Wilshire, D. "The Uses of Myth, Image, and the Female Body in Re-visioning Knowledge," in Jaggar, A. and Bordo, S. eds. *Gender/Body/Knowledge*. New Brunswick, NJ: Rutgers University Press, 1989, pp. 92–114.

Zimmer, H. "Sakti: The Essence of the World." *Parabola*, V. 4, #4, 1980, pp. 33–35.

SORCERESS, IMPERIAL CONCUBINE AND DANCING GIRL
Yunyu Wang

Women and dance have played fundamental and critical roles in Chinese history although the role of women in China is underdocumented. The female position in Chinese society often seems secondary to the male. Likewise, dance, a female pursuit, has suffered from its consideration as a woman's art and has appeared inconsequential. In actuality, the influence of women in Chinese dance has been significant.

Female Dancers in Ancient Chinese History

Throughout antiquity, vivid accounts written by Chinese poets kept alive the spirit and skillful steps of female dancers, yet the scattered literary references reveal little about the personal artistry and social position of female dancers.

The earliest female representation in dance may be the hieroglyphic Chinese character inscribed on a turtle shell unearthed in a ruin from the Ying Dynasty (late Shang, 1600–1100 B.C.E.).[1] The graphic character represents a dancer wearing a costume with ultra-long, billowy sleeves. Although the sex of the dancer cannot be determined from this stylized drawing, the performers of "Long Sleeved Dances" according to various Han Dynasty records were female.

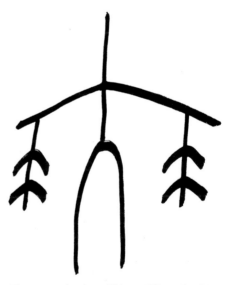

Figure 1 Ancient Chinese Hieroglyphic.

---

[1] The hieroglyphic character is an oracle-bone inscription. The earliest oracle-bone inscriptions that have been discovered date to the Shang (1600–100 B.C.E.). It established the principles and basis for the development of Chinese characters and calligraphy.

In prehistoric times, Chinese exorcist dances such as *Ta Nuo* and *Chueh Ti* imitated animal movements to demonstrate aggression and masculinity. In the Shang Dynasty (16th–11th century B.C.E.) god-worshipping dances were performed by male and female sorcerers (Hsi and Wu respectively), but those dancing the roles of gods, signifying authority and power, were males. The dances served the purpose of controlling and ruling people, and therefore became an indispensable tool.

According to the "Li Yueh Tzu" in the *History of the Han Dynasty*, the Hsia Dynasty (2205–1766 B.C.E.) saw the development of the popular Yu ("theatrical") dance, a showcase for dancers who were masters of facial expression. The elevated social position of dancer/sorcerers appears at that time to have been replaced by a common, lower classification, "Wu Ren" (dancing performer) or "Yu Ren" (theatrical performer). The ritual sorcerers dance was from then on solely for divinities and performed by men while the crowd-pleasing "Yu" dance was performed for humans by both men and women.

In the Han Dynasty (207 B.C.E.–220 A.D.), the Yueh Fu (Institute of Music) was established by the royal government to serve as a national headquarters for music and dance. During this time an extensive archive of folk and court dances was collected at the Institute. One of the most popular dances, the "Long Sleeve Dance," featured slight, supple, wasp-waisted female dancers swinging billowy sleeves. This dance was designed to display the physical ideal of female beauty and emphasized feminine charm for the viewing pleasure of the emperor and noblemen. Verses such as "Emperor Ch'u favors slim waists" or "His palace houses many starvelings" or "tiny waist and slender neck" were understood as literary portraits of female beauty of that era.[2] As one can see in Han paintings, the female dancers of the period had tiny waists, long slim necks and were costumed in robes with extra-long sleeves. This demonstrates the influence of the Ch'u nation. This standard provides a fascinating parallel to the physicality requisite of a Balanchine ballerina.

However, the picture on the whole was grim for dancers. During the four hundred or more years of the former and later Han Dynasties, feudal lords claimed dancers as their possessions who could be given away as gifts during their owners' lifetimes and buried alive with them after their deaths.

During the Tsin Dynasty (265–420 A.D.) the well-to-do and influential kept private dancers in their households whose duty was exclusively to serve their masters. As is recorded in the ancient oral document, *History of the Tsin Dynasty*, Shih Chung, a most affluent landowner, entertained his guests with banquets of everflowing wine and a continuous, dazzling, visual array

---

[2] By Chinese scholar Fa-Jung Han, born in 280 B.C. and died in 233 B.C.

of female dancers. He was known to have the dancers killed when they failed to persuade the guests to drink, an inhuman and bombastic gesture which demonstrated his disregard of human life. While the legendary suicide of Lu-Chu, Shih's concubine, was once praised as an act of devotion and chastity, she was actually "fulfilling her socially allotted duty" as a dancer.

During the Tang Dynasty (618–907 A.D.), China, then a most powerful nation, was trading with various countries. The dances were influenced from abroad. Hu Hsuan was a dance of swirls and jumps originating in K'ang (now the Uzbek Republic) and requiring considerable technique. As illustrated in one of the celebrated Dung Huang murals, dancers of the Hu Hsuan were clothed in padded jackets, tight pants, and tight boots, while their chiffon scarves and embroidered belts flew up in the air. Author Li Zehou notes: "Chinese dances in those days (Tang Dynasty) evolved mainly from a dance of the northern minority nationalities that consisted largely of quick steps and spins called Hu prancing. The jumps went left and right, up and down and were spinning like the wind. The cursive script of the prime Tang, with its vigorous and flexible serpentine lines, its varied continuous loose or compact structure, its sudden and unpredictable changes, its unbridled moods and power is the representation of violent dancing on paper."[3]

Yang Yu-huan, the best loved concubine of Emperor Hsuan Tsung and one of the famous femme fatales in Chinese history, was an accomplished performer of Hu Hsuan. The affection she enjoyed was aptly described by one of the best Tang poets, Pai Chu-i, in his *Song of Eternal Sorrow: All three thousand shares of love given her.*[4] However, when the aged and senile emperor began to lose his political power, the angry populace spared his life while demanding dancer Yang's in his place. At the age of thirty-eight, Yang was strangled in front of him, another outstanding dancer fallen prey to the hideous and bloodthirsty customs affecting the lives of female dancers.

In the literature, firsthand accounts of these dancers' personal sentiments are seldom given, their creativity hardly ever considered. What does exist are songs and poems reflecting the hidden pains and sorrows, and the bitter fate of these dancers. Chinese dance history is enriched by these vivid descriptions. Songs and poems record the impressions of male

---

[3] Li Zehou, *The Path of Beauty — A Study of Chinese Aesthetics*. Morning Glory Publishers, Beijing, China: 1988, p. 179.

[4] "Song of Eternal Sorrow" is a Chinese classic by Pai Chu-i of the Tang Dynasty and published in late Tang, circa 800 A.D.

songwriters and poets. One might ask if they were fully able to interpret the female dancers' inner feelings, aspirations, hopes, and fears.

Nu Shu, or feminine writing, is a special writing style created by women hundreds of years ago in Chiang Yung Hsien in the Hunan Province. Rediscovered in 1956, this special language of feminine anguish created under male suppression is being analyzed and decoded by contemporary scholars. A group of feminist scholars in Taiwan, are attempting a translation of Nu Shu into modern Chinese which might lead to a better understanding of the feminine mind and, consequently, an appreciation of these female dancers of centuries ago.

From the literature as well as from artifacts, we can presume that most dances from the Tang Dynasty did not give priority to individual expression. Folk dance reflected commoners' toil and rituals of worship. Court dances were displays of spectacular technique and won poetic accolades such as "having learnt this in Heaven, looking hardly like a mortal."[5] Owing to the narrow scope of court dancers' lives, their choreographic themes and ideas left much to be desired. As opposed to the spectacles of the court dance, folk dances did disclose peoples lives and wishes. Some folk dances demonstrated affection and courtship, other dances expressed distress in life during wartime or under tyrants and corrupt officials.

Many documents of considerable historic value were either recklessly destroyed or simply lost due to the high-handed oppression of those with political power. In his *Preface to Fu Dance* collected in the *Yueh Chi* of the *History of the Sung Dynasty*, Yang Hung states that "people in Wu suffered under Sun Hao's tyranny and longed to be subjects of Tsin," indicating a common anticipation of hyacinth days while accusing Sun's heartless reign of terror.[6] It is clear that dances were starting to reflect social issues of the time.

In some traditional Chinese paintings, female dancers of various times were portrayed. Two contrasting types deserve special observation. One is the Tang dancer at the peak of that dynasty, a period when the whole nation was unified and enjoying unprecedented power and prosperity. As painted in the Tun Huang murals, Tang ladies are enchantingly plump and elegant, exhibiting an interesting mixture of gentility from the Han heritage (the predominant ethnic group of the Chinese race), and the robust physique of the northern tribes, a physical hybrid brought about by increased trading and cultural contacts.

---

[5] This poem appears on page 31 of *Three Hundred Poems of Tang's Dynasty* published by Li-sing Book Co., Taipei, Taiwan.

[6] This classic was published between 960 and 1127 A.D.

Toward the end of the Ch'ing, or Manchu Dynasty (1644–1911), the last dynasty in China, we see another extreme type of femininity. In this dynasty females were not only seen as the secondary sex, but were bound by the most restrictive decorum in thousands of years. Confined by the "Commandments for Women" and the so-called "feminine virtues," Ch'ing ladies were fated disciples of the sickly, vulnerable look, the practice of foot binding, and a socially prescribed motto "less talents make better women." The "Commandments for Women" are ancient Chinese aphorisms such as: woman should know nothing, but serve man; woman is born to follow and work for father, husband or son. As the imperial reign drew to an end in 1911, traditional dances no longer addressed the people's needs. Dances were transformed into dramatic performances. Since Ch'ing ladies were not allowed to appear in public, actresses as well as female dancers in dramatic performances were replaced by males. During this time, dance by females came to an abrupt and sad halt in China.

Contemporary Chinese Female Dancers

In 1911 China was split in two. Senior dancer Tai Ai-lien was an advocate for contemporary dance on mainland China, while the dance circle in Taiwan was influenced by Japan. In Taiwan Li Tsai-o started teaching ballet in 1943, sometimes also trying her hand at choreographing modern dances. Tai and Li, the first pioneers of contemporary dance, were both female.

Dance in China was either Russian style ballet or Chinese folk dance. The Communist system and perhaps the ethical temperament of the Chinese people prevented this nation from truly embracing Western contemporary dance. Although the Martha Graham technique had been introduced, it wasn't until 1986 that the Kuan Chou Contemporary Dance School was established. This and the introduction of Western instructors, recommended by the American Dance Festival, changed the whole dance climate. Although their dancers had only had a few years of serious study in contemporary dance, a solo piece *The Long Night* by Wang Mei, a female choreographer from China, won acclaim in the gala performance of the 1990 International Dance Conference held in Hong Kong.

In Taiwan, mid-twentieth century choreographers centered their works on political themes. However, they failed to free themselves from a nihilistic mode of expression associated with the political campaign "Retrieve the Mainland." Dance was marginalized and was not deemed a fine art. Male dancers were few and socially unacceptable, while female dancers considered dance either recreation or exercise. Yet despite this unfavorable climate, many female dancers gradually emerged.

Elizabeth Kao became the first head of a university dance department in 1964 at the Chinese Cultural University and trained ninety-five percent of the choreographers and dance educators now in the thirty to forty age group. Not surprisingly, ninety-nine percent of them are female.

In 1972 the first professional contemporary dance troupe, Cloud Gate Dance Theatre, was started by the male choreographer Lin Hwai-min and four female dancers. In the early years the company consisted of six female and two male dancers. After 1976 the ensemble tripled its original size, yet the number of female members stayed three times that of males. Along with Lin, the females did most of the choreography.

Another important contemporary group, New Classic Dance Troupe, which existed from 1975–1978, was directed by female choreographer Liou Feng-Hsueh, who had been trained in physical education. This company, which was drawn from her physical education students, initially had an equal number of male and female dancers, yet the choreographic tasks were undertaken by the female members.

For about ten years the creative predilection of these two predominantly female groups was traditional Chinese motifs. A few dancers from Cloud Gate Dance Theatre tried to explore modern themes with social concerns. They usually did so from their personal experiences. For instance, Chen Shu-gi choreographed *The Bride-to-be* just before her own wedding. From their own experience of moving from the countryside south of Taiwan to Taipei City, Lin Hsiu-wei and Du Pi-tao choreographed *A City Corner*. This work presented young people who got lost in urban indulgence and were overwhelmed by culture shock. In the past six years, due to political openness, the trend of studying abroad, and the influence of visiting dance troupes, different styles and experimental approaches to dance have grown. The young generation strives for a creative breakthrough, as pointed out by Lin Hwai-min in a 1990 article commissioned by the Cultural Development Committee: "Choreographers of the new generation are able to shrug away the stifling pressure of 'nothing but things Chinese' and the nostalgic sentimentality. Taiwan, China, and the Western world all offer friendly room. Tradition and modernity are both natural material with which to create; between the two they do not necessarily see conflicts, and to mix and mingle the two extremes is not a must. They do not need to carry the burden of tradition. The elegance and beauty sought by older choreographers is no longer an absolute accomplishment. 'I have something to say' can be seen as their shared slogan. They can 'talk/dance' in an accusing manner, with sarcasm and mockery, or with grace and tenderness. The things they 'talk/dance' about can be current events, trends, fashions, phenomena, meditation, imagination, or simply 'just movements.' When they 'talk/dance' they are confident in what they say and how they are saying it."[7]

The new group of choreographers, 1987 until the present, numbers about thirty females and ten males. Some of these female choreographers emphasize athleticism, some employ theatrical approaches to depict ugliness and struggles in human nature and society, some are interested in natural rhythmic movement.

Tao Fu-lang, the only choreographer who consistently focuses her creative endeavors on contemporary feminist issues, in 1989 created a thirty minute piece entitled "Females." After receiving a B.A. degree in anthropology at National Taiwan University, Tao started her dance study at Kansas State University. In 1982 she returned to Taiwan with an M.F.A. degree from that university to teach in the National Institute of the Arts and began to give annual performances. These continue through the present. In her 1987 talk with Li Yuen-chen, the head of the feminist movement in Taiwan, Tao mentioned that one of her main themes was "various situations modern females find themselves in ...in a sense I want to use an introspective language which, hopefully, can contribute to the integration of form and content in my work." Of the feminist conscience in Tao's choreography, Li said "it might well open up a whole new perspective for the dance professionals and audiences in Taiwan."[8]

Feminist concerns also appeared in the recent works of male choreographers, Lin Huai-min's *Spring Attire* and Chen Wei-chen's 1990 *Whose Body Is This?* The former deals with male chauvinism and the subconscious maltreatment of females, while the latter depicts violent and dramatic movements which incite sensual feelings in an attempt to unmask feminine contention and hostility. Nevertheless, both male and female choreographers in Taiwan subscribe to a decorum which assumes that no choreographer would deliberately shock or embarrass an audience. Material which, in the West, might be demonstrated graphically is abstracted in the East.

From the perspective of 1991 it appears that the tears and sweat women dancers have shed have not been wasted. Today the situation is a much more balanced one in which female dancer/choreographers are free to work hard and gain proper respect and support from their colleagues and society in general. Chinese female dancers have come a long bittersweet way

---

[7] Hwai-min Lin, *Comment and Prospect of Chinese Culture in 1989*, p. 182.

[8] Personal interview between Ms. Li Yuen-chen and Ms. Tao, 1987.

from their silent devotion to their art centuries ago to their vigorous role in contemporary dance.

Bibliography

Chang, Rehn-shiar. *History of Chinese Dance*. Taipei, Taiwan: Lang-tin Book Co., 1985.

Chiu, Jennifer. *Nu Shu Script — A Clue to Chinese Female Psychology*. Taipei: The Free China Journal. December, 1990.

Jan, Shung-chin. *Research of Ta Nuo*. Taipei: Lang-tin Book Co., 1988.

Jang, Ding-lin. *Research of Chinese Long Sleeves Dance*. Taipei: National Institute of the Arts, 1990.

Jang, Shung. *The Beauty of Women*. Taipei: Lion Arts Magazine, 1978.

Le, Yun. *Female Image in Chinese Traditional Painting*. Taipei: Lion Arts Magazine, 1978.

Liang, An-ber. *Folk Dance of Hang*. Peking: People's Music Publisher, 1975.

Liang, Hsiu-chuan. *Movement Method for the Female Roles for the Chinese Theater*. Taipei: Yuan-liu Chu-pan-she, 1983.

Lin, Hwai-min. *Comment and Prospect of Chinese Culture in 1989*. Taipei: Council for Cultural Planning and Development, 1990.

Lin, Kunt-fan. *The Story of Ancient Chinese Dancers*. Taipei: Lang-tin Book Co., 1986.

Mackerras, Colin, ed. *Chinese Theatre*. Honolulu, University of Hawaii Press, 1983.

Mei, Lan-fang. *Forty Years of Life on the Stage*. Peking: Jen-min Wen-hsueh Ch'u-pan-she, 1957.

Meng, Yao. *History of Chinese Theatre*. Taipei: Chuan-Chi Wen-hsueh Ch'u-pan-she, 1979.

Oh-yin, Wei-ching. *History of Chinese Dance I*. Taipei: Lang-tin Book Co., 1985.

Wang, Kung-wei. *History of Theatre, Music in Shung and Yung*. Taipei: Taiwan Business Printers, 1964.

Wang, Yuan-fu. *Chinese Opera*. Taipei: Twilight Culture Publisher, 1973.

Wang, Yunyu. *The Sleeve Dance Technique Class*. Urbana: University of Illinois Press, 1983.

LIST OF CONTRIBUTORS

Ann Cooper Albright is an associate professor in the dance and theater program at Oberlin College. Combining her interests in dancing and cultural theory, she is involved in teaching dance, performance studies and women's studies. She is a recipient of a 1993 and 1995 Ohio Arts Council Individual Artist Award in Dance Criticism. Her book, *Choreographing Difference: The Body and Identity in Contemporary Dance*, will be published in 1997 by Wesleyan University Press.

Judy Austin has been a member of the Hubbard Street Dance Company, the Gus Giordano Dancers, and Ernst/Watson Dance. She is currently on the faculty of Northwestern University, where she teaches jazz and tap and serves as dance advisor to the Musical Theater Program.

Ann Barzel, Chicago-based dance critic since 1945, is a senior editor for *Dance Magazine* and is widely published internationally. She was a major contributor to *Dance Encyclopedia*, edited by Anatole Chujoy, and formerly on the faculties of the Universities of Chicago and North Carolina. She was a close friend of Catherine and Dorothie Littlefield for the many years that their company was based in Chicago.

Ninotchka Devorah Bennahum, artistic director of Route 66 Dance Company, is currently writing her doctoral dissertation on flamenco performance. Bennahum began a study of gypsy culture of the Iberian penninsula in 1991, creating a video documentary of Andalusian flamenco artists. She is a contributing writer for *Dance Magazine*.

Ananya Chatterjea trained for over fifteen years in Indian classical dance styles in India. She concentrated on Odissi, but has also studied Bharatnatyam, Kathakali, and Manipuri styles. In 1996 she received graduate research awards from both the Committee on Research in Dance and the Society of Dance History Scholars.

Gay Cheney, author of *Basic Concepts In Modern Dance, A Creative Approach*, is professor and graduate director of dance at the University of North Carolina — Greensboro. She continues to be a respectful student of Native American ceremony and cosmology, which deepen her teaching, writing, choreography and work for the Earth.

Roger Copeland teaches at Oberlin College and is a consultant for the National Endowment for the Arts and the PBS "Dance in America" series. He has written for the New York *Times*, the *New Republic, Saturday Review* and many dance publications. His books include *What Is Dance?* and the forthcoming *Cunningham's Legacy: The Nature of Post-Modern Dance*.

Marion Rudin Frank is a licensed psychologist and board-certified medical psychotherapist. She has been in private practice in Philadelphia for twenty years, specializing in relationship and gender issues. She still stretches on her barre and does an occasional plié.

Linda Caruso Haviland is the director of dance at Bryn Mawr College. She has taught children's dance as well as a full range of dance at several colleges and universities. She performed with Zeromoving Company and continues to choreograph and perform with independent choreographers.

Sally Hess performed worldwide as a soloist in her own choreography and with the companies of Jose Limon (*Day on Earth*), Lucas Hoving, Ernestine Stodell, Dan Wagoner (1970–1979), and Remy Charlip. She performs and writes in French and English and serves on the faculties of Princeton University and Swarthmore College.

Billie Kirpich, former director of dance at Radcliffe Collge and the State University of New York at Buffalo, moved to Miami where she founded the Grove Danstheatre. She is the host and star of the nationally award-winning television show, "Exercise with Billie," a program for older adults.

Susan A. Lee, founding director of the Dance Program in the Theatre Department at Northwestern University, holds a joint appointment in the School of Education and Social Policy. Lee is author of *Dance: The Last Hundred Years*, numerous articles on dance and a forthcoming book on dance criticism co-edited with Lynne Anne Blom.

Bella Lewitzky is the artistic director of the internationally renowned Lewitzky Dance Company founded in 1966. She was the founding dean of the School of Dance at the California Institute of the Arts. In 1990, she refused a major grant from the National Endowment of the Arts because grant recipients were required to sign a pledge not to create or show "obscene works." For more than forty years she has been at the forefront of those who guard our constitutional rights of free expression.

Carolyn McConnell wrote her article while an undergraduate at Swarthmore College, where she received a bachelor's degree in philosophy in 1993 and where she was actively involved in the dance program. In the fall of 1994 she began graduate study in philosophy at Johns Hopkins University.

Wendy Perron danced with many choreographers, including Trisha Brown from 1975 to 1978, and began showing her own choreography in the early 1970's. She has performed and taught widely and has been guest choreographer for groups in the U.S. and abroad. She has written on dance and performance extensively and is currently working on a book of quotes from artists of all disciplines.

Stephanie Reinhart, co-director of the American Dance Festival, has worked as an arts administrator since 1969, when she joined the staff for the National Endowment for the Arts. She travels worldwide, lecturing on American modern dance and arts administration. In 1993, she was awarded a Fulbright research grant to study the history of Argentine modern dance.

Julie Sandler teaches dance, movement, anatomy, body therapies and nonverbal communication. She is on the faculties of N.Y.U. School of Visual Arts, the New School for Social Research and the Laban Bartenieff Institute of Movement Studies.

Yunyu Wang is on the faculty at Colorado College and is a certified Labanotation teacher and reconstructor. She danced professionally with Taiwan Cloud Gate Dance Theater between 1971 and 1981. She has served as artistic director of the National Institute of the Arts in Taipei.

Brenda Way trained at the School of American Ballet and is the founder and Artistic Director of ODC/San Francisco. She was the driving force behind the purchase and creation of the New Performance Gallery in San Francisco — her home studio and the site of an extensive dance curriculum and performance program.

Kariamu Welsh Asante is the editor of *African Dance: An Artistic, Historical and Philosophical Inquiry*. She is an associate professor in the department of African American studies at Temple University. She was the founding artistic director of the National Dance Company of Zimbabwe.

Cheryl M. Willis has done extensive research on tap dance history and the role of African American women in this dance form. She is currently a creative movement specialist in the Vancouver public schools in Washington State.

INDEX

This book is part of a series. The publisher will accept continuation orders which may be cancelled at any time and which provide for automatic billing and shipping of each title in the series upon publication. Please write for details.